MIND ASSOCIATION OCCASIONAL SERIES

MACHINES AND THOUGHT

MIND ASSOCIATION OCCASIONAL SERIES

This series consists of occasional volumes of original papers on predefined themes. The Mind Association nominates an editor or editors for each collection, and may co-operate with other bodies in promoting conferences or other scholarly activities in connection with the preparation of particular volumes.

Publications Officer: M. A. Stewart
Secretary: C. Macdonald

Also published in the series

Perspectives on Thomas Hobbes
Edited by G. A. J. Rogers and A. Ryan

Reality, Representation, and Projection
Edited by J. Haldane and C. Wright

Connectionism, Concepts, and Folk Psychology
The Legacy of Alan Turing, Volume II
Edited by A. Clark and P. J. R. Millican

Machines and Thought

The Legacy of Alan Turing

VOL. I

Edited by

P. J. R. MILLICAN

and

A. CLARK

CLARENDON PRESS • OXFORD

1996

Oxford University Press, Walton Street, Oxford OX2 6DP

Oxford New York
Athens Auckland Bangkok Bogota Bombay
Buenos Aires Calcutta Cape Town Dar es Salaam
Delhi Florence Hong Kong Istanbul Karachi
Kuala Lumpur Madras Madrid Melbourne
Mexico City Nairobi Paris Singapore
Taipei Tokyo Toronto
and associated companies in
Berlin Ibadan

Oxford is a trade mark of Oxford University Press

Published in the United States by
Oxford University Press Inc., New York

British Library Cataloguing in Publication Data
Data available

Library of Congress Cataloging in Publication Data
The legacy of Alan Turing / edited by P. Millican and A. Clark.
(Mind Association occasional series)
Contents: v. 1. Machines and thought.
Includes bibliographical references and index.
1. Artificial intelligence. I. Turing, Alan Mathison,
1912–1954. II. Millican, P. (Peter) III. Clark, Andy. IV. Series.
Q335.5.L44 1996 006.3—dc20 96–25418
ISBN 0-19-823593-3 (v. 1)

1 3 5 7 9 10 8 6 4 2

Typeset by Graphicraft Typesetters Ltd., Hong Kong
Printed in Great Britain by
Biddles Ltd., Guildford and King's Lynn

ACKNOWLEDGEMENTS

The editors are grateful for permission to reproduce the following material in this volume:

Donald Michie, 'Turing's Test and Conscious Thought', *Artificial Intelligence* 60 (1993), 1–22, included with the kind permission of Elsevier Science B.V., Amsterdam, the Netherlands.

Robert French, 'Subcognition and the Limits of the Turing Test', *Mind* 99 (1990), 53–65, included with the kind permission of Oxford University Press, Oxford, England.

Clark Glymour, 'The Hierarchies of Knowledge and the Mathematics of Discovery', *Minds and Machines* 1 (1991), 75–95, included with the kind permission of Kluwer Academic Publishers, Dordrecht, the Netherlands.

Herbert Simon, 'Machine as Mind', Kenneth M. Ford, Clark Glymour, and Patrick J. Hayes (eds), *Android Epistemology* (MIT Press, 1995), included with the kind permission of MIT Press.

CONTENTS

Introduction   1
PETER MILLICAN

1. Subcognition and the Limits of the Turing Test   11
   ROBERT M. FRENCH

2. Turing's Test and Conscious Thought   27
   DONALD MICHIE

3. The Turing Test: AI's Biggest Blind Alley?   53
   BLAY WHITBY

4. The Intentional Stance and the Imitation Game   63
   AJIT NARAYANAN

5. Machine as Mind   81
   HERBERT SIMON

6. Minds, Machines, and Gödel: A Retrospect   103
   J. R. LUCAS

7. Human versus Mechanical Intelligence   125
   ROBIN GANDY

8. The Church-Turing Thesis: Its Nature and Status   137
   ANTONY GALTON

9. Measurement and Computational Description   165
   CHRIS FIELDS

10. Beyond Turing Equivalence   179
    AARON SLOMAN

11. The Demise of the Turing Machine in Complexity
    Theory   221
    IAIN A. STEWART

12. A Grammar-Based Approach to Common-Sense
   Reasoning   233
   PETER MOTT

13. Chaos: Its Past, Its Present, but Mostly Its Future   255
   JOSEPH FORD

14. The Hierarchies of Knowledge and the
   Mathematics of Discovery   265
   CLARK GLYMOUR

   Index   293

LIST OF CONTRIBUTORS

CHRIS FIELDS Vice President of Scientific Affairs at the National Center for Genome Resources, Santa Fe

JOSEPH FORD late Regents' Professor in the School of Physics, Georgia Institute of Technology, Atlanta

ROBERT M. FRENCH Research Scientist in the Psychology Department, University of Liège

ANTONY GALTON Lecturer in the Department of Computer Science, University of Exeter

ROBIN GANDY late Reader in Mathematical Logic in the University of Oxford

CLARK GLYMOUR Valtz Family Professor of Philosophy, University of California, and Alumni Professor, Carnegie Mellon University, Pittsburgh

J. R. LUCAS Fellow and Tutor in Philosophy at Merton College, Oxford

DONALD MICHIE Senior Fellow at the Turing Institute, Glasgow, and Professor Emeritus, University of Edinburgh

PETER MILLICAN Senior Lecturer in Philosophy and Computer Studies, University of Leeds

PETER MOTT Lecturer in the School of Computer Studies, University of Leeds

AJIT NARAYANAN Senior Lecturer in Computer Science and Dean of the Faculty of Science, University of Exeter

HERBERT SIMON Richard King Mellon University Professor of Computer Science and Psychology, Carnegie Mellon University

JOOP SCHOPMAN Independent Researcher based at the Faculty of Philosophy, University of Utrecht

MURRAY SHANAHAN Senior Research Fellow in the Department of Computer Science, Queen Mary and Westfield College, University of London

AZIZ SHAWKY Consultant at Knowledge Centre Cibit, Utrecht

CHRISTOPHER J. THORNTON Lecturer in the School of Cognitive and Computing Sciences, University of Sussex

Introduction

PETER MILLICAN

———◆———

This is the first of two volumes of essays in commemoration of
Alan Turing. It is centred on the continuing discussion of his
classic contributions to the theory of artificial intelligence and computer science, and in particular, the three most fundamental and
seminal ideas universally associated with his name: the Turing Test,
the Turing machine, and the Church–Turing thesis.

The Turing Test was first proposed in a paper that was to
become amongst philosophers (or at least those not specializing in
logic and computation) Turing's easily best-known work: 'Computing Machinery and Intelligence', published in *Mind* in 1950. It was
the fortieth anniversary of this publication that brought together,
at the Turing 1990 Colloquium, the impressive interdisciplinary
array of speakers and distinguished invited guests whose contributions, both at the Colloquium itself and subsequently, form the heart
of these two volumes. The level of discussion at the Colloquium
was such as to lead a number of the contributors to wish substan-
tially to revise or extend their papers, and given the significance of
the occasion, the relatively timeless nature of much of the subject-
matter, and the unusual opportunity for mutual response between
researchers across a variety of disciplines, it seemed appropriate
to delay immediate publication for this purpose. We hope that
this has allowed these collections, though conceived at the Turing
Colloquium 1990, to be more than just another conference proceedings, albeit one with an unusually impressive cast of contributors.
Among that cast, it is particularly gratifying to be able to include
two of the earliest and most influential pioneers of artificial intelligence, Donald Michie (who worked side by side with Turing,
codebreaking at Bletchley Park) and the Nobel laureate Herbert
Simon, and also Turing's doctoral student Robin Gandy.

THE TURING TEST AND THE IMITATION OF HUMAN COGNITION

Most of the papers in this volume allude in some way to the famous Turing Test, or the 'imitation game' on which it is based, and several make it a central theme. The idea is very well known: an interrogator is connected by teletype to two respondents, one of which is a human and the other a computer programmed to respond like a human. The interrogator then asks questions of each respondent, with a view to discovering which of them is which. Turing argues that such an imitation game provides a useful criterion of intelligence—if the computer were able to give sufficiently humanlike responses to resist identification in such circumstances, then it would be quite gratuitous to deny that it was behaving intelligently, irrespective of its alleged lack of a soul, an inner perspective, consciousness, or whatever.

Robert French does not dispute the Turing Test's adequacy as a positive criterion of intelligence, but he casts doubt on its usefulness by denying that any computer, intelligent or otherwise, could reasonably be expected to pass it. The problem he identifies is that the responses of any human in the imitation game will manifest numerous 'subcognitive' influences which will be virtually impossible for any respondent to mimic unless it has experienced the world in a humanlike way—the richness of our experience sets up a vast array of subcognitive associations which cannot realistically be formulated explicitly, or represented in a program, but which can be elicited by appropriately designed questions (e.g. 'Rate "Flugly" as the name of a teddy bear, and as the name of a glamorous female movie star'). The upshot is that the Turing Test is too demanding: it 'provides a guarantee not of intelligence but of culturally oriented *human* intelligence'.

Donald Michie's paper further brings out the significance of the subconscious levels of human thought, though he suggests that French's attack on the Turing Test may be slightly uncharitable given that Turing himself set a relatively low hurdle of success in the imitation game—the ability to deceive only to the extent of giving 'an average interrogator' no more than a '70 per cent chance of making the right identification after five minutes of questioning' (it is also worth bearing in mind here the comments that Gandy makes on page 125 regarding Turing's intentions in his famous paper). Michie begins his own discussion by drawing attention to a hitherto little-known 1947 lecture in which Turing proposed a number of trail-blazing ideas which later became quite standard in computer science. Especially relevant here is the notion that advanced computers would need a learning capacity, and in particular the ability to learn from contact with human beings and to 'adapt to their standards'. Michie points out that learning from humans is far from straightforward—typically as humans acquire expertise in a particular domain they become progressively *less* rather than more able to articulate their knowledge, and so effective learning from human experts must in practice involve the computer not just in passive reception of the expert's opinions, but in active induction of the rules being implicitly followed. This reveals a surprising flaw in the Turing Test—questions aimed at eliciting explicit knowledge of these rules could be answered much better by such a 'superarticulate' computer than by the human expert, but it seems odd to judge the machine a failure in the Test when it betrays its non-humanity by a superior cognitive performance.

Blay Whitby agrees with the negative points made by French and Michie regarding the adequacy of the Turing Test when interpreted as an operational definition of intelligence. However he regards this as a serious misinterpretation with unfortunate consequences, suggesting that it has led researchers in artificial intelligence to put far too much emphasis on the imitation of human performance, rather than on the achievement of a proper understanding of the abstract nature of intelligence and on autonomous developments based on such an understanding. He argues that the imitation game can instead more usefully be seen as a persuasive device to encourage a paradigm shift towards the now familiar perspective which distinguishes between the physical and the logical nature of a machine, and which regards these as potentially independent. The game forces the interrogator to judge respondents on the basis of their input–output behaviour rather than their physical characteristics, and it is this shift of perspective, together with a related emphasis on the significance of third-person attitudes rather than intrinsic characteristics in the ascription of 'intelligence', that marks the proper legacy of Turing's paper.

Ajit Narayanan takes up this theme of the importance of third-person attitudes in the ascription of intelligence, and begins from a reinterpretation of the imitation game based on Daniel Dennett's idea of the 'intentional stance'. According to this, the appropriate issue becomes not whether a computer can think, but rather whether it can properly have the intentional stance applied to it—whether its behaviour can usefully be seen as intentionally directed. This, however, is clearly an insufficient condition for consciousness or for any other more full-blooded notion on Dennett's 'ladder of personhood', so Narayanan proceeds to formulate a distinction between the 'representational stance' (concerned with the applicability of terms from a representational framework, based on behaviour alone) and the 'ascriptional stance' (which requires in addition a commitment to some underlying theory of consciousness, considered to be appropriate to the type of entity in question). The latter naturally raises 'meta-ascriptional' questions, concerned with the evaluation of ascription mechanisms, and Narayanan ends by suggesting a new interpretation of the imitation game at this third level.

Herbert Simon does not explicitly discuss the imitation game as such, but he approaches the question of whether machines can think in very much the same spirit as Turing, and is equally robust in the treatment of 'romantic' objections. His argument is two-pronged: on the one hand, he describes a considerable body of evidence, much of it garnered from his own research, that indicates the ways in which human cognitive processing actually operates; on the other, he points to a number of computer programs, again some of them his own, that have succeeded in operating 'intelligently' in strikingly similar ways. He concludes that 'we need not talk about computers thinking in the future tense; they have been thinking (in smaller or bigger ways) for forty years.' Simon's work indicates that the two interpretations of Turing distinguished by Whitby may not be so far apart—here we have investigations into the nature of human intelligence providing essential theoretical groundwork for the achievement of cognitive performances by computers that amount to much more than mere imitation.

A THEORETICAL BARRIER TO COMPUTER THOUGHT?

Though a champion of machine intelligence, Turing was of course one of those responsible (along with Kurt Gödel and Alonzo Church) for turning the world of logic upside down during the

1930s with a series of crucial negative results regarding the theoretical powers of computers and logical systems. In 1961, this irony was exploited by John Lucas in a famous—some would say notorious—paper entitled 'Minds, Machines and Gödel' (in the journal *Philosophy*), where he argued that the essential limits on formal computation implied by such results provided solid proof that human thought, which successfully discovered these limits, cannot be reduced to algorithmic processing, and hence cannot be copied (in at least this crucial respect) by a computer program. Lucas's article provoked a host of replies and 'refutations', and also inspired a number of other notable thinkers (most recently the theoretical physicist Roger Penrose) to pursue a similar line. For this volume he has written a typically forthright and uncompromising 'Retrospect' on the debate, in which he aims to refute his critics and confirm what must be, if successful, the most striking and fundamental conclusion about human nature ever to be drawn from a result in mathematical logic.

Responding to Lucas and Penrose on Turing's behalf, Robin Gandy considers some examples of what might be supposed to be non-algorithmic 'divine spark' thinking in mathematics and logic—for example the proof of Gödel's second theorem. He provides a fascinating insight into what goes on in the mathematician's mind when attempting to grapple with abstract objects such as infinite sequences, but dismisses the idea that the 'spark', when it comes, is really 'divine' or in any other way essentially resistant to mechanical modelling. It may indeed not be strictly *algorithmic*—but that is because it is *fallible* (and hence non-effective, in the technical sense), being based on such trains of thought as 'I see how it goes . . . ', 'Wouldn't it be nice if . . . ', 'This looks rather like that . . . ', and so on, rather than because it is *non-mechanical*. Gandy ends his paper by 'coming down off the fence on both sides', though his vision of the future of computers (as potential mathematical colleagues for example) is strikingly reminiscent of Turing's.

TURING COMPUTABILITY AND THE CHURCH–TURING THESIS

Speculation regarding the existence and potential fruitfulness of non-algorithmic thinking naturally raises issues concerning the scope and limits of what can properly be called algorithmic. And here we come to what is arguably Turing's crowning achievement—the definition of a precise notion of computability in terms of Turing machines, and the application of this to prove the unsolvability of Hilbert's *Entscheidungsproblem*. Here we are not concerned so much with the technical details of Turing's work but with its philosophical implications, and in particular with the question whether he is right to claim that our 'intuitive' concept of effective computability is completely exhausted by Turing machine computability (and the other precise notions of computability that have been proved to be equivalent, such as general recursiveness and λ-definability). This is the famous Church–Turing thesis, and provides the topic of Antony Galton's paper.

Galton explores the difficulties surrounding the interpretation and evaluation of the Church–Turing thesis (CT), some of which spring from its apparent oddity in asserting an equivalence between a precise notion (Turing machine computability) and a vague one (the idea of a computation which is intuitively 'effective'). This raises questions regarding its status: should CT be seen as a conceptual claim, or an empirical assertion, or even instead as a stipulation—a proposal to replace the vague intuitive notion with the precise one? To shed light on these issues Galton adopts a novel approach based on the semi-precise concept of *black-box computability*, which is intended to provide a more tractable substitute for the initutive notion, whilst retaining an appropriate level of indeterminacy. After considering its implications for CT, and a variety of possible conceptual revisions prompted by recent work (e.g. of David Deutsch and Chris Fields on quantum computability, and Iain Stewart's paper in this volume), Galton ends by discussing the relevance of CT to research in artificial intelligence.

Chris Fields, one of those whose earlier work is mentioned by Galton, here addresses the issue of what it is for a process to count as a computation, an issue which clearly has major significance for the interpretation and assessment of the Church–Turing thesis. Fields suggests an intimate connection between computation and measurement: a physical system can be considered as behaving computationally only when its states are measured, and the measurements are interpreted, in particular ways. This has an important implication, because the methods of measurement and interpretation employed by computer science are independent of whether the system under study is natural or an artefact. Fields concludes that whether a system is to count as a computer is a pragmatic question, to be answered by considering the explanatory utility of computational descriptions of its behaviour.

Aaron Sloman covers similar ground to Fields, drawing some similar conclusions. He is concerned to make clear what counts as a 'computational process', where such processes are to be understood as what underlies intelligence. In this sense, he insists, the notion is broader than Turing machine computability, but unfortunately there is no clear way to delineate it, since if our definition is extended to include all the kinds of processes that play a role in intelligence, it will become hard if not impossible to draw any line between computational and non-computational processes without falling into circularity. He therefore recommends abandoning the idea that any precisely defined concept of computation can be the key notion underlying intelligence, and instead recommends the study of a variety of architectures and mechanisms, with the aim of developing a new theory-based taxonomy of cognitive processes.

BEYOND THE TURING MACHINE: NEW HORIZONS

The Turing machine provided the first clear, precise, and determinate specification of a computing machine, and has since proved itself to be an immensely valuable reference point for developments in computability and complexity theory. But Iain Stewart argues that in some important areas of the latter field, at least, the Turing machine has had its day, and could profitably be replaced as an analytical tool by an appropriate formal logic. This makes the representation of a problem more natural, and also its transformation into an executable high-level program. It even has potential pedagogic advantages in demonstrating how the study of complexity theory has genuine relevance to practical computer programs rather than just to the apparently artificial workings of a theoretical Turing machine. Stewart readily concedes, however, that Turing's brainchild will retain its place as a more general unifying concept, given the inability of his own logical treatment to deal with problems of arbitrary complexity.

Peter Mott's paper is in somewhat the same spirit as Stewart's, in that it advocates a move from an artificial to a more natural medium of representation for the treatment of complex problems. Here, however, the field is common-sense reasoning rather than complexity theory, and formal logic now plays the role of target rather than proposed replacement. The traditional Montague paradigm for modelling linguistic reasoning, which Mott opposes, involves the translation of sentences into logical formulae, with inferential operations being performed on those formulae, and conclusions finally being retranslated back into sentences. Mott recommends instead the direct use of natural language as an inferential medium, cutting out the logical middleman by means of what he calls 'grammar-based inference'. This can dramatically reduce the complexity of common-sense reasoning, though admittedly at the cost of some loss of rigour, and it no doubt provides a far more plausible model of how our own reasoning actually takes place. It is also tantalizingly reminiscent of ancient syllogistic logics—raising the intriguing possibility that such logics, rejected in the past because of the alleged complexity and multiplicity of their forms, could ultimately be rehabilitated in the computer age by the recognition that mere linear complexity of forms is quite insignificant compared with the intractable exponential complexity that can result when we try to model reasoning using our traditional formal systems.

Joseph Ford is well known as the 'Evangelist of Chaos', spreading the word of this new scientific 'paradigm' with an enthusiasm and style characteristic of the Southern states. His paper provides an engaging introduction to this exciting field, with useful pointers for those who wish to pursue its potentially dramatic implications for the theories of complexity, computability, and information. Ford particularly draws attention to the important discovery by Greg Chaitin of an information theoretical analogue to Gödel's theorem, proving 'that there exist naturally occurring, simple questions whose answers are so complex they contain more information than exists in all our human logical systems combined.' Physics provides such questions, and Ford examines some of the uncomfortable implications of the new paradigm for physical measurement before suggesting, with the aid of two examples, that chaos may nevertheless provide an ally rather than an enemy in the attempt to tame complexity, enabling us 'to solve incredibly complex problems by letting controlled chaos do the work'. He then provides a brief discussion of the place of chaos in the quantum world (which according to Penrose provides the essential substructure of human intelligence) before concluding with a typically evangelistic coda.

The collection ends with yet another example of work illustrating the great breadth of philosophical ideas taking significant inspiration from Turing. This is the development, pursued by Clark Glymour amongst others, of a mathematical 'theory of discovery'. The extent of Turing's influence here is perhaps surprising, because the famous negative results which he, Gödel, and Church established, by ruling out an algorithmic decision procedure even for the limited domain of first-order logic, may have seemed to close the door on any interesting formal treatment of epistemology. But Glymour sketches how the notion of 'knowledge in the limit', formulated by Gold and Putnam in 1965, has provided the key to open a new and fascinating field of investigation, which builds on the theories of mathematical logic, computation, and recursion, and has potential implications in many areas including not only the philosophy of science, but also artificial intelligence, cognitive neuropsychology, economics, and even, intriguingly, the formal treatment of epistemological relativism.

I

Subcognition and the Limits of the Turing Test

ROBERT M. FRENCH

———•———

INTRODUCTION

Alan Turing, in his original article[1] about an imitation-game definition of intelligence, seems to be making two separate claims. The first, the philosophical claim, is that if a machine could pass the Turing Test, it would necessarily be intelligent. This claim I believe to be correct.[2] His second point, the pragmatic claim, is that in the not-too-distant future it would in fact be possible actually to build such a machine. Turing clearly felt that it was important to establish both claims. He realized, in particular, that if one could rigorously show that *no* machine could ever pass his test, his philosophical point, while still true, would lose a great deal of significance. He thus devoted considerable effort to establishing not only the philosophical claim but also the pragmatic claim.

Ever since his article appeared most philosophers have concentrated almost exclusively on attacking or defending the philosophical claim. There are those who believe that passing the Turing Test constitutes a sufficient condition for intelligence and those who do not. The philosophical importance of this first claim is that it

I especially wish to thank Daniel Dennett and Douglas Hofstadter for their invaluable comments on the ideas and emphasis of this paper. I would also like to thank David Chalmers, Melanie Mitchell, David Moser, and the editor of *Mind* for their remarks.

[1] Alan M. Turing, 'Computing Machinery and Intelligence', *Mind*, 59 (1950), 433–60.

[2] For a particularly clear defence of this view see D. C. Dennett, 'Can Machines Think?', in *How We Know*, ed. Michael Shafto, San Francisco, Calif.: Harper & Row, 1985.

provided a clean and novel test for intelligence that neatly side-stepped the vast philosophical quagmire of the mind–body problem. The philosophical claim translates elegantly into an operational definition of intelligence: whatever *acts* sufficiently intelligent *is* intelligent.

However, in this paper I will take issue with Turing's pragmatic claim, arguing that the very capacity of the Turing Test to probe the deepest, most essential areas of human cognition makes it virtually useless as a real test for intelligence. I strongly disagree with Hubert Dreyfus's claim, for example, that 'as a goal for those actually trying to construct thinking machines, and as a criterion for critics to use in evaluating their work, Turing's test was just what was needed.'[3] We will see that the Turing Test could be passed only by things that have experienced the world as we have experienced it, and this leads to the central point of the present paper, namely, that *the Test provides a guarantee not of intelligence but of culturally-oriented* human *intelligence*.

I establish this consequence of the Turing Test by proposing a first set of 'subcognitive' questions that are explicitly designed to reveal low-level cognitive structure. Critics might object that there is something unfair about this type of question and suggest that it be disallowed. This leads to another important claim of this paper, which is that in fact, there is no way to distinguish questions that are subcognitive from those that are not. Close examination of some of the original questions of the Turing Test reveals that they, too, are subcognitive. In like manner, any sufficiently broad set of questions making up a Turing Test would necessarily contain questions that rely on subcognitive associations for their answers. I will show that it is impossible to tease apart 'subcognitive' questions from ones that are not. From this it follows that the cognitive and subcognitive levels are inextricably intertwined.

It is this essential inseparability of the subcognitive and cognitive levels—and for that matter even the physical and cognitive levels—that makes the Turing Test a test for *human* intelligence, not intelligence in general. This fact, while admittedly interesting, is not particularly useful if our goal is to gain insight into intelligence in general. But if we cannot use the Turing Test to this end, it may

[3] Hubert L. Dreyfus, *What Computers Can't Do: A Critique of Artificial Reason* New York: Harper & Row, 1972: 73.

turn out that the best (or possibly only) way of discussing general intelligence will be in terms of categorization abilities, the capacity to learn new concepts, to adapt old concepts to a new environment, and so on. Perhaps what philosophers in the field of artificial intelligence need is not simply a *test* for intelligence but rather a *theory* of intelligence. The precise elements of this theory are, as they were in 1950 when Turing proposed his imitation-game test, still the subject of much controversy.

ON NORDIC SEAGULLS

Consider the following parable: It so happens that the only flying animals known to the inhabitants of a large Nordic island are seagulls. Everyone on the island acknowledges, of course, that seagulls can fly. One day the two resident philosophers on the island are overheard trying to pin down what 'flying' is really all about.

Says the first philosopher, 'The essence of flying is to move through the air.'

'But you would hardly call this flying, would you?' replies the second, tossing a pebble from the beach out into the ocean.

'Well then, perhaps it means to remain aloft for a certain amount of time.'

'But clouds and smoke and children's balloons remain aloft for a very long time. And I can certainly keep a kite in the air as long as I want on a windy day. It seems to me that there must be more to flying than merely staying aloft.'

'Maybe it involves having wings and feathers.'

'Penguins have both, and we all know how well they fly ... '.

And so on. Finally, they decide to settle the question by, in effect, avoiding it. They do this by first agreeing that the only examples of objects that they are absolutely certain can fly are the seagulls that populate their island. They do, however, agree that flight has something to do with being airborne and that physical features such as feathers, beaks, and hollow bones probably are superficial aspects of flight. On the basis of these assumptions and their knowledge of Alan Turing's famous article about a test for intelligence, they hit upon the Seagull Test for flight. The Seagull

Test is meant to be a very rigorous sufficient condition for flight. Henceforth, if someone says, 'I have invented a machine that can fly', instead of attempting to apply any set of flight-defining criteria to the inventor's machine, they will put it to the Seagull Test. The *only* things that they will certify with absolute confidence as being able to fly are those that can pass the Seagull Test. On the other hand, they agree that if something fails the Test, they will not pass judgement; maybe it can fly, maybe it can not.

The Seagull Test works much like the Turing Test. Our philosophers have two three-dimensional radar screens, one of which tracks a real seagull; the other will track the putative flying machine. They may run any imaginable experiment on the two objects in an attempt to determine which is the seagull and which is the machine, but they may watch them only on their radar screens. The machine will be said to have passed the Seagull Test for flight if both philosophers are indefinitely unable to distinguish the seagull from the machine.

An objection might be raised that some of their tests (for example, testing for the ability to dip in flight) might have nothing to do with flying. The philosophers would reply: 'So what? We are looking for a sufficient condition for flight, not a *minimal* sufficient condition. Furthermore, we understand that ours is a very hard test to pass, but rest assured, inventors of flying machines, failing the Test proves nothing. We will not claim that your machine *cannot* fly if it fails the Seagull Test; it may very well be able to. However we, as philosophers, want to be absolutely certain we have a true case of flight, and the only way we can be sure of this is if your machine passes the Seagull Test.'

Now, of course, the Seagull Test will rightly take bullets, soap bubbles, and snowballs out of the running. This is certainly as it should be. But helicopters and jet airplanes—which *do* fly—would also never pass it. Nor, for that matter, would bats or beetles, albatrosses or hummingbirds. In fact, under close scrutiny, probably only seagulls would pass the Seagull Test, and maybe only seagulls from the philosophers' Nordic island, at that. What we have is thus not a test for flight at all, but rather a test for flight as practised by a Nordic seagull.

For the Turing Test, the implications of this metaphor are clear: an entity could conceivably be extremely intelligent but, if it did not respond to the interrogator's questions in a thoroughly human way, it would not pass the Test. The *only* way, I believe, that it would have been able to respond the questions in a perfectly humanlike manner is to have experienced the world as humans have. What we have is thus not a test for intelligence at all, but rather a test for intelligence as practised by a human being.

Furthermore, the Turing Test admits of no degrees in its sufficient determination of intelligence, in spite of the fact that the intuitive human notion of intelligence clearly does. Spiders, for example, have little intelligence, sparrows have more but not as much as dogs, monkeys have still more but not as much as 8-year-old humans, who in turn have less than adults. If we agree that the underlying neural mechanisms are essentially the same across species, then we ought to treat intelligence as a continuum and not just as something that only humans have. It seems reasonable to ask a good test for intelligence to reflect, if only approximately, those differences in degree. It is especially important in the study of artificial intelligence that researchers not treat intelligence as an all-or-nothing phenomenon.

SUBCOGNITIVE QUESTIONS

Before beginning the discussion of subcognitive questions, I wish to make a few assumptions that I feel certain Turing would have accepted. First, I will allow the interrogator to poll humans for the answers to some of the questions prior to posing them during the imitation game itself. (I will call the humans who are polled the 'interviewees'.) I also want to make explicit an assumption that is tacit in Turing's article, namely that the human candidate and the interrogator (and, in this case, the interviewees) are all from the same culture and that the computer will be attempting to pass as an individual from that culture. Thus, if ever the computer replies, 'I don't speak English' or something of the sort, the interrogator will immediately deduce, rightly, that the other candidate is the human being. Finally, while I believe that it is *theoretically* possible to build a machine capable of experiencing the world in a manner indistinguishable from a human being— a machine that can fall off bicycles, be scratched by thorns on roses, smell sewage, and taste strawberries—, I will assume that no computer is now, or will in the foreseeable future be, in a position to do so.

I will designate as *subcognitive* any question capable of providing a window on low-level (i.e. unconscious) cognitive structure. By 'low-level cognitive structure' I am referring, in particular, to the subconscious associative network in human minds that consists of highly overlapping activatable representations of experience. This is the level currently being explored by new approaches to cognitive modelling.[4]

The first class of questions is explicitly designed to reveal low-level cognitive structure (and I think everyone will agree that they do so). I will respond to the anticipated objection that these explicitly subcognitive questions are unfair by following up with another set of questions that seem, at first glance, to be at a higher cognitive level than the first set. These questions will turn out, under closer examination, to be subcognitive also. I will conclude with a final set of questions that seem uncontestably to be innocent high-level cognitive questions but that will be just as hard as the others were for the computer to answer in the way a human would.

ASSOCIATIVE PRIMING

This first set of questions is based on current research on associative priming, often called semantic facilitation. The idea is the following. Humans, over the course of their lives, develop certain associations of varying strength among concepts. By means of the so-called lexical decision task it has been established[5] that it requires less time to decide that a given item is a word when that item is

---

[4] Three different approaches that all address subcognitive issues can be found in: J. A. Feldman and D. H. Ballard, 'Connectionist Models and Their Properties', *Cognitive Science*, 6(1982), 205–54; D. R. Hofstadter and the Fluid Analysis Research Group, *Fluid Concepts and Creative Analogies*, New York: Basic Books (1995); D. Rumelhart and J. McClelland (eds.), *Parallel Distributed Processing*, Cambridge, Mass.: Bradford/MIT Press, 2 vols, 1986.

[5] A particularly relevant, succinct discussion of associative priming can be found in J. R. Anderson, *The Architecture of Cognition*, Cambridge, Mass.: Harvard University Press, 1983, ch. 3: 86–125. In this chapter Anderson makes reference to the classic work on facilitation by Meyer and Schvaneveldt (D. E. Meyer and R. W. Schvaneveldt, 'Facilitation in Recognizing Pairs of Words: Evidence of a Dependence between Retrieval Operations', *Journal of Experimental Psychology* (1971), 227–34).

preceded by an associated word. If, for example, the item 'butter' is preceded by the word 'bread', it would take significantly less time to recognize that 'butter' was a word than had an unassociated word like 'dog' or a nonsense word preceded it.

The Turing Test interrogator makes use of this phenomenon as follows. The day before the Test, she selects a set of words (and non-words), runs the lexical decision task on the interviewees and records average recognition times. She then comes to the Test armed with the results of this initial test, asks both candidates to perform the same task she ran the day before, and records the results. Once this has been done, she identifies as the human being the candidate whose results more closely resemble the average results produced by her sample population of interviewees.

The machine would invariably fail this type of test because there is no a priori way of determining associative strengths (i.e. a measure of how easy it is for one concept to activate another) between *all* possible concepts. Virtually the only way a machine could determine, even on average, all of the associative strengths between human concepts is to have experienced the world as the human candidate and the interviewees had.

A further example might help to illustrate the enormous problem of establishing the associative weights between concepts in an a priori manner. Certain groups of concepts, say, the steps in baking a cake, are profoundly sequential in nature. The associative strengths between sequentially related concepts involved in baking a cake (opening the flour bin, breaking the eggs, mixing the flour and eggs, putting the mixture in the oven, setting the oven temperature, removing a baked cake) are profoundly dependent on the human experience of cake-baking. Even if we made the assumption that concepts like 'removing a cake from an oven', 'breaking eggs', 'setting oven temperature', and so on could be explicitly programmed into our computer, the associative strengths among these concepts would have to reflect the temporal order in which they normally occurred in human experience if the machine were to pass the Turing Test. We would have to be able to set these strengths in an a priori manner, not only for category sequences associated with cake-baking, but also between the concepts of *all* the concept sequences experienced by humans. While this may be theoretically possible, it would certainly seem to be very implausible.

Now, suppose a critic claims that these explicitly subcognitive questions are unfair because—ostensibly, at least—they have nothing to do with intelligence; they probe, the critic says, a cognitive level well below that necessary for intelligence and therefore they should be disallowed. Suppose, then, that we obligingly disallow such questions and propose in their stead a new set of questions that seem, at first glance, to be at a higher cognitive level.

RATING GAMES

Neologisms will form the basis of the next set of questions, which we might call the Neologism Rating Game. Our impressions involving made-up words provide particularly impressive examples of the 'unbelievable number of forces and factors that interact in our unconscious processing of even . . . words and names only a few letters long'.[6]

Consider the following set of questions, all having a totally high-level cognitive appearance:

On a scale of 0 (completely implausible) to 10 (completely plausible), please rate:

- 'Flugblogs' as a name Kellogg's would give to a new breakfast cereal
- 'Flugblogs' as the name of a new computer company
- 'Flugblogs' as the name of big, air-filled bags worn on the feet and used to walk on water
- 'Flugly' as the name a child might give its favourite teddy bear
- 'Flugly' as the surname of a bank accountant in a W. C. Fields movie
- 'Flugly' as the surname of a glamorous female movie star

The interrogator will give, say, between fifty and one hundred questions of this sort to her interviewees,[7] who will answer them. Then,

---

[6] D. R. Hofstadter, 'On the Seeming Paradox of Mechanizing Creativity', in *Metamagical Themas*, New York: Basic Books, 1985: 526–46.

[7] Even though Turing did not impose a time constraint in his original formulation of the imitation game, he did claim that 'in about fifty years' time [i.e. by the year 2000] it will be possible to programme computers . . . to make them play the imitation game so well that an average interrogator will not have more than 70%

as before, she will give the same set of questions to the two candidates and compare their results to her interviewees' averaged answers. The candidate whose results most closely resemble the answers given by the polled group will almost certainly be the human.

Let us examine a little more closely why a computer that had not acquired our full set of cultural associations would fail this test. Consider 'Flugblogs' as the name of a breakfast cereal. It is unquestionably pretty awful. The initial syllable 'flug' phonetically activates (unconsciously, of course) such things as 'flub', 'thug', 'ugly', or 'ugh!', each with its own aura of semantic connotations. 'Blogs', the second syllable, activates 'blob', 'bog', and other words, which in turn activate a halo of other semantic connotations. The sum total of this spreading activation determines how we react, at a conscious level, to the word. And while there will be no precise set of associated connotations for all individuals across a culture, on the whole there is enough overlap to provoke *similar* reactions to given words and phrases. In this case, the emergent result of these activations is undeniable: 'Flugblogs' would be a lousy name for a cereal (unless, of course, the explicit *intent* of the manufacturer is to come up with a perverse-sounding cereal name!).

What about 'Flugly' as a name a child might give its favourite teddy bear? Now *that* certainly sounds plausible. In fact, it's kind of cute. But, on the surface at least, 'Flugblogs' and 'Flugly' seem to have quite a bit in common; if nothing else, both words have a common first syllable. But 'Flugly', unlike 'Flugblogs', almost certainly activates 'snugly' and 'cuddly', which would bring to mind feelings of cosiness, warmth, and friendship. It certainly also activates 'ugly', which might normally provoke a rather negative feeling, but, in this case, there are competing positive associations of vulnerability and endearment activated by the notion of children and things that children like. To see this, we need look no further than the tale of the Ugly Duckling. In the end, the positive associations seem to dominate the unpleasant sense of 'ugly'. The

chance of making the right identification after five minutes of questioning' (p. 442). In current discussions of the Turing Test, the duration of the questioning period is largely ignored. In my opinion, one reasonable extension of the Turing Test would include the length of the questioning period as one of its parameters. In keeping with the spirit of the original claim involving a five-minute questioning period, I have tried to keep the number of questions short although it was by no means necessary to have done so.

outcome of this subcognitive competition means that 'Flugly' is perceived by us as being a cute, quite plausible name for a child's teddy bear. And yet, different patterns of activations rule out 'Flugly' as a plausible name for a glamorous female movie star.

Imagine, for an instant, what it would take for a computer to pass this test. To begin with, there is no way it could look up words like 'flugly' and 'flugblogs': they do not exist. To judge the appropriateness of any given word (or, in this case, nonsense words) in a particular context requires taking unconscious account of a vast number of culturally acquired, competing associations triggered initially by phonetic resemblances. And, even though one might succeed in giving a program a certain number of these associations (for example, by asking subjects questions similar to the ones above and then programming the results into the machine), the space of neologisms is virtually infinite. The human candidate's reaction to such made-up words is an emergent result of myriad subcognitive pressures, and unless the machine has a set of associations similar to those of humans both in degree and in kind, its performance in the Rating Game would necessarily differ more from the interviewees' averaged performance than would the human candidate's. Once again, a machine that had not experienced the world as we have would be unmasked by the Rating Game, even though the questions comprising it seemed, at least at the outset, so cognitively high-level in nature.

If, for some reason, the critics were still unhappy with the Neologism Rating Game using made-up words, we could consider a variation on the game, the Category Rating Game,[8] in which all of the questions would have the form: 'Rate Xs as Ys' (0 = 'could be no worse', 10 = 'could be no better') where X and Y are any two categories. Such questions give every appearance of being high-level cognitive questions: they are simple in the extreme and rely not on neologisms but on everyday words. For example, we might have, 'Rate *dry leaves* as *hiding places*'. Now, clearly no definition of 'dry leaves' will ever include the fact that piles of dry autumn leaves are wonderful places for children to hide in and, yet, few among us would not make that association upon seeing the juxtaposition of those two concepts. There is therefore some overlap, however implausible this might seem a priori, between

---

[8] This variation of the Rating Game was suggested to me by Douglas Hofstadter.

the categories of 'dry leaves' and 'hiding places'. We might give dry leaves a rating of, say, 4 on a 10-point scale. Or, another example, 'Rate *radios* as *musical instruments*'. As in the previous example, people do not usually think of radios as musical instruments, but they do indeed have some things in common with musical instruments: both make sounds; both are designed to be listened to; John Cage once wrote a piece in which radios were manipulated by performers; etc. Once again, therefore, there is some overlapping of these two categories; as a musical instrument, therefore, we might give a radio a rating of 3 or even 4 on a 10-point scale.

The answer to any particular rating question is necessarily based on how we view the two categories involved, each with its full panoply of associations, acquired through experience, with other categories. A list of such questions might include:

- 'Rate *banana splits* as *medicine*'
- 'Rate *grand pianos* as *wheelbarrows*'
- 'Rate *purses* as *weapons*'
- 'Rate *pens* as *weapons*'
- 'Rate *jackets* as *blankets*'
- 'Rate *pine boughs* as *mattresses*'

Just as before, it would be virtually impossible to explicitly program into the machine all the various types and degrees of associations necessary to answer these questions like a human.

Other variations of the Rating Game could be invented that would have the same effect. We could, for example, have a Poetic Beauty Rating Game where we would ask for ratings of beauty of various lines of poetry.[9] For a computer to do as well as a human on this test, it would either have to have experienced our life and language *as we had* or contain a theory of poetic beauty that included necessary and sufficient conditions for what constituted a beautiful line of poetry. Few would seriously argue that such an experience-independent theory was possible.

Or a Joke Rating Game: 'On a scale of 0 to 10 rate how funny you find each of the following jokes' followed by a list of jokes. Again, capturing the necessary and sufficient conditions for humour

[9] In fact, the interrogator in Turing's original article does indeed conduct a line of questioning about a particular turn of phrase in one of Shakespeare's sonnets.

would seem to require a grounding in all of human experience. Most jokes depend on a vast network of associative world knowledge ranging from the most ridiculous trivia, through common but little-commented-upon aspects of human experience, to the most significant information about current events. So here again is an example of where a computer, in order to appreciate humour as we did and thereby fool the Turing Test interrogator, would almost certainly have had to experience life and language as we had.

A final variation: the Advertising Rating Game. 'Given the following product: X, rate the following advertising slogan Y for that product.' Once again, it is hard to imagine any theory that could provide necessary and sufficient conditions for catchy advertising slogans. Good advertising slogans, like good jokes and good lines of poetry, are perceived as good because of the myriad subconscious pressures and associations gathered in a lifetime of experiencing the world.

THE IMPOSSIBILITY OF ISOLATING THE PHYSICAL LEVEL FROM THE COGNITIVE LEVEL

One of the tacit assumptions on which Turing's proposed test rests is that it is possible to isolate the 'mere' (and thus unimportant to the essence of cognition) physical level from the (essential) cognitive level. This is the reason, for example, that the candidates communicate with the interrogator by teletype, that the interrogator is not permitted to see them, and so on. Subcognitive questions, however, will always allow the interrogator to 'peek behind the screen'. The Turing Test is really probing the associative concept (and sub-concept) networks of the two candidates. These networks are the product of a lifetime of interaction with the world which *necessarily involves* human sense organs, their location on the body, their sensitivity to various stimuli, etc. Consider, for example, a being that resembled us precisely in all physical respects except that its eyes were attached to its knees. This physical difference alone would engender enormous differences in its associative concept network compared to our own. Bicycle-riding, crawling on the floor, wearing various articles of clothing (e.g. long pants), and negotiating crowded hallways would all be experienced in a vastly different way by this individual.

The result would be an associative concept network that would be significantly—and detectably by the Turing Test—different from our own. Thus, while no one would claim that the physical location of eyes had anything essential to do with intelligence, a Turing Test could certainly distinguish this individual from a normal human being. The moral of the story is that the physical level is *not* disassociable from the cognitive level. When Dreyfus says that no one expects an intelligent robot to be able to 'get across a busy street. It must only compete in the more objective and disembodied areas of human behaviour, so as to be able to win at Turing's game',[10] he, like Turing, is tacitly accepting that such a separation of the physical and the cognitive levels is indeed possible. This may have seemed to be the case at first glance but further examination shows that the two are inextricably intertwined.

CAN THE TURING TEST BE APPROPRIATELY MODIFIED?

Any reasonable set of questions in a Turing Test will necessarily contain subcognitive questions in some form or another. Ask enough of these questions and the computer will become distinguishable from the human because its associative concept network would necessarily be unlike ours. And thus the computer would fail the Turing Test.

Is it possible to modify the rules of the Turing Test in such a way that subcognitive questions are forbidden? I think not. The answers to subcognitive questions emerge from a lifetime of experience with the minutiae of existence, ranging from functionally adaptive world-knowledge to useless trivia. The sum total of this experience with its extraordinarily complex interrelations is what defines human intelligence and this is what Turing's imitation game tests for. What we would really like is a test for (or, lacking that, a theory of) intelligence *in general*. Surely, we would not want to limit a Turing Test to questions like, 'What is the capital of France?', or 'How many sides does a triangle have?' If we admit that intelligence in general must have *something* to do with categorization, analogy-making, and so on, we will of course

---

[10] Dreyfus, *What Computers Can't Do*, 78.

want to ask questions that test these capacities. But these are the very questions that will allow us, unfailingly, to unmask the computer.

THE RELEVANCE OF SUBCOGNITIVE FACTORS

There remains the question of the *relevance* of these subcognitive factors that, as I believe I have shown, make it essentially impossible for a machine that has not experienced the world as we have to pass the Turing Test. Are these factors irrelevant to intelligence—just as a seagull's dipping in flight is irrelevant to flying in general—or are they a necessary substrate of intelligence? An initial part of my response is that a *human* subcognitive substrate is definitely not necessary to intelligence in general. The Turing Test tests precisely for the presence of a human subcognitive substrate and this is why it is limited as a test for general intelligence.

On the other hand, I believe that *some* subcognitive substrate is necessary to intelligence. I will not present a detailed defence of this view in this paper for two reasons: first, such a defence is beyond the scope of this paper, the goal of which has only been to discuss the limits of the Turing Test as a tool for determining intelligence, and second, the necessity of a subcognitive substrate for intelligence has been compellingly argued elsewhere.[11] Some ideas of the defence will, however, be briefly presented below.

There is little question that intelligence relies on an extraordinarily complex network of concepts with various degrees of overlap. Philosophers from Wittgenstein[12] to Lakoff[13] have shown that the boundaries of concepts are extraordinarily elusive things to pin down. It is probably impossible, even in principle, to describe categories in an absolute, objective manner. 'Apples', for example, are almost always members of the category 'food', but what about 'grass', or 'shoes'? If you have not eaten for ten days, 'shoes' might well fall into your category of 'food'. But could something

---

[11] Hofstadter, 'Waking Up from the Boolean Dream, *or*, Subcognition as Computation', in *Metamagical Themas*, 631–65.

[12] Ludwig Wittgenstein, *Philosophical Investigations*, New York: Macmillan, 1958.

[13] George Lakoff, *Women, Fire and Dangerous Things*, Chicago: University of Chicago Press, 1987.

like 'the Spanish Inquisition' ever be considered 'food'? (Of course. Consider the following statement by a professor about to give an extraordinarily long lecture on medieval methods of torture: 'The meat of the first three hours of this lecture will be medieval torture in general. And if none of you has fallen asleep by then, we'll have the Spanish Inquisition for dessert.')[14] This is not a point to be taken lightly, for the associative overlap of categories essential to intelligence (and creativity) frequently occurs near the blurry boundaries of categories. And, to repeat, these boundaries are virtually impossible to define in an objective, context-independent way. Most of our thought processes are intimately tied to the associative overlap of categories. One particular example is analogy-making. Considered by many to be a *sine qua non* of intelligent behaviour, it relies heavily on the ability to see two apparently unrelated situations as members, however obliquely, of the same category.

If we can view categories as being composed of many tiny (subcognitive) parts that can overlap with the subcognitive parts of other categories, we can go a long way to explaining these associative phenomena. If, on the other hand, we deny the relevance of subcognitive factors in intelligence, we are left with the daunting, perhaps impossible, task of explicitly defining *all* of the possible attributes of each particular category in every conceivable context. It is, therefore reasonable to conclude that all intelligence has a subcognitive substrate. In particular, this implies that an intelligent computer would have to possess such a substrate, though there is no reason to believe that this substrate would be identical to our own.

CONCLUSION

In conclusion, the imitation game proposed by Alan Turing provides a very powerful means of probing humanlike cognition. But when the Test is actually used as a real test for intelligence, as certain philosophers propose, its very strength becomes a weakness. Turing invented the imitation game only as a novel way of looking at the question 'Can machines think?' But it turns out to

---

[14] This example is due to Peter Suber.

be so powerful that it is really asking: 'Can machines think exactly like human beings?' As a real test for intelligence, the latter question is significantly less interesting than the former. The Turing Test provides a sufficient condition for human intelligence but does not address the more important issue of intelligence in general.

I have tried to show that only a computer that had acquired adult human intelligence by experiencing the world as we have could pass the Turing Test. In addition, I feel that any attempt to 'fix' the Turing Test so that it could test for intelligence in general and not just human intelligence is doomed to failure because of the completely interwoven and interdependent nature of the human physical, subcognitive, and cognitive levels. To gain insight into intelligence, we will be forced to consider it in the more elusive terms of the ability to categorize, to generalize, to make analogies, to learn, and so on. It is with respect to these abilities that the computer will always be unmasked if it has not experienced the world as a human being has.

2

Turing's Test and Conscious Thought

DONALD MICHIE

———◆———

INTRODUCTION

Although its text is now available,[1] there is little awareness of a remarkable lecture delivered to the London Mathematical Society on 20 February 1947. The lecturer was Alan Turing. His topic was the nature of programmable digital computers, taking as his exemplar the 'Automatic Computing Engine' (ACE) then under construction at the National Physical Laboratory. At that time no stored-program machine was yet operational anywhere in the world. So each one of his deeply considered points blazes a trail—logical equivalence to the Universal Turing machine of hardware constructions such as the ACE, the uses of variable-length precision, the need for large paged memories, the nature of 'while' loops, the idea of the subroutine, the possibility of remote access, the automation of I/O, and the concept of the operating system. Turing then considers the eventual possibility of automating the craft of programming, itself scarcely yet invented. He further discusses the forms of predictable resistance to such automation among those whom today we call DP (data-processing) staff:

They may be unwilling to let their jobs be stolen from them in this way. In that case they would surround the whole of their work with mystery

In preparing and revising this review I was assisted by facilities at the Turing Institute, Glasgow, UK, and from Virginia Polytechnic Institute and State University during tenure of a C. C. Garvin Endowed Visiting Professorship. I owe thanks to colleagues at both these institutions, and also to the referees for their helpful criticisms. I also had the great benefit of comments on an early draft from Professor Colwyn Trevarthen and from Dr Patricia Churchland, both of whom pointed me to relevant materials and sources.
[1] B. E. Carpenter and R. W. Doran (eds.), *A. M. Turing's Ace Report and Other Papers* (MIT Press, Cambridge, Mass., 1986).

and make excuses, couched in well chosen gibberish, whenever any dangerous suggestions were made. (p. 121)

We then read

[t]his topic [of automatic programming] naturally leads to the question as to how far it is possible in principle for a computing machine to simulate human activities [p.121],

and the lecturer launches into the theme which we know today as artificial intelligence (AI).

Turing put forward three positions:

POSITION 1. *Programming could be done in symbolic logic and would then require the construction of appropriate interpreters.*
POSITION 2. *Machine learning is needed so that computers can discover new knowledge inductively from experience as well as deductively.*
POSITION 3. *Humanized interfaces are required to enable machines to adapt to people, so as to acquire knowledge tutorially.*

I reproduce relevant excerpts below, picking out particular phrases in bold type.

1. *Turing on logic programming*

I expect that digital computing machines will eventually stimulate a considerable interest in **symbolic logic and mathematical philosophy**. . . . in principle one should be able to communicate in any symbolic logic, provided that the machine were given instruction tables which would enable it to **interpret that logical system**. (p. 122)

2. *Turing on machine learning*

Let us suppose we have set up a machine with certain initial instruction tables, so constructed that these tables might on occasion, if good reason arose, **modify those tables**. One can imagine that after the machine had been operating for some time, the instructions would have altered out of all recognition, but nevertheless still be such that one would have to admit that the machine was still doing very worthwhile calculations. Possibly it might still be getting results of the type desired when the machine was first set up, but in a much more efficient manner. In such a case one would have to admit that the progress of the machine had not been foreseen when its original instructions were put in. It would be like a pupil who had learnt much from his master, but had **added much more by his own work**. (pp. 122–3)

3. *Turing on cognitive compatibility*

No man adds very much to the body of knowledge; why should we expect more of a machine? Putting the same point differently, the machine must be allowed to have **contact with human beings** in order that it may **adapt itself to their standards**. (p. 124)

AI's inventory of fundamental ideas due to Turing would not be complete without the proposal which he put forward three years later in the philosophical journal *Mind*, known today as the 'Turing Test'. The key move was to define intelligence *operationally*, i.e. in terms of the computer's ability, tested over a typewriter link, to sustain a simulation of an intelligent human when subjected to questioning. Published accounts usually overstate the scope proposed by Turing for his 'imitation game', presenting the aim of the machine's side as successful deceit of the interrogator throughout a lengthy dialogue. But Turing's original imitation game asked only for a rather weak level of success over a relatively short period of interrogation.

I believe that in about fifty years' time it will be possible to programme computers, with a storage capacity of about 10^9, to make them play the imitation game so well that an average interrogator will not have more than 70 per cent chance of making the right identification [as between human and computer] after five minutes of questioning. (p. 442)

Presumably the interrogator has no more than $2\frac{1}{2}$ minutes of question-putting to bestow on each of the remote candidates, whose replies are not time-limited. We have to remind ourselves that—in spite of subsequent misstatements, repeated and amplified in a recent contribution to *Mind* by Robert French[2]—the question which Turing wished to place beyond reasonable dispute was *not* whether a machine might think at the level of an intelligent human. His proposal was for a test of whether a machine could be said to think at all.

SOLIPSISM AND THE CHARMED CIRCLE

Notwithstanding the above, French's paper has important things to say concerning the role played by 'subcognitive' processes in

---

[2] R. M. French, 'Subcognition and the Limits of the Turing Test', in this volume, pp. 11–26.

intelligent thought. He points out that 'any sufficiently broad set of questions making up a Turing Test would necessarily contain questions that rely on subcognitive associations for their answers' (p. 54).

The scientific study of cognition has shown that some thought processes are intimately bound up with consciousness while others take place subliminally. Further, as French reminds us, the two are interdependent. Yet other contributors to the machine intelligence discussion often imply a necessary association between consciousness and all forms of intelligence, as a basis for claiming that a computer program could not exhibit intelligence of any kind or degree. Thus John R. Searle[3] recently renewed his celebrated 'Chinese Room' argument against the possibility of designing a program that, when run on a suitable computer, would show evidence of 'thinking'. After his opening question 'Can a machine think?', Searle adds: 'Can a machine have conscious thoughts in exactly the same sense that you and I have?' (p. 20). Since a computer program does nothing but shuffle symbols, so the implication goes, one cannot really credit it with the kinds of sensations, feelings, and impulses which accompany one's own thinking—e.g. the excitement of following an evidential clue, the satisfaction of following a lecturer's argument, or the 'Aha!' of subjective comprehension. Hence however brilliant and profound its responses in the purely intellectual sense recognized by logicians, a programmed computing system can never be truly intelligent. Intelligence would imply that suitably programmed computers can be *conscious*, whereas we 'know' that they cannot be.

In his 1950 *Mind* paper Turing considered arguments of this kind, citing Jefferson's Lister Oration for 1949:

Not until a machine can write a sonnet or compose a concerto because of thoughts and emotions felt, and not by the chance fall of symbols, could we agree that machine equals brain—that is, not only write it but know that it had written it. No mechanism could feel (and not merely artificially signal, an easy contrivance) pleasure at its successes, grief when its valves fuse, be warmed by flattery, be made miserable by its mistakes, be charmed by sex, be angry or depressed when it cannot get what it wants. (pp. 445–6)

[3] J. R. Searle, 'Is the Brain's Mind a Computer Program?' *Scientific American*, 262 (1990), 20–5.

Jefferson's portrayal of conscious thought and feeling here compounds two aspects which are today commonly distinguished, namely on the one hand self-awareness, and, on the other, empathic awareness of others, sometimes termed 'intersubjectivity'. Turing's comment on Jefferson disregards this second aspect, and addresses only the first. The relevant excerpt from the *Mind* paper is:

4. *Turing on the argument from consciousness*

According to the most extreme form of this view [that thought is impossible without consciousness] the only way by which one could be sure that a machine thinks is to *be* the machine and to feel oneself thinking. One could then describe these feelings to the world, but of course no one would be justified in taking any notice. Likewise according to this view the only way to know that a *man* thinks is to be that particular man. It is in fact the solipsist point of view. It may be the most logical view to hold but it makes communication of ideas difficult. A is liable to believe 'A thinks but B does not' whilst B believes 'B thinks but A does not'. Instead of arguing continually over this point it is usual to have the polite convention that everyone thinks. (p. 446)

After a fragment of hypothetical dialogue illustrating the imitation game, Turing continues:

I think that most of those who support the argument from consciousness could be persuaded to abandon it rather than be forced into the solipsist position. They will then probably be willing to accept our test. (p. 447)

He thus contributes a fourth position to the previous list.

POSITION 4. *To the extent that possession of consciousness is not refutable in other people, we conventionally assume it. We should be equally ready to abandon solipsism for assessing thinking in machines.*

Turing did not suggest that consciousness is irrelevant to thought, nor that its mysterious nature and the confusions of educated opinion on the subject should be ignored. His point was simply that these mysteries and confusions do not have to be resolved before we can address questions of intelligence. Then and since, it has been the AI view that purely solipsistic definitions based on subjectively observed states are not useful. But Turing certainly underestimated the potential appeal of a more subtle form of solipsism generalized to *groups* of agents so as to avoid the dilemma which he posed. Following Daniel C. Dennett,[4] I term this variant the 'charmed circle' argument. A relationship with the notion of intersubjectivity, or socially shared consciousness[5] can be brought out by revising the above-quoted passage from Turing along some such lines as 'the only way by which one could be sure that a machine thinks is to be a member of a charmed circle which has accepted that machine into its ranks and can collectively feel itself thinking.' It is indeed according to just such social pragmatics that this issue is likely to be routinely adjudicated in the coming era of human–computer collaborative groups (see later).

But note that in the first of the two quoted passages concerning the argument from consciousness, the concluding sentence becomes truer to human society if rephrased: 'it is usual to have the polite convention that everyone *who is regarded as a person* thinks.' Turing's uncorrected wording, quite unintentionally I believe, pre-judges whether the polite convention would have led Aristotle to concede powers of intelligent thought to women, or Australian settlers to Tasmanian aborigines, or nineteenth-century plantation owners to their slaves. Nor, conversely, would Turing necessarily have wished to withhold the polite convention if someone asserted: 'My dog is a real person, and intelligent too.' In his above-cited contribution on consciousness to the *Oxford Companion to the Mind,* Daniel Dennett[6] puts the point well:

How do creatures differ from robots, real or imagined? They are organic-ally and biologically similar to *us,* and we are the paradigmatic conscious creatures. This similarity admits of degrees, of course, and one's intui-tions about which sorts of similarity count are probably untrustworthy. Dolphins' fishiness subtracts from our conviction, but no doubt should not. Were chimpanzees as dull as sea-slugs, their facial similarity to us would no doubt nevertheless favour their inclusion in the charmed circle. If house-flies were about our size, or warm-blooded, we'd be much more

---

[4] D. C. Dennett, 'Consciousness', in R. L. Gregory (ed.), *The Oxford Compan-ion to the Mind* (Oxford University Press, Oxford, 1987).

[5] See C. Trevarthen, 'The Tasks of Consciousness: How Could the Brain Do Them?' *Brain and Mind,* Ciba Foundation Series 69 (NS) (Excerpta Medica/Elsevier North-Holland, Amsterdam, 1979); id., 'Split-Brain and the Mind', in R. L. Gregory (ed.), *The Oxford Companion to the Mind* (Oxford University Press, Oxford, 1987).

[6] Dennett, 'Consciousness'.

confident that when we plucked off their wings they felt pain (*our* sort of pain, the kind that matters). (p. 161)

At the outset of his paper Turing does briefly consider what may be termed the argument from dissimilarity. He dismisses the idea of 'trying to make a "thinking machine" more human by dressing it up in artificial flesh', and commends the proposed typewriter link as sidestepping a line of criticism which he sees as pointless. He evidently did not foresee the use of similarity to define charmed circles of sufficient radius to deflect the accusation of narrow solipsism. In view of the absence from his discussion of all reference to shared aspects of conscious thought, he would probably have seen it as an evasion.

The 'charmed circle' criterion disallows intelligence in any non-living vehicle—so long as one is careful to draw the circle appropriately. But the idea of inanimate intelligence is in any case a difficult one to expound, for human intelligence is after all a product of the evolution of animals. This partly explains Turing's simplifying adoption of an engineering, rather than a scientific, scenario for his purpose. But the notion of performance trials conducted by a doubting client also sorted naturally with Turing's temperamental addiction to engineering images. Although himself conspicuously weak in purely mechanical skills, he startled his associates with a flow of highly original practical innovations, home-built and usually doomed. The same addiction was also discernible at the abstract level, where his gifts were not hampered by problems of physical implementation—notably in that most unlikely of purely mathematical constructions, the Universal Turing Machine itself.

CONSCIOUSNESS IN ARTEFACTS

Searle himself is not insensitive to the appearance of special pleading. In his earlier quoted *Scientific American* article[7] he writes:

I have not tried to show that only biologically based systems like our brains can think. Right now those are the only systems we know for a fact can think, but we might find other systems in the universe that can produce conscious thoughts, and we might even come to be able to create thinking systems artificially. I regard this issue as up for grabs. (p. 21)

[7] Searle, 'Is the Brain's Mind a Computer Program?'

With these words he seems to accept the possibility of conscious thought in machines. But we must remember that John Searle's objection relates only to *programmed* machines or other symbol shufflers. According to the Searle canon, (i) 'thinking' implies that the system is conscious, and (ii) consciousness is not possible in a programmed device which can only shuffle symbols. What if *two* 'other systems in the universe' are found with identical repertoires of intellectual behaviours, including behaviour suggestive of conscious awareness? If one of the systems is implemented entirely in circuitry and the other in software, then Searle gives the benefit of the doubt to the first as a thinking system, but withholds it from the second as not being 'really' conscious. What is to be done if some laboratory of the future builds a third system by faithfully reimplementing the entire circuitry of the first as software, perhaps microcoded for speed? Not only the functionality of the first machine would be reproduced, but also its complete and detailed logic and behavioural repertoire. Yet a strict reading of Searle forces the conclusion that, although the scientifically testable attributes of conscious thought would be reconstructed in the new artefact, an intangible 'something' would be lost, namely 'true' consciousness. The latter *could* in principle be synthesized in circuitry (see Searle: 'we might even come to be able to create thinking systems artificially'), but not in software or other forms of symbol shuffling.

There is in this a counterpoint to earlier reflections by the Nobel prizewinning neuroscientist Sir John Eccles,[8] who held, like Searle today, that a being's claim to be conscious may legitimately be ignored on grounds of knowing that being's interior mechanisms:

We can, in principle, explain all . . . input–output performance in terms of activity of neuronal circuits; and consequently, consciousness seems to be absolutely unnecessary! . . . as neurophysiologists we simply have no use for consciousness in our attempts to explain how the nervous system works. (p. 164)

But for Eccles it was the 'activity of neuronal circuits' rather than Searle's shuffling of symbols that permitted appearances of consciousness to be discounted. Eccles has subsequently changed his

---

[8] J. C. Eccles (1964), cited in R. W. Sperry, 'Consciousness and Causality', in R. L. Gregory (ed.), *The Oxford Companion to the Mind* (Oxford University Press, Oxford, 1987).

view,[9] which we now see as having defined the limits of neuro-physiology prematurely. In the same way Searle's in-principle exclusion of possible future AI artefacts risks prematurely defining the limits of knowledge-based programming. Like Eccles, Searle produces no workable definition of consciousness.

To rescue such positions from metaphysics, we must hope that a suitable Searle Test will be forthcoming to complement Turing's.

SUBARTICULATE THOUGHT

In earlier generations students of intelligent behaviour generally ignored the phenomenon of consciousness. Some from the behaviourist camp denied that there was anything for the term to name. Turing's impact on psychology has been to move the study of cognition towards increasingly computation-oriented models. One of the ways in which these formulations differ from those of behaviourism is in allotting an important role to those aspects of consciousness which are susceptible of investigation, including investigation *via* verbal report. But as new findings have multiplied, an awareness has grown of the complementary importance of other forms of thought and intelligence. Dennett[10] remarks as follows:

[T]he cognitive psychologist marshals experimental evidence, models, and theories to show that people are engaged in surprisingly sophisticated reasoning processes of which they can given no introspective account at all. Not only are minds accessible to outsiders; some mental activities are more accessible to outsiders than to the very 'owners' of those minds! (p. 162)

Although having no access to these mental activities in the sense of direct awareness of their operations, the explicitly conscious forms of mental calculation enjoy intimate and instant access to their fruits. In many cases, as illustrated below with the problem of conjecturing the pronunciation of imaginary English words, access to the fruits of subliminal cognition is a necessity, even though conscious awareness of the cognitive operations themselves is not.

---

[9] See K. R. Popper and J. C. Eccles, *The Self and Its Brain* (Routledge & Kegan Paul, London, 1977). [10] Dennett, 'Consciousness'.

The Turing Test's typewriter link with the owners of two candidate minds gives no direct access to the class of 'silent' mental activity described by Dennett. In the form put forward by Turing, the Test can directly detect only those processes which are susceptible of introspective verbal report. Does this then render it obsolete as a test of intelligence in machines?

The regretful answer is 'Yes'. The Test's didactic clarity is today suffering erosion from developments in cognitive science and in knowledge engineering. These have already revealed two dimensions of mismatch, even before questions of intersubjectivity and socially expressed intelligence are brought into the discussion:

(i) inability of the Test to bring into the game thought processes of kinds which humans can perform but cannot articulate, and
(ii) ability of the Test to detect and examine a particular species of thought process ('cognitive skills') in a suitably programmed machine through its self-articulations; similar access to human enactments of such processes is not possible because they are typically subarticulate.

Concerning (i), the idea that mental processes below the level of conscious and articulate thought are somehow secondary was dispatched with admirable terseness by A. N. Whitehead in 1911:

It is a profoundly erroneous truism . . . that we would cultivate the habit of thinking what we are doing. The precise opposite is the case. Civilisation advances by extending the number of important operations which we can perform without thinking about them.[11]

Moreover, although subcognitive skills can operate independently of conscious thought, the converse is by no means obvious. Indeed the processes of thought and language are dependent on such skills at every instant. The laboriously thought-out, and articulate, responses of the beginner are successively replaced by those which are habitual and therefore effortless. Only when a skilled response is blocked by some obstacle is it necessary to 'go back to first principles' and reason things out step by step.

It is understandable that Turing should have sought to separate intelligence from the complications and ambiguities of the conscious/unconscious dichotomy, and to define this mental quality

[11] A. N. Whitehead, *An Introduction to Mathematics*, 1911.

in terms of communication media which are characteristic of the academic rather than, say, the medical practitioner, the craftsman, or the explorer. But his Test has paid a price for the simplification. At the very moment that a human's mastery of a skill becomes most complete, he or she becomes least capable of articulating it and hence of sustaining a convincing dialogue *via* the imitation game's remote typewriter. Consider, for example, the following.

A particularly elaborate cognitive skill is of life-and-death importance in Micronesia, whose master navigators undertake voyages of as much as 450 miles between islands in a vast expanse of which less than two-tenths of one per cent is land. We read in Hutchins's contribution to Gentner and Stevens's *Mental Models*:[12]

Inasmuch as these navigators are still practicing their art, one may well wonder why the researchers don't just ask the navigators how they do it. Researchers do ask, but it is not that simple. As is the case with any truly expert performance in any culture, the experts themselves are often unable to specify just what it is they do while they are performing. Doing the task and explaining what one is doing require quite different ways of thinking. (p. 200)

We thus have the paradox that a Micronesian master navigator, engaging in dialogue, let us suppose, via a typewriter link with the aid of a literate interpreter, would lose most marks precisely when examined in the domain of his special expertise, namely long-distance navigation.

PROCEDURAL INFRASTRUCTURE OF DECLARATIVE KNOWLEDGE

The Turing Test seems at first sight to sidestep the need to implement such expertise by only requiring the machine to display general ability rather than specialist skills, the latter being difficult for their possessors to describe explicitly. But the display of intelligence and thought is in reality profoundly dependent upon some of these. Perhaps the most conspicuous case is the ability to express oneself in one's own language. Turing seems to have assumed that by the time that a fair approach to mechanizing intelligence had

---

[12] E. Hutchins, 'Understanding Micronesian Navigation', in D. Gentner and A. Stevens (eds.), *Mental Models* (Erlbaum, Hillsdale, NJ, 1983), 191–225.

been achieved, this would somehow bring with it a certain level of linguistic competence, at least in the written language. Matters have turned out differently. Partly this reflects the continuing difficulties confronting machine representation of the semantics and pragmatics (i.e. the 'knowledge' components) of discourse, as opposed to the purely syntactic components. Partly it reflects the above-described inaccessibility to investigators of the laws which govern what everyone knows how to do.

In spoken discourse, we find the smooth and pervasive operation of linguistic rules by speakers who are wholly ignorant of them! Imagine, for example, that the administrator of a Turing Test were to include the following, adapted from Philip Johnson-Laird's *The Computer and the Mind*:[13]

Question: How do you pronounce the plurals of the imaginary English words: 'platch', 'snorp', and 'brell'?

A human English speaker has little difficulty in framing a response over the typewriter link.

Answer: I pronounce them as 'platchez', 'snorpss', and 'brellz'.

The linguist Morris Halle[14] has pointed out that to form these plurals a person must use unconscious principles. According to Allen *et al.*,[15] subliminal encoding of the following three rules would be sufficient:

(1) If a singular noun ends in one of the phonetic segments /s/, /z/, /sh/, /zh/, /ch/, or /j/, then add the *ez* sound.
(2) If a singular noun ends in one of the phonetic segments /f/, /k/, /p/, /t/, or /th/, then add the *ss* sound.
(3) In any other case, add the *z* sound.

What about a machine? In this particular case programmers acquainted with the phonetic laws of English 's' pluralizations might have forearmed its rule base. But what about the scores of

[13] P. N. Johnson-Laird, *The Computer and the Mind* (Harvard University Press, Cambridge, Mass., 1988).
[14] M. Halle, 'Knowledge Unlearned and Untaught: What Speakers Know about the Sounds of Their Language', in M. Halle, J. Bresnan, and G. A. Miller (eds.), *Linguistic Theory and Psychological Reality* (MIT Press, Cambridge, Mass., 1978).
[15] J. Allen, M. S. Hunnicutt, and D. Klatt, *From Text to Speech: The MITalk System* (Cambridge University Press, Cambridge, 1987).

other questions about pronunciation against which they could not conceivably have forearmed it, for the sufficient reason that phonetic knowledge of the corresponding unconscious rules has not yet been formulated? Yet a human, *any* English-speaking human capable of typewriter discourse, would by contrast shine in answering such questions.

If account is taken of similar domains of discourse ranging far from linguistics, each containing thousands of subdomains within which similar 'trick questions' could be framed, the predicament of a machine facing interrogation from an adversarial insider begins to look daunting. We see in this a parable of futility for the attempt to implement intelligence solely by the declarative knowledge-based route, unsupported by skill-learning. A version of this parable, expensively enacted by the Japanese Fifth Generation, is discussed in my contribution[16] to Rolf Herken's *The Universal Turing Machine*.

Among the brain's various centres and subcentres only one, localized in the dominant (usually the left) cerebral hemisphere, has the ability to reformulate a person's own mental behaviour as linguistic descriptions. It follows that Turing's imitation game can directly sample from the human player only those thought processes accessible to this centre. Yet as Hutchins reminds us in the context of Micronesian navigation, and Johnson-Laird in the context of English pronunciation, most highly developed mental skills are of the verbally *inaccessible* kind. Their possessors cannot answer the question 'What did you do in order to get that right?'

This same hard fact was recently and repeatedly driven home to technologists by the rise and fall in commercial software of the 'dialogue-acquisition' school of expert systems construction. The earlier-mentioned disappointment which overtook this school, after well-publicized backing from government agencies of Japan and other countries, could have been avoided by acceptance of statements to be found in any standard psychological text. In John Anderson's *Cognitive Psychology and Its Implications*[17] the chapter on development of expertise speaks of the *autonomous stage* of skill acquisition:

[16] D. Michie, 'The Fifth Generation's Unbridged Gap', in R. Herken (ed.), *The Universal Turing Machine* (Oxford University Press, Oxford, 1988).

[17] J. R. Anderson, *Cognitive Psychology and Its Implications* (Freeman, New York, 3rd edn., 1990).

Because facility in the skill increases, verbal mediation in the performance of the task often disappears at this point. In fact, the ability to verbalize knowledge of the skill can be lost altogether. (p. 260)

Against this background, failure of attempts to build large expert systems by 'dialogue acquisition' of knowledge from the experts can hardly be seen as surprising. It is sufficient here to say that many skills are learned by means that do not require prior description, and to give a concrete example from common experience. For this I have taken from M. I. Posner's *Cognition: An Introduction*[18] an everyday instance which can easily be verified:

If a skilled typist is asked to type the alphabet, he can do so in a few seconds and with a very low probability of error. If, however, he is given a diagram of his keyboard and asked to fill in the letters in alphabetic order, he finds the task difficult. It requires several minutes to perform and the likelihood of error is high. Moreover, the typist often reports that he can only obtain the visual location of some letters by trying to type the letter and then determining where his finger would be. These observations indicate that experience with typing produces a motor code which may exist in the absence of any visual code. (p. 25)

Imagine, then, a programming project which depends on eliciting a skilled typist's knowledge of the whereabouts on an unlabelled keyboard of the letters of the alphabet. The obvious short cut is to ask him or her to type, say, 'the quick brown fox jumps over the lazy dog' and record which keys are typed in response to which symbols. But you must *ask* the domain experts what they know, says the programmer's tribal lore, not learn from what they actually do. Even in the typing domain this lore would not work very well. With the more complex and structured skills of diagnosis, forecasting, scheduling, and design, it has been even less effective. Happily there is another path to machine acquisition of cognitive skills from expert practitioners, namely: analyse what the expert does, *then* ask him what he knows. As reviewed elsewhere,[19] a new craft of rule induction from recording what the expert does is now the basis of commercial operations in Britain, America, Scandinavia, continental Europe, and Japan.

[18] M. I. Posner, *Cognition: An Introduction* (Scott, Foresman, Glenview, Ill., 1973).
[19] D. Michie, 'Methodologies from Machine Learning in Data Analysis and Software', *Computer Journal*, 34/6 (1991), 559–65.

Psychologists speak of 'cognitive skill' when discussing intens-ively learned intuitive know-how. The term is misleading on two counts. First, the word 'cognitive' sometimes conveys a connota-tion of 'conscious', inappropriate when discussing intuitive pro-cesses. Second, the term carries an implication of some 'deep' model encapsulating the given task's relational and causal structure. In actuality, just as calculating prodigies are commonly ignorant of logical and number-theoretical models of arithmetic, so skilled practitioners in other domains often lack developed mental models of their task environments. I follow French[20] in using the term 'subcognitive' for these procedurally oriented forms of operational knowledge.

Knowledge engineers sometimes call subcognitive know-how 'compiled knowledge', employing a metaphor which misdirects attention to a conjectured top-down, rather than data-driven, route of acquisition. But whichever acquisition route carries the main traffic, collectively, as remarked in the passage from Whitehead, such skills account for the preponderating part, and a growing part as our technical culture advances, of what it is to be an intelli-gent human. The areas of the human brain to which this silent corpus is consigned are still largely conjectural and may in large part even be subcortical. A second contrast between articulate and inarticulate cerebral functions is that between the verbally silent (usually the right) cerebral hemisphere, and the logical and articu-late areas located in left hemisphere. Right-brain thinking notably involves spatial visualization and is only inarticulate in the strict sense of symbolic communication: sublinguistic means of convey-ing mood and intent are well developed, as also are important modalities of consciousness. For further discussion the reader is referred to Popper and Eccles[21]—see also later in this paper.

THE SUPERARTICULACY PHENOMENON

Two dimensions were earlier identified along which the Turing Test can today be seen as mismatched to its task, even if we put aside forms of intelligence evoked in inter-agent co-operation which

[20] French, 'Subcognition and the Limits of the Turing Test'.
[21] Popper and Eccles, *The Self and Its Brain*.

the Test does not address at all. The first of these dimensions reveals the imitation game's inability to detect, in the human, thought processes of kinds which humans cannot articulate. We now turn to the second flaw, namely that the Test can catch in its net thought processes which the machine agent *can* articulate, but should not if it is to simulate a human.

What is involved is the phenomenon of machine 'superarticulacy'. A suitably programmed computer can inductively infer the largely unconscious rules underlying an expert's skill from samples of the expert's recorded decisions. When applied to new data, the resulting knowledge-based systems are often capable of using their inductively acquired rules to justify their decisions at levels of completeness and coherence exceeding what little articulacy the largely intuitive expert can muster. In such cases a Turing Test examiner comparing responses from the human and the artificial expert can have little difficulty in identifying the machine's. For so skilled a task, no human could produce such carefully thought-out justifications! A test which can thus penalize important forms of intelligent thought must be regarded as missing its mark. In my Technology Lecture at the London Royal Society,[22] I reviewed the then-available experimental results. Since that time, Ivan Bratko and colleagues[23] have announced a more far-reaching demonstration, having endowed clinical cardiology with its first certifiably complete, correct, and fully articulate, corpus of skills in electrocardiogram diagnosis, machine-derived from a logical model of the heart. In a Turing imitation game the KARDIO system would quickly give itself away by revealing explicit knowledge of matters which in the past have always been the preserve of highly trained intuition.

Of course a clever programming team could bring it about that the machine was as subarticulate about its own processes as we humans. In a cardiological version of the Turing Test, Bratko and his colleagues could enter a suitably crippled KARDIO system. They would substitute a contrived error rate in the system's clinical

[22] D. Michie, 'The Superarticulacy Phenomenon in the Context of Software Manufacture', *Proceedings of the Royal Society, London*, A 405 (1986), 185–212; also in D. Partridge and Y. Wilks (eds.), *The Foundations of Artificial Intelligence* (Cambridge University Press, Cambridge, 1990), 411–39.

[23] I. Bratko, I. Mozetic, and N. Lavrac, *Kardio: A Study in Deep and Qualitative Knowledge for Expert Systems* (MIT Press, Cambridge, Mass., 1989).

decisions for KARDIO's near-zero level. In place of KARDIO's impeccably knowledgeable commentaries, they might supply a generator of more patchy and incoherent, and hence more true-to-life explanations. At the trivial level of arithmetical calculation, Turing anticipated such 'playing dumb' tactics.

It is claimed that the interrogator could distinguish the machine from the man simply by setting them a number of problems in arithmetic. The machine would be unmasked because of its deadly accuracy. The reply to this is simple. The machine . . . would not attempt to give the *right* answers to the arithmetic problems. It would deliberately introduce mistakes in a manner calculated to confuse the interrogator. (p. 448)

But at levels higher than elementary arithmetic, as exemplified by KARDIO's sophisticated blend of logical and associative reasoning, surely one should judge a test as blemished if it obliges candidates to demonstrate intelligence by concealing it!

CLASSICAL AI AND RIGHT-BRAIN INTELLIGENCE

Findings from 'split-brain' studies have identified the coexistence in the two cerebral hemispheres of separate and under normal conditions mutually co-operating centres of mental activity. The deconnected right hemisphere (surgically separated from the left) is relatively weak in the faculties of logic and language, and is usually incapable of verbal report. Description of it as a centre of 'consciousness' may therefore be questioned. But Roger Walcott Sperry, cited by Popper and Eccles in their book *The Self and Its Brain*,[24] regards it as

a conscious system in its own right, perceiving, thinking, remembering, reasoning, willing, and emoting, all at a characteristically human level. . . . Though predominantly mute and generally inferior in all performances involving language or linguistic or mathematical reasoning, the minor hemisphere is nevertheless the superior cerebral member for certain types of tasks. If we remember that in the great majority of tests it is the disconnected left hemisphere that is superior and dominant, we can review quickly now some of the kinds of exceptional activities in which it is the minor hemisphere that excels. First, of course, as one would predict, these are all nonlinguistic nonmathematical functions. Largely they involve the

[24] Popper and Eccles, *The Self and Its Brain*.

apprehension and processing of spatial patterns, relations and transformations. They seem to be holistic and unitary rather than analytic and fragmentary, and orientational more than focal, and to involve concrete perceptual insight rather than abstract, symbolic, sequential reasoning. (p. 325)

One should add in particular that the right hemisphere supports the recognition and appreciation of music and pictures—both important forms of human communication and cultural transmission. In his book with Karl Popper, John Eccles refers to a case reported by Gott of surgical excision of the right hemisphere, which 'occurred in a young woman who was a music major and an accomplished pianist. After the operation there was a tragic loss of her musical ability. She could not carry a tune but could still repeat correctly the words of familiar songs' (p. 338).

In their survey of these questions, Popper and Eccles distinguish self-consciousness, located in the left hemisphere, from other forms of consciousness. In Dialogue V, Popper says:

I can't help feeling . . . that self-consciousness is somehow a higher development of consciousness, and possibly that the right hemisphere is conscious but not self-conscious, and that the left hemisphere is both conscious and self-conscious. It is possible that the main function of the corpus callosum is, so to speak, to transfer the conscious—but not self-conscious—interpretations of the right hemisphere to the left, and of course, to transfer something in the other direction too. (p. 484)

The corpus callosum is the two-way connecting bundle between the cerebral hemispheres. It consists of some hundreds of millions of nerve fibres, estimated to carry a total traffic of 4×10^9 impulses per second. It is this massive high-speed highway which has been surgically interrupted in the human subjects studied under the name 'split-brain'.

Imagine now that Turing's Test were one day to be passed by a machine simulating the kind of intelligence which remained intact in Gott's young woman patient after her operation. It is in this kind of intelligence that AI scientists have so far demonstrated most interest and success. After seeing the imitation game mastered under the special condition that the human player (as Gott's woman patient) functions in left-brain-only mode, a critic may declare that what we *now* need is a machine that can be certificated for possession of right-brain mental skills. Such a requirement would surely overwhelm the combined efforts of the world's computing community into the indefinite future. The following reasons for intractability come to mind.

The isolated right brain is rated by Eccles as 'having a status superior to that of the non-human primate brain'. Without a linguistic link, a first step would need to be implementation of the kind of versatile trainability on which a shepherd relies in developing intelligent behaviour in his sheep-dog. 'Special testing methods with non-verbal expression', to use words taken from Sperry, are used for clinical study of human subsymbolic thinking. Equivalent methods would need to be developed for work with artificial right-brain intelligences. Imagination reels at the thought of the prodigies of innovative mechanical and electronic engineering required to build a mobile artefact which could be programmed to compete in international sheep-dog trials, or, say, which could support the behaviour required of a dumb but capable robot footman! There is a persistent suggestion that Turing (to quote the words of an anonymous informant) 'also considered a robotics-style test, not one involving "deception" of a human examiner; rather, it involved seeing to what extent the robot could succeed in the completion of a range of tasks by acting appropriately in a natural range of environments.' There is a point of historical interest here. Although I cannot confirm this account from personal recollection, it fits in with a tale which I have related elsewhere[25] of Turing's early post-war days at NPL: 'Turing', his colleagues said, 'is going to infest the countryside with a robot which will live on twigs and scrap-iron!' Such things are still in the far future of the art of rule-based programming. Even the proprioceptive control of a single robot limb at present constitutes an almost crushing challenge. H. McIlvaine Parsons'[26] proposals are in the same direction, and contain much of interest.

Perhaps the symbolic school of AI should consider a treaty with their neural net and connectionist colleagues. Each party might renounce its claim to the other's hemispheric area, and concentrate on the cognitive functions which lie within its competence. This

---

[25] D. Michie, Editorial introduction to A. M. Turing's chapter 'Intelligent Machinery', in B. Meltzer and D. Michie (eds.), *Machine Intelligence*, 5 (Edinburgh University Press, Edinburgh).

[26] H. M. Parsons, 'Turing on the Turing Test', in W. Karwowski and M. Rahimi (eds.), *Ergonomics of Hybrid Automated Systems II* (Elsevier, Amsterdam, 1990).

said, the time is nevertheless ripe for a symbolically oriented foray into one particular silent area, namely the inductive extraction of articulate models from behavioural traces of inarticulate skills.

CONSCIOUSNESS AND HUMAN–COMPUTER INTERACTION

Only the dominant hemisphere is logically and linguistically equipped to respond to Turing's Test. But the other hemisphere's functions include complementary forms of thought and intelligences. To complicate matters, a person's stream of awareness becomes available to others only when that person's (left-brain) discourse draws upon selected traces of conscious experience in memory. Moreover such traces partly consist of after-the-event rationalizations and confabulations. Possibly one of the needs catered for by the editing process is mnemonic. Another may be the need to explain one's feelings and/or actions to self and others. Such possibilities are consistent with Trevarthen's[27] account in *The Oxford Companion to the Mind*:

The brain is adapted to create and maintain human society and culture by two complementary conscious systems. Specialized motives in the two hemispheres generate a dynamic partnership between the intuitive, on the one side, and the analytical or rational, on the other, in the mind of each person. This difference appears to have evolved in connection with the human skills of intermental co-operation and symbolic communication. (p. 746)

As with scientific publication from an experienced laboratory, what appears in conscious recollection seems to be not so much a panoptic video of everything that went on, but rather a terse documentary, edited to highlight and establish each main conclusion. This view of the matter has survived without serious challenge since its formulation by William James[28] just a century ago:

[We] see that the mind is at every stage a theatre of simultaneous possibilities. Consciousness consists in the comparison of these with each other,

---

[27] C. Trevarthen, 'Split-Brain and the Mind', in R. L. Gregory (ed.), *The Oxford Companion to the Mind* (Oxford University Press, Oxford, 1987).

[28] W. James, *The Principles of Psychology* (Dover, New York, 1950; first published 1890).

the selection of some, and the suppression of the rest by the reinforc-
ing and inhibiting agency of attention. The highest and most elaborated
mental products are filtered from the data chosen by the faculty next
beneath, out of the mass offered by the faculty below that, which mass
in turn was sifted from a still larger amount of yet simpler material, and
so on. The mind, in short, works on the data it receives very much as a
sculptor works on his block of stone. In a sense the statue stood there from
eternity. But there were a thousand different ones beside it, and the sculptor alone is to thank for having extricated this one from the rest. (p. 288)

James's image of the sculptor postulates selective data destruction.
Recent laboratory studies summarized by Dennett and Kinsbourne[29]
indicate a slightly different metaphor. Rather than the sculptor's
block of stone, Dennett proposes the writer's 'multiple drafts' as a
model of conscious recollection—for a comprehensive account, see
his *Consciousness Explained*.[30] As far as can be, the mind's inbuilt
editor squeezes parallel streams of perception into a single 'story
line', *not refraining even from rearranging temporal sequences*. The
following account comes from Dennett and Kinsbourne's paper.

The cutaneous 'rabbit'. . . . The subject's arm rests cushioned on a table,
and mechanical square-wave tappers are placed at two or three locations
along the arm, up to a foot apart. A series of taps in rhythm are delivered
by the tappers, e.g. 5 at the wrist followed by 2 near the elbow and then
3 more on the upper arm. The taps are delivered with interstimulus
intervals between 50 and 200 msec. So a train of taps might last less than
a second, or as much as two or three seconds. The astonishing effect is
that the taps seem to the subjects to travel in regular sequences over
equidistant points up the arm—as if a little animal were hopping along
the arm. Now *how did the brain know* that after the 5 taps to the wrist,
there were going to be some taps near the elbow? The experienced 'depar-
ture' of the taps from the wrist begins with the second tap, yet in catch
trials in which the later elbow taps are never delivered, all five wrist taps
are felt at the wrist in the expected manner. The brain obviously cannot
'know' about a tap at the elbow until after it happens. Perhaps, one might
speculate, the brain delays the conscious experience until after all the taps
have been 'received' and then, somewhere upstream of the seat of consciousness (whatever that is), *revises* the data to fit a theory of motion,
and sends the edited version on to consciousness.

---

[29] D. C. Dennett and M. Kinsbourne, 'Time and the Observer: The Where and
When of Consciousness in the Brain', *Behavioral and Brain Sciences*, 15 (1992),
183–201.
[30] D. C. Dennett, *Consciousness Explained* (Little, Brown & Co., Boston, 1992).

We guide the compressions and filterings, and manage the unavoidable distortions of the story-building, with the aid of an intellectual tool developed expressly for the purpose, the notion of causality—absent, as Russell[31] was the first to point out, from the explicit formulations of classical physics. This notion can be seen as a cognitive device for trivializing the computations while extracting the story that we can most easily understand. It follows that cause and effect may be differently attributed by different rational observers of the same events. R. E. Ornstein[32] in his *The Psychology of Consciousness* quotes from an Islamic tale:

'What is Fate?' Nasrudin was asked by a scholar.
'An endless succession of intertwined events, each influencing the other.'
'That is hardly a satisfactory answer. I believe in cause and effect.'
'Very well,' said the Mulla, 'look at that.' He pointed to a procession passing in the street.
'That man is being taken to be hanged. Is that because someone gave him a silver piece and enabled him to buy the knife with which he committed the murder; or because someone saw him do it; or because nobody stopped him?' (p. 75)

DESIGN PRAGMATICS OF INTELLIGENT AWARENESS

To many, the incommunicable (and less testable) experiences seem even more vitally important than the communicable aspects of consciousness. But for detecting and measuring intelligence in *other* agents we have to substitute for the full concept a restricted notion of 'operational awareness', i.e., the testable aspect. This notion is easier to integrate into scientific usage. Moreover, news from the market-place indicates an unexpected application in the technology of graphical user interfaces for personal computers and workstations. Developments are in train in the laboratories of a number of large corporations for animated figures to appear on the screen. These personal agents are programmed to simulate awareness and intelligent interest, articulately guiding the interactive user through the operating system. Nicholas Negroponte,

[31] B. Russell, 'On the Notion of Cause', *Proceedings of the Aristotelian Society*, 13(1913), 1–26.
[32] R. E. Ornstein, *The Psychology of Consciousness* (Harcourt, Brace & Jovanovich, 1977, 96; 1st edn., Freeman, New York, 1972).

who directs MIT's Media Lab, remarked in the *Byte* magazine of December 1989: 'Today, the PC is driven by the desktop metaphor, but that scenario will disappear and be replaced by a theatrical metaphor. Users literally will see on their screens little *expert agents* who will do things for them'[33].

It seems possible, then, that the software industry may come to be a more exacting designer and taskmaster of imitation games than Turing's or any other academically conceived test of machine intelligence. If the graphically displayed figures fail to muster a sufficiently convincing show of conscious awareness, users will no doubt complain to the manufacturers that their agents do not understand them. To address customer dissatisfaction of this kind, such agents will need programs capable of signalling not only coherent attention, but intentions and feelings. Negroponte's 'little expert agents' must convey the motives of a teacher, or they will fail.

Conversely, simulated agents may arouse complaints that their displayed awareness, although attentive, is stilted and socially obtuse. The dimension of *social* intelligence has been noticeably absent from most discussions. Yet present-day workstation designers envisage networking environments for multiway co-operation among members of mixed task groups. Humans and machines are expected to pool diverse specialist skills in a common attack on each problem. Social intelligence by definition escapes through the net of one-on-one testing by dialogue. A version of the imitation game which can assess this form of intelligence needs to have the examiner communicate with *teams*—teams of humans, of knowledge-based robots, and (most interestingly) teams of mixed composition. Some of the design considerations go quite deep. In assessing co-operative behaviours we have to analyse, suitably translated into the realm of robot intelligence, such intimate inter-agent skills as committee work, co-operative construction of artefacts, and the collective interaction of classmates with each other and with teachers.

For forty years AI has followed the path indicated by the original form of the Test. It is no longer premature to consider extended modalities, designed to assess creative thought, subliminal and

---

[33] *Byte Magazine*, 14/13 (1989), in 'The Wizards of the Media Lab', by Janet J. Bannon, 360.

'silent' forms of expertise, social intelligence, and the ability of one intelligent agent to teach another and in turn be taught.

THE IMITATION GAME IN REVIEW

Let us now look back on the relation of conscious thought to Turing's imitation game.

(i) Turing left open whether consciousness is to be assumed if a machine passes the Test. Some contemporary critics only attribute 'intelligence' to conscious processes. An operational interpretation of this requirement is satisfied if the examiner can elicit from the machine *via* its typewriter no less evidence of consciousness than he or she can elicit *via* the human's typewriter. We thus substitute the weaker (but practical) criterion of 'operational awareness', and ask the examiner to ensure that this at least is tested.

(ii) In addition to strategies based on an intelligent agent's deep models ('understanding', 'relational knowledge') we find intrinsically different strategies based on heuristic models ('skill', 'know-how'). The outward and visible operations of intelligence depend critically upon integrated support from the latter, typically unconscious, processes. Hence in preparing computing systems for an adversely administered Turing Test, developers cannot dodge attempting to implement these processes. The lack of verbal report associated with them in human experts can be circumvented in some cases by computer induction from human decision examples. In others, however, the need for exotic physical supports for input–output behaviour would present serious engineering difficulties.

(iii) Conversely, where inductive inference allows knowledge engineers to reconstruct and incorporate the needed skill-bearing rules, it becomes possible to include a facility of introspective report which not uncommonly out-articulates the human possessors of these same skills. Such 'superarticulacy' reveals a potential flaw in the Turing Test, which could distinguish the machine from the human player on the paradoxical ground of the machine's *higher* apparent level of intelligent awareness.

(iv) In humans, consciousness supports the functions of communicating with others, and of predicting their responses. As a next step in user-friendly operating systems, graphically simulated 'agents' endowed with pragmatic equivalents of conscious awareness are today under development by manufacturers of personal computers and workstations. At this point AI comes under pressure to consider how emotional components may be incorporated in models of intelligent communication and thought.

(v) Extensions to the Turing Test should additionally address yet more subtle forms of intelligence, such as those involved in collective problem solving by co-operating agents, and in teacher–pupil relations.

(vi) By the turn of the century, market pressures may cause the designers of workstation systems to take over from philosophers the burden of setting such goals, and of assessing the degree to which this or that system may be said to attain them.

3

The Turing Test: AI's Biggest Blind Alley?

BLAY WHITBY

———◆———

INTRODUCTION

Alan Turing's 1950 paper, 'Computing Machinery and Intelligence',[1] and the 'Turing Test' suggested in it are rightly seen as inspirational to the inception and development of artificial intelligence (AI). However, inspiration can soon become distraction in science, and it is not too early to begin to consider whether or not the Turing test is just such a distraction. What will be argued is that this is indeed the case with the Turing Test and AI.

AI has had an intimate relationship with the Turing Test throughout its brief history. The view of this relationship presented in this paper is that it has developed more or less as follows:

1950–66: A source of inspiration to all concerned with AI.

1966–73: A distraction from some more promising avenues of AI research.

1973–90: By now a source of distraction mainly to philosophers, rather than AI workers.

1990 onwards: Consigned to history.[2]

One conclusion that is implied by this view of the history of AI and Turing's 1950 paper is that for most of the period since its

---

I am grateful to Professor Aaron Sloman for his comments on an early draft of this paper.

[1] A. M. Turing, 'Computing Machinery and Intelligence', *Mind*, 59/236: 433–60. I shall assume familiarity with the text of this paper throughout.

[2] The (somewhat arbitrary) dates in this history are derived from the first publications describing ELIZA (1966) and PARRY (1973) and the Turing 1990 Colloquium.

publication it has been a distraction. While not detracting from the brilliance of the paper and its central role in the philosophy of AI, it can be argued that Turing's 1950 paper, or perhaps some strong interpretations of it have, on occasion, hindered both the practical development of AI and the philosophical work necessary to facilitate that development. Thus one can make the claim that, in an important philosophical sense, 'Computing Machinery and Intelligence' has led AI into a blind alley from which it is only just beginning to extract itself.

One main source of this distraction has been the common, yet mistaken reading of 'Computing Machinery and Intelligence' as somehow 'showing' that one can attempt to build an intelligent machine without a prior understanding of the nature of intelligence. If we can, by whatever means, build a computer-based system which deceives a human interrogator for a while into suspecting that it might be human, then we have solved the many philosophical, scientific, and engineering problems of AI! This simplistic reading has, of course, proved both false and misleading in practice. The key to this misreading would seem to be the mistaken view that Turing's paper contains an adequate operational definition of intelligence. A later section of this paper suggests an interpretation of 'Computing Machinery and Intelligence' and of the 'imitation game' in their historical context. This interpretation does not imply the existence of an operational definition of intelligence.

That 'Computing Machinery and Intelligence' was almost immediately read as providing an operational definition of intelligence is witnessed by the change from the label 'imitation game' to 'Turing Test' by commentators. Turing himself was always careful to refer to 'the game'. The suggestion that it might be some sort of test involves an important extension of Turing's claims. This is not some small semantic quibble, but an important suggestion that Turing's paper was being interpreted as closer to an operational test than he himself intended.

It will be argued in the remainder of this paper that this general misreading of Turing's 1950 paper has led to the currency of three mistaken assertions, namely:

(1) Intelligence in computing machinery is (or is nearly or includes) being able to deceive a human interlocutor.

(2) The best approach to the problem of defining intelligence is through some sort of operational test, of which the imitation game is a paradigm example.

(3) Work specifically directed at producing a machine which could perform well in the imitation game is genuine (or perhaps even useful) AI research.

This paper will not pursue the falsity of assertions (1) and (2) in any great detail. On claim (1) it should be sufficient to remark that the comparative success of ELIZA[3] and programs like it at deceiving human interlocutors could not be held to indicate that they are closer to achieving intelligence than more sophisticated AI work. Other writers have convincingly attacked claim (2) on the grounds that the imitation game does not test for intelligence, but rather for other items such as cultural similarity.[4]

Instead this paper focuses on assertion (3) and the effect of this assertion on the history of AI. The claim is that work directed at success in the Turing Test is neither genuine nor useful AI research. In particular, the point will be stressed that, irrespective of whether or not Turing's 1950 paper provided one, the last thing that AI has needed since 1966 is an operational definition of intelligence.

Few, if any, philosophers and AI researchers would assent to claim (3) stated boldly. However, the influence of Alan Turing and his 1950 paper on the history of AI has been so profound that such mistaken claims can have a significant influence at a 'subconscious' (or more properly a subcultural) level.

In any case, the passing of more than forty years gives sufficient historical perspective to enable us to begin to debate the way in which 'Computing Machinery and Intelligence' has influenced the development of AI. The basic theme of this paper is that the influence of Turing's 1950 paper has been largely unfortunate. This is not through any fault of the paper, but is rather a consequence of the historical circumstances which obtained at the time of its writing and some of the pressures which have affected the subsequent development of AI.

---

[3] J. Weizenbaum, 'ELIZA—A Computer Program for the Study of Natural Language Communication between Man and Machine', *Communications of the A.C.M.*, 9/1: 36–45.

[4] See e.g. R. French (in this volume, pages 11–26) and D. Michie (in this volume, pages 27–51).

SOME CONSEQUENCES OF MISINTERPRETATION OF 'COMPUTING MACHINERY AND INTELLIGENCE'

The main consequence of perceiving intelligence in terms of some sort of imitation of human performance, such as success in the imitation game, is that AI research and experiment has paid far too much attention to the development of machinery and programs which seek directly or indirectly to imitate human performance. It might, at first, be thought that this was inevitable since human behaviour is the only practical clue to the nature of intelligence which is readily available. However, this is a mistaken view. We know so very little about the nature of human intelligence that we cannot produce a definition which is of use to an AI engineer. Such a definition would have to make no direct reference to either humans or machines.

This focus of AI research on imitation of human performance has at least three unfortunate consequences. First, it does not seem to have been very productive. Secondly, as I have argued at length elsewhere,[5] it is unlikely to lead to profitable or safe applications of AI. New technology is generally taken up quickly where there is a clear deficiency in existing technologies and very slowly, if at all, where it offers only a marginal improvement over existing technologies. Even an amateur salesman of AI should be able to see that researchers should be steered away from programs that imitate human beings. The old quip about there being no shortage of natural intelligence contains an important truth. There are many safe, profitable applications for AI, but programs inspired by the imitation game are unlikely to lead towards them. This sort of research is more likely to produce interesting curiosities such as ELIZA than working AI applications.

A third unfortunate consequence is the way in which the myth that intelligence can be operationally defined as some sort of imitation of human beings has apparently exempted both philosophers and AI researchers from the rather difficult task of providing the sort of definition of intelligence which would be of use to AI. To be useful in AI research any definition of intelligence needs to be independent of human capabilities. This is for a number of reasons. Among these are the lack of a clear understanding of

[5] B. R. Whitby, *AI: A Handbook of Professionalism*, Ellis Horwood, Chichester (1988), ch. 1.

human intellectual abilities and the lack of an uncontroversial framework within which such understanding might be achieved. Human psychology as a study is divided into factions which do not agree on basic methodological questions or on the definition of basic terms. It is not the purpose of this paper to be critical of human psychology, but simply to observe that human psychology is not, and is not for some time likely to be, in a position to provide AI with the theoretical basis which would turn it from a form of research into a form of engineering.

In various other places,[6] an analogy has been developed between AI and artificial flight. One feature of this analogy which is relevant here is the way in which direct imitation of natural flight proved a relatively fruitless avenue of research. It is true that many serious aviation pioneers did make a detailed study of bird flight, the most notable being Otto Lilienthal; but it must be stressed that working aircraft were developed by achieving greater understanding of the principles of aerodynamics. The Wright brothers were extremely thorough and precise scientists. They succeeded because they were thorough in their experimental methods, whereas others had failed because they were too hasty to build aircraft based upon incomplete theoretical work. There may be some important lessons for AI research in the methodology of the Wrights.[7]

It is also importantly true that our understanding of bird flight has stemmed from our knowledge of aerodynamics and not the reverse.[8] If there were an imitation game type of test for flight we would probably still not be able to build a machine which could pass it. Some aircraft can imitate some features of bird flight such

---

[6] e.g. in B. R. Whitby, ibid., ch. 2. and in M. Yazdani and B. R. Whitby 'Artificial Intelligence: Building Birds out of Beer Cans', *Robotica*, 5(1987): 89–92.

[7] There are two features of the Wright's methodology which contrast sharply with other contemporary experimenters and which may have relevance to AI. First, they spent a good deal of time looking at the work, both successful and unsuccessful, of previous aviation experimenters. They developed a coherent account of these successes and failures. Secondly and surprisingly, unlike most of their contemporaries they had a full appreciation of the need to control any aircraft in addition to simply getting it airborne. See e.g. D. Mondey (ed.), *The International Encyclopaedia of Aviation*, Octopus, London (1977), 38–49.

[8] In 1928 the first successful soaring flight was made in a glider; the aircraft climbing in the rising air of a thermal. Birds had been observed doing so for centuries, but at this time many biologists maintained that they could do so by virtue of the air trapped within the hollow bones of their wings being expanded by the heat of the sun. In this case a young pilot was able to overturn biological theory by performing the same feat.

as a glider when soaring in a thermal, but totally convincing imitation does not exist. We do not know how to build a practical ornithopter (an aircraft which employs a birdlike wing-flapping motion) but this is not of any real importance. Some of the purposes for which we use artificial flight, such as the speedy crossing of large distances, are similar to the purposes for which natural flight has evolved, but others, such as controlling the re-entry of spacecraft, are radically different. It is clear that AI, if it is to be a useful technology, should undergo a similar development. Many of the most useful applications for AI will be in areas which in no way replace or imitate natural intelligence. It is quite probable that we will never build a machine which could pass the Turing Test in its entirety, but this may well be because we can see little use for such a machine; indeed it could have dangerous side-effects.

What is needed is a definition of intelligence which does not draw on our assumed intuitive knowledge of our own abilities. Such knowledge is at best vague and unreliable, and there may be Gödel-like[9] reasons for believing that we do not fully understand our own capabilities. Some writers have made tentative approaches to such a definition[10] and perhaps some common features are beginning to emerge, among which are that any intelligent entity must be able to form clearly discernible goals. This is a feature which is not suggested by the Turing Test nor possessed by programs which have reputedly done well in the imitation game, such as ELIZA, DOCTOR,[11] and PARRY.[12]

In considering AI as an engineering enterprise—concerned with the development of useful products—the effects of the imitation game are different but equally misleading. If we focus future work in AI on the imitation of human abilities, such as might be required to succeed in the imitation game, we are in effect building 'intellectual statues' when what we need are 'intellectual tools'. This may prove to be an expensive piece of vanity. In other words,

---

[9] See e.g. J. R. Lucas, 'Minds Machines and Gödel', *Philosophy*, 36(1961): 112–27 and in this volume, pp. 103–24.

[10] e.g. R. C. Schank, *Explanation Patterns*, Lawrence Erlbaum, London (1986) and M. Yazdani (ed.), *Artificial Intelligence*, Chapman & Hall, London, 263.

[11] For the claim that DOCTOR passed the 'Turing Test' see D. Michie, *On Machine Intelligence*, Ellis Horwood, Chichester (2nd edn., 1986), 241–2.

[12] K. M. Colby, F. D. Hilf, Sylvia Weber, and H. C. Kraemer, 'Turing-Like Indistinguishability Tests for the Validation of a Computer Simulation of Paranoid Processes', in *Artificial Intelligence*, 3(1972): 199–222.

there is no reason why successful AI products should relate to us as if they were humans. They may instead resemble a workbench which enables a human operator to achieve much more than he could without it, or perhaps be largely invisible to humans in that they operate automatically and autonomously.

A MORE USEFUL INTERPRETATION OF 'COMPUTING MACHINERY AND INTELLIGENCE'

If we are not to read Turing's 1950 paper as providing an operational definition of intelligence, what are we to make of it? There has, of course, been a preponderance of interpretations which stress the use of the imitation game as a test for intelligence or the ability to think. In fact in the reported discussions about his work in the all too brief three years before his death in 1953, Turing seems to have allowed this sort of interpretation to have played a significant part.[13] It is possible to explain Turing's toleration of such interpretations of the paper as something more than the desire for a good argument.

There is little point in being sidetracked into a discussion of Turing's actual intention at the time of his writing. This is, probably correctly, known in literary criticism as 'the intentionalist fallacy'. What matters is the way in which the paper has been and is to be interpreted. However, in order to explain the first part of a better interpretation, it is necessary to set the paper in its historical context. The 1950 paper was in many ways based upon a report written for the National Physics Laboratory in August 1948.[14] This in turn, although ostensibly a technical report, drew together Turing's speculations on the possibility of building an intelligent machine which had been carried on in conversation at least as far back as 1940 at Bletchley Park.

During this period Turing (among others) was leading what Thomas Kuhn has christened a 'paradigm shift'.[15] This paradigm shift involved an understanding of what we would now call the

---

[13] For the best account of this brief period see A. Hodges, *Alan Turing, The Enigma of Intelligence*, Unwin, London (1983), 413–46.

[14] Eventually published (though perhaps incorrectly dated) in B. Meltzer and D. Michie (eds.), *Machine Intelligence* 5, Edinburgh University Press.

[15] T. S. Kuhn, *The Structure of Scientific Revolutions*, University of Chicago Press (2nd edn., 1970).

logical and physical aspects of certain types of systems. The wartime work at Bletchley Park was crucial to the development of this paradigm shift, as Turing was one of the few men who could fully appreciate what the Polish cryptanalysts had done in the years immediately preceding 1939, in discovering how the *physical* nature of the Enigma coding machine could be deduced from the *logical* nature of its output. This work also involved the building of further *physical* machines such as the Colossi to assist in the deciphering of the intercepted traffic, that is, the *logical* output of another machine. The whole of computing is founded upon this understanding of the way in which physical and logical systems can be direct counterparts of each other. However, the fact that we all understand this now should not distract us from the fact that in 1940 only a few men of vision were capable of appreciating its importance. By 1950 this paradigm shift had spread more widely in computing and the sciences, but not to philosophy or the general public.

Thus a crucial part of 'Computing Machinery and Intelligence' is devoted to pursuing the philosophical implications of applying this paradigm shift to the question of whether or not machines can think. In the imitation game Turing picks a man and a woman because they would be obviously physically different. Turing assumes that the general public would have no difficulty in appreciating that there are physical differences between participants in the imitation game. However, the observer is denied any access to the physical attributes of the participants in the imitation game and instead must try to deduce these from their logical output via a teletype. In a way it is Enigma revisited, but with human beings. Just as the wartime cryptanalysts had to deduce the physical nature of the Enigma coding device by observing logical patterns in its output, so the observer in the imitation game must attempt to distinguish the physical differences between the participants by discerning differing patterns of output.

When a machine is introduced into the game the observer is again forced to view it in terms of its logical output. Turing does not need to take a view on how successful the observer might be in distinguishing the man from the woman. He simply suggests that when a machine is introduced into the game and achieves comparable levels of success in producing indistinguishable output then we can no longer attach much importance to physical differences between women, men, and machines. What Turing managed creatively to show was that the paradigm shift in which he had a leading role could be applied to the familiar question: 'Can a machine think?' The imitation game contrived a method, understandable to a wide audience, of showing what Turing and a few others had already clearly grasped: that observable physical features have a subordinate role in answering such questions.

The remaining portion of a useful interpretation of 'Computing Machinery and Intelligence' is more relevant today. It also explains the continuing appeal of the Turing Test to present-day writers. This is because 'Computing Machinery and Intelligence' clearly illustrates the importance of human attitudes in determining the answers to questions such as 'can machines think?'

Ascribing the label 'intelligent' is not a purely technical exercise; it involves a number of moral and social dimensions. Human beings consider themselves obligated to behave in certain ways toward intelligent items.

To claim that the ascription of intelligence has moral and social dimensions is not merely to claim that it has moral and social consequences. It may well be the case that certain moral and social criteria must be satisfied before such an ascription can be made. In a sense it is true that we feel more at ease in ascribing intelligence (and sometimes even the ability to think) to those entities with which we can have an interesting conversation than with radically different entities. It is this feature of the ascription of intelligence which makes the use of any sort of operational test of intelligence with human beings so unattractive.

These moral and social dimensions to the ascription of intelligence are also covered by 'Computing Machinery and Intelligence'. Turing wanted to ask (although he obviously could not answer) the question: 'What would be the human reaction to the sort of machine which could succeed in the imitation game?' If, as Turing clearly believed, digital computers could, by the end of the century, succeed in deceiving an interrogator 70 per cent of the time, how would we describe such a feat? This is not primarily a technical or philosophical question, but rather a question about human attitudes. As Turing himself observed, the meaning of words such as 'thinking' can change with changing patterns of usage. Although sampling human attitudes as a method of answering the question 'can a machine think?' is rejected in the first paragraph of 'Computing

Machinery and Intelligence', we can read the entire paper as primarily concerned with human attitudes. The contrivance of the imitation game was intended to show the importance of human attitudes, not to be an operational definition of intelligence.

Given this interpretation of the paper, it is not surprising that Turing tolerated a certain amount of misinterpretation of the role of the imitation game. The paper itself was partly an exercise in testing and changing human attitudes. Turing fully expected it to provoke a certain amount of controversy. However, in the fourth decade of research in AI this sort of controversy is no longer productive.

CONCLUSIONS

After the passage of over forty years it is safe to assume that not only will Turing's prediction of machines succeeding in the imitation game by the end of the century not come about, but also that it probably never will be achieved. There would be little practical use for a machine aimed specifically at success in the imitation game. Furthermore, examination of AI products from a 1990s perspective prompts a high degree of cynicism about the possibility of success in the imitation game being simply an emergent property of computers with sufficient memory and performance.

It should be clear that at this stage in the development of AI there is nothing to be gained by clinging to the notion of the imitation game as an operational test for intelligence. It is now clear that we need AI for a number of practical purposes, including making computing machinery more useful. To imagine, for whatever reason, that this involves making computers more like human beings may well be a distracting vanity.

In conclusion it is worth repeating that the last thing needed by AI *qua* science is an operational definition of intelligence involving some sort of comparison with human beings. The need here is for an account of intelligence which makes no direct reference to either humans or machines. This is analogous to the account provided by the science of aerodynamics in the field of artificial flight. AI *qua* engineering should not be distracted into direct copying of human performance and methods. There is no reason to assume either that this is an easy task, or that it is likely to produce useful products.

4

The Intentional Stance and the Imitation Game

AJIT NARAYANAN

———————◆———————

1. THE INTENTIONAL STANCE AND INTENTIONAL SYSTEMS

In *Brainstorms* Dennett (1981) proposes the following six conditions, each of which is necessary, of 'personhood'. Although Dennett is concerned with 'moral personhood', rather than personhood as such, he believes that metaphysical personhood is a necessary condition of moral personhood. The six conditions are: rationality, intentionality, stance, reciprocity, verbal communication, and consciousness. The first three (rationality, intentionality, and stance) are used for defining *intentional system*:

An intentional system is a system whose behavior can be . . . explained and predicted by relying on ascriptions to the system of *beliefs* and *desires* (and other intentionally characterized features—what I will call *intentions* here, meaning to include hopes, fears, intentions, perceptions, expectations, etc.). . . . We ascribe beliefs and desires to dogs and fish and thereby predict their behavior, and we can even use the procedure to predict the behavior of some machines. . . . By *assuming* the [chess-playing] computer has certain beliefs (or information) and desires (or preference functions) dealing with the chess game in progress, I can calculate—under auspicious circumstances—the computer's most likely next move, *provided I assume that the computer deals rationally with these beliefs and desires*. The computer is an intentional system in these instances not because it has any particular intrinsic features, and not because it really and truly has beliefs and desires (whatever that would be), but just because it succumbs to a certain *stance* adopted toward it, namely the intentional stance, the stance that proceeds by ascribing intentional predicates under the usual constraints to the computer, the stance that proceeds by considering the computer as a rational practical reasoner. (Dennett, 1981: 271–2, emphasis added)

The second condition of the first three, interdependent conditions is that of intentionality, i.e. the ascription to the system of beliefs and desires. Although Dennett does not state explicitly how such ascription is possible, he clearly depends on the sort of ascription mechanism formulated by Strawson in his book, *Individuals* (Strawson, 1959). For instance, when outlining the six conditions, or 'themes' as he calls them, Dennett writes:

The second theme is that persons are beings to which states of consciousness are attributed, or to which psychological or mental or *intentional predicates*, are ascribed. Thus Strawson identifies the concept of a person as 'the concept of a type of entity such that *both* predicates ascribing states of consciousness *and* predicates ascribing corporeal characteristics' are applicable. (Dennett, 1981: 269–70, emphasis added)

The first condition is that persons are *rational beings*. Dennett unpacks this condition in two ways. First, he appeals to the rules of logic:

The assumption that something is an intentional system is the assumption that it is rational; that is, one gets nowhere with the assumption that entity x has beliefs $p, q, r, \ldots$ unless one also supposes that x believes what follows from $p, q, r, \ldots$; otherwise there is no way of ruling out the prediction that x will, in the face of its beliefs $p, q, r \ldots$ do something utterly stupid, and, if we cannot rule out *that* prediction, we will have acquired no predictive power at all. So whether or not the animal is said to *believe* the *truths* of logic, it must be supposed to *follow* the *rules* of logic. (Dennett, 1981: 10–11, emphasis added)

The second way of unpacking the notion of rationality is to provide some sort of status for the beliefs that a rational being holds. Dennett appeals to Griffiths (1962–3) at this point:

For the concept of belief to find application, two conditions . . . must be met: (1) In general, normally, more often than not, if x believes p, p is true. (2) In general, normally, more often than not, if x avows that p, he believes p [and, by (1), p is true]. Were these conditions not met, we would not have rational, communicating systems; we would not have believers or belief-avowers. (Dennett, 1981: 18)

Taken together, these first three conditions, namely, rationality, intentionality, and stance, define intentional systems. Dennett states:

So defined, intentional systems are obviously not all persons. We ascribe beliefs and desires to dogs and fish and thereby predict their behavior, and we can even use the procedure to predict the behavior of some machines. (Dennett, 1981: 271)

Dennett claims that there are certain advantages implied in his account of intentional systems, the main one being:

The concept of an intentional system is a relatively uncluttered and unmetaphysical notion, abstracted as it is from questions of the composition, constitution, consciousness, morality, or divinity of the entities falling under it. Thus, for example, it is much easier to decide whether a machine can be an intentional system than it is to decide whether a machine can *really* think, or be conscious, or morally responsible. (Dennett, 1981: 16, emphasis added)

The remaining three conditions of personhood are briefly these. Whereas the first three conditions are mutually interdependent in that they are not ordered, the remaining three are ordered. The fourth condition is *reciprocity*. For Dennett, a person must be able to reciprocate the stance, and this is best achieved by requiring that an intentional system itself adopt the intentional stance towards other objects. This in turn can be achieved by allowing an intentional system to ascribe beliefs, desires, and intentions about beliefs, desires, and intentions:

An intentional system S would be a second-order intentional system if among the ascriptions we make to it are such as *S believes that T desires that p*, *S hopes that T fears that q*, and reflexive cases like *S believes that S desires that p*. (Dennett, 1981: 273)

The difference between animals and humans, according to Dennett, is that 'it is hard to think of a case where an animal's behavior was so sophisticated that we would need to ascribe second-order intentions to it in order to predict or explain its behavior' (Dennett, 1981: 273).

The fifth condition is the capacity for *verbal communication*, and Dennett turns to Grice's theory of 'non-natural' meaning (Grice, 1957). The final condition for personhood is *consciousness*, and for this Dennett appeals to Frankfurt (1971), who developed the notion of 'reflective self-evaluation'.

2. REINTERPRETING THE IMITATION GAME

One of the interesting aspects of Dennett's views is that the 'Turing Test' implied by the imitation game can be reinterpreted in a modern light. That is, when Turing asks whether an intelligent machine can be imagined to fool the human interrogator as often as the man does in the original version of the game, this can be interpreted along intentional stance lines: 'Will the interrogator use the intentional stance with the intelligent computer as frequently as with the human?' If the answer is 'Yes', all that has been agreed to, for both human and computer, is the ascription of intentional and mental terms which are useful explanatory and predictive devices. There is no need to infer anything to do with the mind, or with consciousness. For example, it could be argued that the adoption of the intentional stance is justified on the basis of a short and concise statement being provided with the help of an intentional term, instead of a long technical description of the computer's program and physical characteristics.

Hence, the modern interpretation consists of arguing that, *even if* a machine successfully passes the test, the machine does not really think, or is really conscious or intelligent. The argument implies that the question, 'Can machines think?', after being replaced by the imitation game, should in turn be replaced by the question, 'Can machines have intentional stances applied to them?', which if answered positively implies nothing about mental or conscious matters. (Interestingly, Turing does not seem to have used the term 'Turing Test' himself. See Narayanan (1988, ch. 1) for evidence that Turing did not originally intend his imitation game to be a test as such, although he may not have objected to such an interpretation subsequently.) Where humans differ from machines (and dogs and cats, for example), according to Dennett's framework, is that there are three further rungs in the ladder of personhood which humans can climb, but machines (and dogs and cats) cannot.

Tempting as this scenario is, it is not clear that Dennett's ladder of personhood can support such an interpretation. It must be remembered that the intentional stance is just one step in the ladder, in that Dennett argues that being an intentional system is not a sufficient condition for being a person and thereby having consciousness. But if either, or both, of the other two, interdependent conditions—intentionality based on a Strawsonian mechanism, and rationality—themselves introduce consciousness (the sixth condition) then there is no longer a stepped approach.

3. INTERDEPENDENCE, OR CIRCULARITY?

If a Strawsonian ascription framework is really being appealed to by Dennett as the provider of the second condition, then the question arises as to how the second condition is going to cope with the following characteristic of intentional predicates (or, more generally, what Strawson calls *P-predicates* for *person*-predicates):

[T]hough not all P-predicates are what we would call 'predicates ascribing states of consciousness' (e.g. 'going for a walk' is not), they may be said to have this in common, that *they imply the possession of consciousness on the part of that to which they are ascribed.* (Strawson, 1959: 105, emphasis added)

This makes it appear that consciousness is at least necessary for intentionality, not the other way around as in Dennett's scheme. That is, the important point is whether in the act of ascribing an intentional predicate to an object consciousness is being ascribed to that object, or whether the object already possesses consciousness and the mechanism only deals with the justification of a certain ascription. Strawson himself writes:

There would be no question of ascribing one's own states of consciousness, or experiences, to anything, *unless* one also ascribed, or were ready and able to ascribe, states of consciousness, or experiences, to other individual entities *of the same logical type* as that thing to which one ascribes one's own states of consciousness. (Strawson, 1959, 104: emphasis added)

That is, for Strawson it appears that if humans ascribe a state of consciousness or intentional predicate to another individual, that other individual must be of the same type as humans, namely an entity with consciousness (a person). (Strawson goes on to outline three different types of P-predicate, but this is not important here.) What the ascription mechanism does is to provide justification for the ascription of *particular* mental states and intentional predicates, and in the case of both this is done with the assumption that the other individual is conscious. What is in question is *which* state of consciousness that individual is in, not whether that individual has consciousness. But consciousness is introduced only in the sixth condition.

Dennett's strategy therefore fails to take into account that a Strawson-like mechanism necessarily implies consciousness on the part of that to which mental and intentional predicates are ascribed, and so cannot have the implication of consciousness removed arbitrarily from these predicates. In short, the application of intentional terms to intentional systems (IS) *per se* assumes the application of intentional terms to humans as intentional systems (HIS)—as required by a Strawsonian framework—whereas Dennett's ladder specifies that the application of intentional terms to HIS assumes the application of intentional terms to IS.

To summarize and conclude the argument, a possible weakness has been identified in the original version of Dennett's thesis as consisting of the appeal to a Strawsonian ascription mechanism in the second condition, when consciousness does not play a full part in Dennett's ladder of personhood until the sixth condition. This led Dennett to propose that terms which have implications of consciousness have two uses: one at a high level in his ladder of personhood, where the terms do indeed convey their full implication of consciousness on the part of that to which they are ascribed (i.e. persons), and another at the lower level of the intentional stance, where the terms do not convey their full implication of consciousness on the part of that to which they are applied. The latter use is, according to Dennett, justified by the intentional stance, whereby such terms are used depending on a stance adopted towards the entity in question. The application of such predicates without consciousness implications is then justified on the basis of explanatory and predictive ease. This, in turn, is based on the pragmatic consideration that the adoption of the intentional stance allows for a short and concise statement to be provided with the help of an intentional term, instead of a long technical description of the computer's program and physical characteristics. This is supported by an appeal to the rationality of the system, and a system is rational if it 'follows the truths of logic'. Following the truths of logic needs to be described without the use of intentional terms, but following a truth of logic (according to some rules) seems intrinsically bound up with having beliefs about the truths of logic, i.e. rationality. But Dennett has not adequately identified the circumstances under which the logically necessary implication of consciousness can be separated from terms involving rationality.

Now, '*x* believes, or thinks, or concludes that *y*' *does* convey some implication of consciousness on the part of *x*, as a Strawson-type account confirms, without the need to know what sort of entity x is. Is there another way to explain what happens when mental terms are used with reference to computers?

4. THE REPRESENTATIONAL STANCE

What is missing from the picture so far is some reference to *representations*. A representation, along classical lines, can be considered as a formal system consisting of a vocabulary of symbols and a set of rules for manipulating these symbols. Representations exist in natural language understanding systems, vision systems, learning systems, and reasoning systems, for example. Representations in this classical sense will contain symbols, and some of these symbols may be 'sees', 'understands', 'decides', and so on. The proposal here is that meaning of these symbols is not intentional but fixed by the role of that symbol in rule-manipulation and its relationship with other symbols.

A representational architecture is a technical term for describing the processes whereby symbols are mapped onto each other. Although a representational architecture may be internalized by a system, the system designers and implementors need not commit themselves to an intentional interpretation of symbols which also have intentional sense. The intentional sense is stripped away if designers and implementors ground the meaning of such symbols in the overall processes of the representational architecture (e.g. one symbol causing another to appear or disappear). The difference between a representational symbol and an intentional symbol of the same name is that the representational symbol stands or falls in its relationship with other symbols and processes of the architecture, whereas an intentional symbol does not. An intentional symbol may stand or fall in virtue of the intentional state it purports to denote existing or not existing. A representational symbol on the other hand will stand or fall in virtue of the symbolic state it is in leading to system success at a task, or system failure and/or inconsistency. The criterion is system performance in relation to what the system is required to do, in the case of representational symbols.

For example, the rule '*unstack:* (*clear X*) (*on X Y*) → (*clear X*) (*ontable X*) (*clear Y*)' specifies the unstacking of a block, X. Given a start state of (*clear a*) (*on a b*), the application of this rule will lead to a final state where (*clear a*) (*ontable a*) (*clear b*). The final state contains a symbolic sequence which achieves, as far as the system specification of *unstack* is concerned, a state in which a block has been unstacked. The success of this final state depends on whether the symbols in the final representational state stand in a relationship with each other such that the specification of *unstack* has been achieved given the start state.

Given this approach, a *representational stance* consists of the application of terms, taken from a particular representational framework, to entities such as computers, dogs, cats, clocks, cars, typewriters, and so on. For instance, the sentence '*x* decides where to sit in the restaurant' may be unpacked as an example of a representational stance towards *x*, where the behaviour of *x* at a particular moment is claimed to be such that a term from a representation of some sort is applicable to *x*. The word 'decide', which usually has intentional sense, is used in the representational stance sentence without that intentional sense, provided that it is made clear that what is being appealed to is some representation where the term 'decide' has a particular technical or theoretical meaning. That is, the term 'decide' is grounded not in the usual understanding of the term but in some representation, where the representation has lost the term's intentional sense but nevertheless the term has some sense according to the representation. In the above example, the sentence may have used a term which is taken directly from the representation (a script, for instance, or at least some abstract representation of one). However, it is also possible to use terms in such sentences which do not appear directly in the representation. For instance, the sentence, '*x* decides on its next chess move', may be an example of the representational stance where the term 'decide' could be *derived* from the terms used in the representation. The chess-playing program may contain no reference to 'decide' anywhere, yet the behaviour of the program is such that the term 'decide' has been derived somehow by the person who has adopted the representational stance. For instance, the explanation could be that from a higher level within the representation certain lower-level features are currently being manipulated by various rule-governed processes, where the lower-level features comprise a set which can be labelled 'decide'.

The notions of explanation and prediction can now be unpacked with regard to system performance. In the case of a direct term, the representational stance sentence is an *explanation* (*prediction*) provided that the adopter can ground the term in some representation which includes that term as one of its terms, with the implication that the system behaviour of the entity *is* (*will be*) subsumed in some sense by that representation. In the case of a derived term, the representational stance is an explanation (prediction) provided that the adopter can somehow *substitute* some features of a representation (e.g. another term based on an abstraction of lower-level features, some control structure, some design feature) for that term, with the implication that the system behaviour of the entity is (will be) subsumed in some sense by what is offered.

In both cases, the appeal to a particular, pre-existing representation need not be necessary for the adoption of a representational stance. That is, someone could use a term in a representational stance which cannot then be grounded or derived because no appropriate representation exists, or the adopter is not aware of one. Nevertheless, the *justification* for, and not explanation of or prediction from, the representational stance sentence can be expressed along the lines that the adopter implies (in the sense of 'presupposes' or 'assumes') that there *may* be some representation available which provides an explanation for, or a prediction from, terms used in the sentence which usually have intentional sense but in this case do not. For instance, 'My car is reluctant to get going this morning' may be an example of the representational stance where the adopter has no particular representation in mind but nevertheless is making the claim that, if there is one, a grounding or substitution can be made. Hence, the representational stance can be adopted on the basis of a *hypothetical* representation. The non-existence of a particular, suitable representation does not prevent someone from adopting such a stance.

An attempt is being made here to capture the intuitive appeal of sentences which use intentional terms but where there may be no necessary commitment to *ascribing* consciousness on the part of that to which such terms are *applied*. The representational stance, as just characterized, appeals to a representational architecture, either real or hypothetical, within which terms gain their 'meaning' in virtue of their relationship to other symbols in the representational architecture, where such relationships are determined by symbol-manipulating rules, for example.

5. THE ASCRIPTIONAL STANCE

Such use of intentional terms is to be distinguished from their use where some commitment to consciousness is implied (in the sense of being presupposed or assumed). This introduces *ascription mechanisms*, where consciousness on the part of entities to which intentional terms and mental predicates are ascribed is implied (presupposed, assumed). Hence, ascription mechanisms are concerned with the nature, and degree, of consciousness that is bestowed on, or assumed of, entities which already (logically) possess consciousness. Ascription mechanisms will be characterized according to the type and range of mental predicates and intentional terms which can be ascribed to a variety of entities. Ascription mechanisms will in turn be underpinned by some theory of consciousness, where an account is provided of what degree of consciousness is to be assumed of various entities by the ascription.

In short, the *ascriptional stance* (or redefined intentional stance) consists of issuing sentences where intentional terms and mental predicates are ascribed to entities by means of a certain ascription mechanism. The sense of the terms and predicates will be fixed by the ascription mechanism which in turn will be grounded in some theory of consciousness.

The point of the ascriptional stance can now be simply put as follows. Whereas the representational stance could not care whether a representation is used for representing the behaviour of humans, machines, dogs, cats, and so on, since it is only the system behaviour (as it 'conforms' in some sense to the representation) which is under examination, the ascriptional stance has precisely the effect of *separating* such entities and classifying them according to the success or otherwise of the ascription, depending on what the underlying theory of consciousness implies of such entities. According to this account, ascription mechanisms *could* use the same intentional term or mental predicate with different meanings. For instance, the sentence '*x* decides where to sit down in the restaurant' could mean something very different when used with regard to a human, a robot, and a dog, i.e. there could be three different senses ascribed by the associated ascription mechanisms, where each is supported by some suitable theory of consciousness.

Just as before, the notions of explanation and prediction can be unpacked with regard to the ascriptional stance. In the case of a mental predicate or intentional term, the ascriptional stance sentence is an *explanation* (*prediction*) provided that the adopter can ground the term in some ascription mechanism which includes that term as one of the terms it can ascribe. The implication or assumption is that the consciousness of the entity is such that other mental predicates or intentional terms which belong to the same or related type, as specified by the ascription mechanism, *can be* (*will be*) ascribed by the same ascription mechanism.

Again, the appeal to a *particular*, pre-existing ascription mechanism need not be necessary for the adoption of an ascriptional stance. That is, someone could use a term in an ascriptional stance which cannot then be grounded or derived because no appropriate ascription mechanism exists, or the adopter is not aware of one. Nevertheless, the *justification* for the ascriptional stance sentence can be expressed along the lines that the adopter implies (in the sense of 'presupposes' or 'assumes') that there *may* be some ascription mechanism available which provides explanations for, or predictions from, terms used in the sentence which have intentional sense. The important characteristic of both the representational and ascriptional stances, as now portrayed, is the way they can be adopted *hypothetically*. For instance, 'My computer is reluctant to provide a solution to this question' is, with regard to the ascriptional stance, essentially of the general form: 'If there is some ascription mechanism for ascribing intentional terms and mental predicates to a computer of a certain sort, then I am somehow justified in claiming that it is reluctant to provide solutions to questions.' That is, the claim is that the term 'reluctant' is one of the terms that can be applied by the ascription mechanism, if there is one.

6. APPLICATION AND ASCRIPTION

One interesting side-effect here is that AI researchers who want to ascribe something more than representations to entities such as computers must be careful in their ascription methods. For example, researchers may use a term in a way that assumes one type of ascription mechanism (say, a restricted type of human ascription mechanism) in order to ascribe that term to a computer, then use the general implication of consciousness on the part of the computer to ascribe a variety of different mental predicates and intentional terms on the basis of another type of ascription mechanism (say, a full-fledged human ascription mechanism). Also, an AI researcher may use the representational stance in order to *apply* to a program or computer a theoretical or technical term based in a representation and then, wrongly, use the same term (or terms related to it by an ascription mechanism) as if the terms can be *ascribed* by some form of ascriptional stance, thereby bestowing, by sleight of hand, some degree of consciousness on the part of the computer (or program). The ascriptional stance, as now defined, can prevent such tricks by requiring that all ascription mechanisms be classified according to the type to which they belong, and that once one particular ascription mechanism is used the same one (or one related somehow in type) must be used for other mental predicates and intentional terms falling under that (or related) type. Ascription of terms is therefore distinguished from application of terms, according to the proposed framework, in that ascription necessarily bestows some degree of consciousness on the part of that to which they are ascribed. The precise nature and content of consciousness is a matter for the ascription mechanism and its supporting theory of consciousness. What is not in question is *whether* the entity is conscious.

Once again the attempt is being made here to capture the intuitive feeling that when an intentional term or mental predicate is ascribed to another entity whose nature and degree of consciousness is in doubt, this is a form of experimenting with intentional and mental terms to see how far an ascription mechanism can be pushed without breaking down. For instance, if someone says, from the ascriptional stance, 'My computer is reluctant to play chess today', it is quite in order for the conversation to proceed along the lines of, say, someone else responding 'Your computer was quite happy to play chess with me yesterday', where the conversation proceeds *on the assumption of computer-consciousness*; yet, the success or failure of the conversation does not necessarily depend on the two individuals agreeing or disagreeing on the precise nature of a particular ascription mechanism, and hence on a particular theory of computer consciousness. The point of the conversation, in this case, could well be for the two individuals involved in the conversation to see where they begin to agree or disagree on what other intentional and mental terms can be ascribed to the computer, and in this way the two individuals can begin to identify the relationships possible between various intentional and mental terms—relationships which may then form the basis for identifying the sorts of conceptual scheme (and hence implicit theories of consciousness) being adopted by one or both individuals. To return to an earlier point, the reason why '*x* believes, or thinks, or concludes that *y*' usually carries some implication of consciousness is that by default it is assumed that *x* is conscious, i.e. the sentence is an example of the ascriptional stance (as opposed to the representational stance) adopted towards *no particular entity*.

So far, there has been no claim concerning whether representations are at level one and ascription mechanisms at level two in some hierarchy or other. Instead, the representational stance and the ascriptional stance have been identified as different spheres of activity. If these spheres of activity are indeed hierarchically organized in the sense that the ascriptional stance is above the representational stance, what are the implications for a third level?

7. THE META-ASCRIPTIONAL STANCE

Since the second level—the ascriptional stance—is concerned with *individual* ascription mechanisms using possibly different types of mental predicates, the third level logically should concern itself with evaluating different *types* of ascription mechanism. If this third level exists, the *meta-ascriptional* level, it would consist in part of the meta-activity of examining and identifying similarities and differences between ascription mechanisms. One task at this level would be to identify the implications of adopting one type of ascription mechanism that is used with one type of conscious entity for another type of conscious entity. Similarly, another task would be to identify the implications of adopting one type of ascription mechanism with regard to two different types of conscious entity. These tasks would have many implications for the relativity of conceptual schemes, the substance of reality including individuals and events, the nature of truth and justification, and the role of language, for instance. But it would be at this level that the degree of overlap could be measured in the application of a mental or intentional predicate to two entities belonging to two different types (e.g. human and computer).

Here would seem to be a good place to locate two of Dennett's original six conditions: reciprocity and verbal communication. Namely, it is likely that one of the ways that ascription mechanisms at the second level can be evaluated is, from a level above, to look for abstract features such as reciprocity and what is involved in ascribing language terms to others, as well as to humans. Although a Gricean formulation (Grice, 1957, 1968) may not be *necessary* at this level, something like it is certainly possible, provided it is accepted that consciousness is already introduced at the lower level. At this level also can be placed general theories of consciousness. For instance, Searle's proposal (Searle, 1987) can be reinterpreted as claiming that, no matter which ascription mechanism is chosen at the second level, they all share the common property that justification for the ascription of intentional and mental predicates is based on neural and biological considerations of the brain (i.e. on the notion of *causal power of the brain*).

8. THE IMITATION GAME REINTERPRETED

If the third level proposed above exists, here is another interpretation of the imitation game, this time from the viewpoint of the redefined hierarchy and the modified view of stance:

The question, 'Can machines think?', is now a question at the third level, asking whether there is a level two (ascriptional) stance of a certain type which can be used for the ascription of mental predicates to computers of a certain type.

The reason why this is a third level question is that it can be answered in several ways, including the following:

(a) Humans and a certain type of computer are of the same type and so have the same mental predicates ascribable to them. Hence, *all* the mental predicates ascribable to humans are ascribable to computers of that type, and vice versa.

(b) There is some overlap between humans and a certain type of computer which allows *some* mental predicates to be ascribed to both.

(c) *Certain* predicates can be equally ascribed to entities belonging to a variety of types (including humans and computers) but these predicates do not assume full person status on the part of that to which they are ascribed.

(*d*) Finally, certain types of predicate can only be ascribed to certain entities, i.e. there is no overlap between humans and any type of computer.

The reason why Turing considered the original question 'too meaningless to deserve discussion' can now be hypothesized, from the three-level framework above, to be that, with so many possible answers available, some level three (meta-ascription) specification was required in order to cut down on the number of possibilities at level two. His reformulation of the question, the imitation game, can be interpreted as an attempt to provide an indication of what particular level two (ascriptional) stances would look like once humans, and computing machines of a certain type, were hypothesized *at the third level* to be of the same type with regard to mental and intentional predicates. In other words, his reformulation was along the lines of (*a*) above.

If this interpretation is essentially correct, there is yet another way of looking at the remainder of his paper. His 'Objections' can be interpreted as attempts to provide greater detail, at the second level, of how such predicates could be applied to computing machines in the first place. These attempts had different degrees of success. For instance, the Mathematical Objection, the Argument from Consciousness, Lady Lovelace's Objection, and the Argument from Informality of Behaviour are essentially arguments of the form: 'If this objection can be raised against ascribing mental and intentional predicates to computing machines, then it can be raised against ascribing such predicates to humans also.' The Argument from Various Disabilities is the objection, at level three but also with implications for level two, that it may not be possible for all the mental predicates ascribable to humans to be ascribed to computers also. However, Turing's response, now reinterpreted, is that even if this were the case, some degree of consciousness is being ascribed by or through other mental predicates when ascribed to computers of a certain type at level two. Finally, the part of his paper which deals with the notions of Turing machine and quintuples is an attempt to provide, at level one, some indication of the formalisms and representations necessary for describing the functional behaviour of machines.

9. CONCLUSION

A threefold classification has been proposed of how talk about intelligent, thinking entities is possible. At one level—the level of representations—a representational stance can be adopted which, whilst allowing talk about an entity in terms which are theory-bound, i.e. terms which have a particular technical meaning given a certain representation, bestow no implication of consciousness or thought on the part of the entity to which such terms are applied. The justification for the application of terms at this level will typically be in the form of demonstrating how the application of the terms is warranted because of the nature of the representation as well as, typically, the internal processes and outward behaviour of the entity. Also, the representational stance can be adopted on the basis of a hypothetical representation, i.e. a representation which may or may not exist. The adoption of such a stance at this level leads to a limited form of prediction and explanation.

At another level—the level of ascriptions—an ascriptional stance can be adopted which, whilst allowing talk about an entity in terms which assume consciousness and thought, i.e. terms which have a particular intentional or mental sense given a certain ascription mechanism, may not necessarily bestow the same degree of consciousness to that entity as for a person (in Strawson's sense). The justification for the ascription of terms at this level will usually be in the form of appealing to a particular theory of consciousness, in which the ascription (rather than application) of such terms is warranted because of the nature of the theory of consciousness. Also, the ascriptional stance can be adopted on the basis of a hypothetical ascription mechanism and hypothetical theory of consciousness which may or may not exist. The adoption of such a stance at this level leads to a limited form of ascriptional prediction and explanation.

The third level—the level of meta-ascriptions—is concerned with what particular ascription mechanisms at the second level look like, e.g. what they have in common, what the assumptions are concerning the degree of consciousness implied, and what various intentional and mental terms have in common. One question which arises at this level concerns the different ascription mechanisms implied by a particular theory of consciousness, as well as a particular ascription mechanism shared by different theories of consciousness.

The main difference between Dennett's proposal and the one above can now be summarized as follows. Whereas Dennett claims that prediction and explanation of, say, a chess-playing computer *assume rationality of design* (but not necessarily perfect rationality) with no implication of consciousness on the part of the chess-playing computer, the claim here is that prediction and explanation in this case *assume consciousness* (but not necessarily human consciousness) with no necessary commitment to any particular ascription mechanism. The adopter of the ascriptional stance here is assuming that there may be an ascription mechanism of some sort which justifies the ascription of the intentional or mental term. One of the roles of the ascriptional stance is therefore to allow an individual to explore the conceptual schemes, and hence views of reality, of others. This is best achieved by pitching the level of exploration fairly high—at the level of theories of consciousness.

REFERENCES

Dennett, D. C. (1981), *Brainstorms*, Harvester Press, Brighton.

Frankfurt, H. G. (1971), 'Freedom of the Will and the Concept of a Person', *Journal of Philosophy*, 68: 5–20.

Grice, H. P. (1957), 'Meaning', *Philosophical Review*, 66: 377–88.

—— (1968), 'Utterer's Meaning, Sentence-Meaning, and Word-Meaning', *Foundations of Language*, 4: 225–42.

Griffiths, A. P. (1962–3), 'On Belief', *Proceedings of the Aristotelian Society*, 68: 167–86.

Narayanan, A. (1988), *On Being a Machine*: i. *Formal Aspects of Artifical Intelligence*, Ellis Horwood, Chichester.

Searle, J. R. (1987), 'Minds and Brains without Programs', in C. Blakemore and S. Greenfield (eds.), *Mindwaves*, Blackwell, Oxford.

Strawson, P. F. (1959), *Individuals*, Methuen, London.

5

Machine as Mind

HERBERT A. SIMON

———◆———

The title of my talk is broad enough to cover nearly anything that might be relevant to a collection memorializing A. M. Turing. However, many, if not most, relevant matters have been debated at length for a number of years—some of them for forty—or are being addressed by others in this volume. For that reason, I will omit discussion of the Turing Test, and mention Searle's Chinese Room only briefly. Instead, starting with the human mind and what psychological research has learned about it, I will proceed to draw lessons from cognitive psychology about the characteristics we must bestow upon computer programs when we wish those programs to think.

I speak of 'mind' and not 'brain'. By mind I mean a system that produces thought, viewed at a relatively high level of aggregation: say, at or above the level of elementary processes that require 100 milliseconds or more for their execution. At that level, little or nothing need be said about the structure or behaviour of individual neurons, or even small assemblages of them. Our units will be larger and more abstract.

It is well known that the language and representation best adapted to describing phenomena depends on the level of aggregation at which we model them. Physicists concerned with quarks and similar particles on minute temporal and spatial scales do not use the same vocabulary of entities and processes as geneticists describing how DNA informs protein synthesis.

Whatever our philosophical position with respect to reduction, it is practically necessary to build science in levels. The phenomena at each level are described in terms of the primitives at that level, and these primitives become, in turn, the phenomena to be described and explained at the level next below.

The primitives of mind, at the level I wish to consider, are symbols, complex structures of symbols, and processes that operate on symbols (Newell and Simon, 1976). The simplest among these processes require tens to hundreds of milliseconds for their execution. Simple recognition of a familiar object takes at least 500 milliseconds. At this level, the same software can be implemented with radically different kinds of hardware—protoplasm and silicon among them.

My central thesis is that at this level of aggregation conventional computers can be, and have been, programmed to represent symbol structures and carry out processes on those structures in a manner that parallels, step by step, the way the human brain does it. The principal evidence for my thesis are programs that do just that. These programs demonstrably think.

It has been argued that a computer simulation of thinking is no more thinking than a simulation of digestion is digestion. The analogy is false. A computer simulation of digestion is not capable of taking starch as an input and producing fructose or glucose as outputs. It deals only with symbolic or numerical quantities representing these substances.

In contrast, a computer simulation of thinking thinks. It takes problems as its inputs and (sometimes) produces solutions as its outputs. It represents these problems and solutions as symbolic structures, as the human mind does, and performs transformations on them like those the human mind does. The materials of digestion are chemical substances, which are not replicated in a computer simulation. The materials of thought are symbols—patterns, which can be replicated in a great variety of materials (including neurons and chips), thereby enabling physical symbol systems fashioned of these materials to think. Turing was perhaps the first to have this insight in clear form, more than forty years ago (Turing, 1950).

NEARLY DECOMPOSABLE SYSTEMS

The successive levels in the architecture of nature are not arbitrary (Simon, 1981). Most complex systems are hierarchical and *nearly decomposable*. Consider a building divided into rooms, which are, in turn, divided into cubicles. Starting from a state of radical temperature disequilibrium—every cubic foot of space being momentarily at quite a different temperature from the adjoining spaces—within a matter of minutes the temperature within each cubicle will approach some constant value, a different value for each cubicle. After a somewhat longer time, all the cubicles in a given room will reach a common temperature. After a still longer interval, all the rooms in the building will reach a common temperature.

In a hierarchical system of this kind, we do not have to consider the behaviour at all levels simultaneously. We can model the cubicles, the rooms, and the building semi-independently. In the short run, we can analyse the changes in individual cubicles while disregarding their interaction with the other cubicles. In the middle run, we can analyse the individual rooms, replacing the detail of each cubicle by its average temperature. For the longer run, we can consider the building as a whole, replacing the detail of each room by its average temperature.

In layered hierarchical systems of this kind each subcomponent has a much higher rate of interaction with the other subcomponents in the same component than it does with subcomponents outside that component. Elsewhere (Simon, 1981) I have shown how the behaviour of nearly decomposable systems can be analysed mathematically, and why, from an evolutionary standpoint, we should expect most of the complex systems that we find in nature to be nearly decomposable.

For present purposes, what is important about nearly decomposable systems is that we can analyse them at a particular level of aggregation without detailed knowledge of the structures at the levels below. These details do not 'show through' at the next level above; only aggregate properties of the more microscopic systems affect behaviour at the higher level. In our temperature example, only the average temperatures of the cubicles affect the changes in temperature in the rooms, and only the average temperatures of the rooms are relevant to the course of equilibration of the building as a whole.

Because mind has shown itself to behave as a nearly decomposable system, we can model thinking at the symbolic level, with events in the range of hundreds of milliseconds or longer, without concern for details of implementation at the 'hardware' level, whether the hardware be brain or computer.

THE TWO FACES OF AI

AI can be approached in two ways. First, we can write smart programs for computers without any commitment to imitating the processes of human intelligence. We can then use all of the speed and power of the computer, and all of its memory capacity, unconcerned with whether people have the same computational speed and power, or the same memory capacity.

Alternatively, we can write smart programs for computers that do imitate closely the human processes, forgoing the computer's capacities for rapid processing of symbols and its almost instantaneous memory storage. We can slow the computer down to human speeds, so to speak, and test whether it can absorb the cunning that will permit it to behave intelligently within these limitations.

Chess-playing programs illustrate the two approaches. DEEP-THOUGHT is a powerful program that now plays chess at grandmaster level, and can defeat all but a few hundred human players. It demonstrably does not play in a humanoid way, typically exploring tens of millions of branches of the game tree before it makes its choice of move. There is good empirical evidence (De Groot, 1965) that human grandmasters seldom look at more than 100 branches on the tree. By generally searching the *relevant* branches, they make up with chess knowledge for their inability to carry out massive searches.

However, DEEPTHOUGHT by no means 'explores all possibilities'. 'All possibilities' would mean at least 10^{50} branches, 10^{40} times more than the program can manage, and obviously more than any computer, present or prospective can explore. DEEP-THOUGHT exercises a certain degree of selectivity in the branches it explores, but more important, it halts its explorations about a dozen ply deep—far short of the end of the game—and applies an evaluation function to measure the relative goodness of all the positions it reaches. A great deal of chess knowledge, supplied by the human programmers, is incorporated in the evaluation function. Hence DEEPTHOUGHT's chess prowess rests on a combination of brute force, unattainable by human players, and extensive, if 'mediocre', chess knowledge.

Consider now a much earlier program, MATER (Baylor and Simon, 1966) which is not nearly as good a chessplayer as DEEPTHOUGHT. In fact, MATER is a specialist designed only to exploit those game positions where an immediate mating combination (possibly a quite deep one) might be hidden. MATER has shown substantial ability to discover such mating combinations—rediscovering many of the most celebrated ones in chess history. What is more interesting, MATER ordinarily looks at fewer than 100 branches of the tree in order to accomplish this. It is as selective in its search as human players are in these kinds of situations, and in fact, it looks at nearly the same parts of the game tree as they do.

We can go even farther in comparing MATER with human players. For these kinds of positions (where a possible checkmate lurks), MATER uses the same rules of thumb to guide its search and select promising lines that human masters use. It examines forceful moves first, and it examines first those branches along which the opponent is most constrained. These heuristics, while powerful, do not always lead to the shortest mate. We have found at least one historical instance (a game between Edward Lasker and Thomas) in which both human player and computer required an extra move because the shortest path to a checkmate did not satisfy these heuristics—did not correspond with the most plausible search path.

The remainder of my remarks are concerned with programs that are intelligent in more or less humanoid ways—that carry out only modest computations to perform their tasks. These programs resemble MATER rather than DEEPTHOUGHT. This does not mean that programs for AI should always be built in this way, but my aim here is to consider machine as mind rather than to celebrate the achievements of rapid computation.

THE VIEW FROM PSYCHOLOGY

Selective heuristic search

How does intelligence look to contemporary cognitive psychology? I have already mentioned one fact that has been verified repeatedly in the laboratory—human problem solvers do not carry out extensive searches. Even examining 100 possibilities in a game tree stretches human memory and patience. Since many of the spaces in which people solve problems are enormous (I have mentioned the figure of 10^{50} for chess), 'trying everything' is not a viable search strategy. People use knowledge about the structure of the problem space to form heuristics that allow them to search extremely selectively.

Recognition: the indexed memory

A second important fact is also well illustrated by the game of chess. A chess grandmaster can play fifty or more opponents 'simultaneously', moving from board to board and seldom taking more than a few seconds for each move. If the opponents are not stronger than experts, say, the grandmaster will win almost every game, although his play will perhaps be only at master level. This demonstrates that much of grandmasters' knowledge (not all of it) is accessed by recognition of cues on the board, for in simultaneous play they have no time for deep analysis by search (Chase and Simon, 1973).

Grandmasters, questioned on how they play simultaneous games, report that they make 'standard' developing moves until they notice a feature of the board that indicates a weakness in the opponent's position (doubled pawns, say). Noticing this feature gives access to information about strategies for exploiting it. The grandmaster's memory is like a large indexed encyclopedia (with at least 50,000 index entries). The perceptually noticeable features of the chessboard (the cues) trigger the appropriate index entries and give access to the corresponding information. This information often includes relevant strategies.

Solving problems by responding to cues that are visible only to experts is sometimes called solving them by 'intuition'. A better label would be 'solving by recognition'. Intuition consists simply in noting features in a situation that index useful information. There is no mystery in intuition, or at least no more mystery than there is in recognizing a friend on the street and recalling what one knows about the friend.

In computers, recognition processes are generally implemented by productions: the condition sides of the productions serving as tests for the presence of cues, the action sides holding the information that is accessed when the cues are noticed. Hence it is easy to build computer systems that solve problems by recognition, and indeed recognition capability is the core of most AI expert systems.

The number, 50,000, suggested above as the number of features a grandmaster can recognize on a chessboard, has been estimated empirically, but only by indirect means (Simon and Gilmartin, 1973). One's confidence rises that the figure is approximately correct on noting that it is roughly comparable to the native language vocabularies of college graduates (usually estimated at 50,000 to 100,000 words).

Items that, by their recognizability, serve to index semantic memory are usually called 'chunks' in the psychological literature. Generalizing, we hypothesize that an expert in any domain must acquire some 50,000 familiar chunks (give or take a factor of four). Although existing expert systems for computers are not this large, the figure is not a daunting one.

By way of footnote, extensive data show that it takes at least ten years of intensive training for a person to acquire the information (presumably including the 50,000 chunks) required for world-class performance in any domain of expertise. This has been shown for chess-playing, musical composition, painting, piano-playing, swimming, tennis, neuropsychological research, research in topology, and other fields (Bloom, 1985; Hayes, 1989). Mozart, who began composing at four, produced no world-class music before at least the age of 17, thirteen years later. Child prodigies are not exempt from the rule.

Seriality: the limits of attention

Problems that cannot be solved by recognition generally require the application of more or less sustained attention. Attention is closely associated with human short-term memory. Symbols that are attended to—the inputs, say, to an arithmetic calculation—must be retained during use in short-term memory, which has a capacity of only about seven chunks, a limit that is based on extensive experimental data (Simon, 1976). The need for all inputs and outputs of attention-demanding tasks to pass through short-term memory essentially serializes the thinking process. Generally, we can only think of one thing at a time. (Sometimes, by time-sharing, we can think of two, if they are not too complex. Light conversation and driving are compatible activities for most people when the traffic is not too heavy!)

Hence, whatever parallel processes may be going on at lower

(neural) levels, at the symbolic level the human mind is fundamentally a serial machine, accomplishing its work through temporal sequences of processes, each typically requiring hundreds of milliseconds for execution.

In contrast, the evidence is equally strong that the sensory organs, especially the eyes and ears, are highly parallel systems. We are confronted with a hybrid system, the sensory (and possibly perceptual) processes operating in parallel, and the subsequent symbolic processes (after patterns of stimuli have been recognized and chunked) serially.

Within the limits of present knowledge there is a no-man's-land between the parallel and serial components of the processor, whose exact boundaries are not known. For example, there are implementable schemes that execute all processing down to the point of recognition in parallel (e.g. so-called Demon schemes), but there are also workable serial recognition systems (e.g. EPAM: Feigenbaum and Simon, 1984; Richman and Simon, 1989). The available evidence does not make a clear choice between these alternatives.

The architecture of expert systems

Psychology, then, gives us a picture of the expert as having a sensory system that is basically parallel in structure, interfaced with a cognitive system that is basically serial. Somewhere in the imprecise boundary between the two is a mechanism (serial or parallel or both) capable of recognizing large numbers (hundreds of thousands) of patterns in the domain of expertise, and of obtaining access through this recognition to information stored in short-term memory. The information accessed can be processed further (using heuristic search) by a serial symbol-processing system.

Recognition takes approximately a half second or second (Newell and Simon, 1972). The individual steps in search also require hundreds of milliseconds, and search is highly selective, the selectivity based on heuristics stored in memory. People can report orally the results of recognition (but not the cues used in the process) and are aware of many of the inputs and outputs of the steps they take in search. It appears that they can report most of the symbols that reside temporarily in short-term memory (i.e. the symbols in the focus of attention).

One reason for thinking that this structure is sufficient to produce expert behaviour is that AI has now built many expert systems, capable of performing at professional levels in restricted domains, using essentially the architecture we have just described. In general, the AI expert systems (e.g. systems for medical diagnosis) have fewer 'chunks' than the human experts, and make up for the deficiency by doing more computing than people do. The differences appear to be quantitative, not qualitative: human and computer experts alike depend heavily upon recognition, supplemented by a little capacity for reasoning (i.e. search).

THE MATTER OF SEMANTICS

It is sometimes claimed that the thinking of computers, symbolic systems that they are, is purely syntactical. Unlike people, it is argued, computers do not have intentions and their symbols do not have semantic referents. The argument is easily refuted by concrete examples of computer programs that demonstrably understand the meanings (at least some of the meanings) of their symbols, and that have goals, thus exhibiting at least two aspects of intention.

Consider, first, a computer-driven van, of which we have an example on our university campus, equipped with television cameras and capable of steering its way (slowly) along a winding road in a nearby park. Patterns of light transmitted through the cameras are encoded by the computer program as landscape features: for example, the verge of the road. The program, having the intention of proceeding along the road and remaining on it, creates internal symbols that denote these features, interprets them, and uses the symbols to guide its steering and speed control mechanisms.

Consider, second, one of the commercially available chess-playing programs that use an actual chess board on which the opponent moves the men physically, and which senses these moves and forms an internal (symbolic) representation of the chess position. The symbols in this internal representation denote the external physical pieces and their arrangement, and the program demonstrates quite clearly, by the moves it chooses, that it intends to beat its opponent.

There is no mystery about what 'semantics' means as applied to the human mind. It means that there is a correspondence, a relation of denotation, between symbols inside the head and objects (or relations among objects) outside. In particular, the brain is (sometimes) able to test whether sensory signals received from particular objects identify those objects as the meanings of particular symbols (names). And the human brain is sometimes able to construct and emit words, phrases, and sentences whose denotation corresponds to the sensed scene.

There is also no mystery about human intentions. In certain circumstances, for example, a human being senses internal stirrings (usually called hunger) that lead him or her to seek food. In other circumstances, other stirrings create the goal of defeating an opponent in chess. Now the two computer programs I described above also have goals: in the one case to drive along a road, in the other case to win a chess game. It would not be hard to store both programs in the same computer, along with input channels that would, from time to time, switch its attention from the one goal to the other. Such a system would then have not a single intention, but a capacity for several, even as you and I.

It may be objected (and has been) that the computer does not 'understand' the meanings of its symbols or the semantic operations on them, or the goals it adopts. This peculiar use of the word 'understand' has something to do with the fact that we are (sometimes) *conscious* of meanings and intentions. But then, my evidence that you are conscious is no better than my evidence that the road-driving or chess-playing computers are conscious.

Moreover, in formal treatments of semantics, consciousness has never been one of the defining characteristics; denotation has. What is important about semantic meaning is that there be a correspondence (conscious or not) between the symbol and the thing it denotes. What is important about intention is that there be a correspondence (conscious or not) between the goal symbol and behaviour appropriate to achieving the goal in the context of some belief system.

Finally, Searle's Chinese Room parable does not prove that computer programs cannot understand Chinese, but only that the particular program Searle described does not understand Chinese. Had he described a program that could receive inputs from a sensory system and emit the symbol 'cha' in the presence of tea, and 'bai cha' in the presence of hot water, we would have to admit that it understood at least a *little* Chinese. And the vocabulary and grammar could be extended indefinitely. Later, I will describe a computer program, devised by Siklóssy (1972), that learns language in exactly this way (although the connection with external senses was not implemented).

'ILL-STRUCTURED' PHENOMENA

Research on human thinking has progressed from relatively simple and well-structured phenomena (e.g. rote verbal learning, solving puzzles, simple concept attainment) to more complex and rather ill-structured tasks (e.g. use of natural language, learning, scientific discovery, visual art). 'Ill-structured' means that the task has ill-defined or multidimensional goals, that its frame of reference or representation is not clear or obvious, that there are no clear-cut procedures for generating search paths or evaluating them—or some combination of these characteristics.

When a problem is ill-structured in one or more of these senses, a first step in solving it is to impose some kind of structure that allows it to be represented—that is, symbolized—at least approximately, and attacked in this symbolized form. What does psychology tell us about problem representations: their nature, and how they are constructed for particular problems?

Forms of representation

We do not have an exhaustive taxonomy of possible representations, but a few basic forms show up prominently in psychological research. First, situations may be represented in words or in logical or mathematical notations. All of these representations are basically propositional, and are more or less equivalent to a set of propositions in some formal logic. Propositional representation immediately suggests that the processing will resemble logical reasoning or proof.

When problems are presented verbally, the propositional translation of these words may be quite literal, or may comprise only the semantic content of the input without preserving syntactic details. In both cases we will speak of propositional representation. There is a great deal of psychological evidence that input sentences are seldom retained intact, but that, instead, their semantic content is usually extracted and stored in some form.

Second, situations may be represented in diagrams or pictures ('mental pictures'). Internally, a picture or diagram can be represented by the equivalent of a raster of pixels (e.g. the cerebral image associated with the direct signals from the retina), or by a network of nodes and links that capture the components of the diagram and their relations. Possibly there are other ways (e.g. as the equations of analytic geometry), but these two have been given most consideration by psychologists. A picture or diagram amounts to a *model* of the system, with processes that operate on it to move it through time or to search through a succession of its states.

Most psychological research on representations assumes, explicitly or implicitly, one of the representations mentioned in the preceding paragraphs: propositional, raster-like 'picture', or node-link diagram, or some combination of them. All of these representations are easily implemented by computer programs.

Equivalence of representations

What consequences does the form of representation have for cognition? To answer that question, we must define the notion of *equivalence of representations*. Actually, we must define two notions: informational equivalence and computational equivalence (Larkin and Simon, 1987). Two representations are *informationally* equivalent if either one is logically derivable from the other—if all the information available in the one is available in the other. Two representations are *computationally* equivalent if all the information *easily* available in the one is easily available in the other, and vice versa.

'Easily' is a vague term, but adequate for our purpose. Information is easily available if it can be obtained from the explicit information with a small amount of computation—small relative to the capacities of the processor. Thus, defining a representation includes specifying the primitive processes, those that are not further analysed and that can be carried out rapidly.

Representations of numerical information in Arabic and Roman numerals, respectively, are informationally equivalent, but not computationally equivalent. It may be much easier or harder to find the product of two numbers in the one notation than in the other. Similarly, representations of the same problem, on the one hand as a set of declarative propositions in PROLOG, and on the other hand as a node-link diagram in LISP, are unlikely to be computationally equivalent (Larkin and Simon, 1987). It may be far easier to solve the problem in the one form than in the other, say, easier by heuristic search than by resolution theorem proving.

Representations used by people

There is much evidence that people sometimes use 'mental pictures' to represent problems, representations that have the properties of rasters or of node-link networks (Kosslyn, 1980). There is little evidence that they use propositions in the predicate calculus to represent them, or operate on their representations by theorem-proving methods. Of course engineers, scientists, and others do represent many problems with mathematical formalisms, but the processes that operate upon these formalisms resemble heuristic search much more than they do logical reasoning (Larkin and Simon, 1987; Paige and Simon, 1966).

Research on problem-solving in algebra and physics has shown that subjects typically convert a problem from natural language into diagrams, and then convert the latter into equations. A direct translation from language to equations seems to take place, if at all, only in the case of very simple familiar problems. AI models of the diagramatic representations that problem-solvers use in these domains can be found in Larkin and Simon (1987) and Novak (1977).

Evidence is lacking as to whether there exists a 'neutral' semantic representation for information that is neither propositional nor pictorial. At least in simple situations, much information is readily transformed from one representation to the other. For example, in one common experimental paradigm subjects are presented with an asterisk above or below a plus sign, and simultaneously, with a sentence of the form, 'The star is above/below the plus' (Clark and Chase, 1972). The subject must respond 'true' or 'false'. Before responding, the subject must, somehow, find a common representation for the visual display and the sentence—converting one into the other, or both into a common semantic representation. But the experiments carried out in this paradigm do not show which way the conversion goes. From the physics and algebra experiments we might conjecture that, for most subjects, the internal (or semantic) representation is the diagramatic one, but we must be careful in generalizing across tasks.

I have barely touched on the evidence from psychology about the representations used by people in their problem-solving activities. The evidence we have throws strong doubt on any claim of hegemony for either propositional or pictorial representations. If either tends to be dominant, it is probably the pictorial (or diagrammatic) rather than the propositional. The evidence suggests strongly that, whatever the form of representation, the processing of information almost always resembles heuristic search rather than theorem proving.

We can only conjecture that these preferences have something to do with computational efficiency. I have elsewhere spelled out some of the implications of the computational inequivalence of representations for such issues as logic-programming versus rule-based computation.

Insight problems

Problems that tend to be solved suddenly, with an 'aha!' experience, often after a long period of apparently fruitless struggle, have attracted much attention. Can we say anything about the mystery of such insightful processes? Indeed, we can. We can say enough to dissipate most or all of the magic.

One problem of this kind is the 'Mutilated Draughtboard'. We are given an ordinary draughtboard of 64 squares, and 32 dominoes, each domino exactly covering two adjoining squares of the board. Obviously we can cover the entire board with the 32 dominoes. Now we cut off the north-west square and the south-east square of the board, and ask whether the remaining 62 squares can be covered exactly by 31 dominoes (Kaplan and Simon, 1990).

Subjects generally attack this problem by attempting coverings, and persist for an hour or more, becoming increasingly frustrated as they fail to achieve a solution. At some point they decide that a covering is impossible, and switch their effort to proving the impossibility. They recognize that to do this they need a new problem representation, but unfortunately people do not appear to possess a general-purpose generator of problem representations. It is not enough to say, 'I need a new representation'. How do you go about constructing it?

Some subjects do, after a shorter or longer time, succeed in constructing a new representation, and then solve the problem in a few minutes. The new representation records the *number* of squares of each colour, and the *number* of each colour that is covered by a single domino. The geometric arrangement of the squares, a central feature of the original representation, is simply ignored. But since the mutilated draughtboard has two more squares of one colour than of the other, and since dominoes, no matter how many, can cover only the same number of squares of each colour, the impossibility of a covering is immediately evident.

The power of the abstraction is obvious, but how do subjects achieve it? Experiments show that they achieve it when their attention focuses on the fact that the remaining uncovered squares, after unsuccessful attempts at covering, are always the same colour. How the attention focus comes about is a longer story, which I won't try to tell here, but which is quite understandable in terms of ordinary mechanisms of attention.

Much remains to be done before we understand how people construct their problem representations and the role those representations play in problem-solving. But we know enough already to suggest that the representations people use—both propositional and pictorial—can be simulated by computers. Diagramatic representations of the node-link type are naturally represented in list-processing languages like LISP. Rasters pose a more difficult problem, for we must define appropriate primitive processes to extract information from them. Finding such processes is more or less synonymous with developing efficient programs for visual pattern recognition.

THE PROCESSING OF LANGUAGE

Whatever the role it plays in thought, natural language is the principal medium of communication between people. What do we know about how it is processed and how it is learned?

Some programs that understand language

Enormous amounts of research on language have been done within the disciplines of linguistics and psycholinguistics. Until quite recent times, the greater part of that research was focused on lexical issues, syntax, and phonetics, seldom straying beyond the boundaries of the individual sentence. Without disputing the importance of this activity, it might be argued that far more has been learned about the relation between natural language and thinking from computer programs that use language inputs or outputs to perform concrete tasks.

For example, I have already mentioned Novak's ISAAC program, which extracts the information from natural-language descriptions of physics problems, and transforms it into an internal 'semantic' representation suitable for a problem-solving system. In somewhat similar manner, Hayes and Simon's (1974) UNDERSTAND program reads natural-language instructions for puzzles and creates internal representation ('pictures') of the problem situations, and interpretations of the puzzle rules for operating on them.

Systems like these give us specific models of how people extract meaning from discourse with the help of semantic knowledge they already hold in memory. For example, Novak's (1977) system interprets the natural-language input using schemas that encapsulate its knowledge about such things as levers and masses, and assembles this knowledge into a composite schema that pictures the problem situation.

At a more abstract level, UNDERSTAND extracts knowledge from prose about the objects under discussion, the relations among them, and the ways of changing these relations. It uses this information to construct a system of internal nodes, links, and processes that represent these objects, relations, and operations. In simple puzzle situations, UNDERSTAND can go quite a long way with a minimum of semantic knowledge, relying heavily on syntactic cues.

Acquiring language

Of equal importance is the question of how languages are acquired. Siklóssy (1972) simulated the process of language acquisition, guided by I. A. Richards' plan for learning language by use of pictures. Siklóssy's program, called ZBIE, was given (internal representations of) simple pictures (A dog chasing a cat, A hat on a woman's head). With each picture, it was given a sentence describing the scene. With the aid of a carefully designed sequence of such examples, it gradually learned to associate nouns with the objects in the pictures, and other words with their properties and the relations.

ZBIE was tested in novel situations whose components were familiar, by requiring it to construct sentences describing these new situations. It learned the fundamentals of a number of European languages, including the appropriate conventions for word order.

Will our knowledge of language scale?

These are just a few illustrations of current capabilities for simulating human use and acquisition of language. Since all of them involve relatively simple language with a limited vocabulary, it is quite reasonable to ask how they would scale up to encompass the whole vast structure of a natural language as known and used by a native speaker. We do not know the answer to this question—and won't know it until it has been done—but we should not overemphasize the criticality of the scaling-up issue. When we wish to understand basic physical phenomena, we do not look for complex real-world situations in which to test them, but instead design the simplest conceivable laboratory situations in which to demonstrate and manipulate them.

Even in classical mechanics, physicists are far from a full understanding of the three-body problem, much less the behaviour of n bodies, where n is a large number. Most scientific effort goes into the study of toy systems rather than the study of a complex 'real world'. We usually understand the mechanisms that govern the complex world long before we are able to calculate or simulate the behaviour of that world in detail.

Similarly, to demonstrate an understanding of human thinking, we do not need to model thinking in the most complex situations we can imagine. It is enough for most purposes that our theory explain the phenomena in a range of situations that would call for genuine thinking in human subjects. Research has already met that criterion for language processing.

DISCOVERY AND CREATIVITY

We should not be intimidated by words like 'intuition' that are often used to describe human thinking. We have seen that 'intuition' usually simply means problem solving by recognition, easily modelled by production systems. We have also seen that the 'insight' that leads to change in representation and solution of the mutilated draughtboard problem can be explained by mechanisms of attention focusing. What about 'creative' processes? Can we give an account of them too?

Making scientific discoveries is generally adjudged to be both ill-structured and creative. As it is also a very diverse activity, with many aspects, a theory that explains one aspect might not explain others. Scientists sometimes examine data to discover regularities—scientific laws, and new concepts for expressing the laws parsimoniously. They sometimes discover new scientific problems or invent new ways of representing problems. They sometimes deduce new consequences from theories.

Scientists sometimes conceive of mechanisms to explain the empirical laws that describe phenomena. They sometimes develop and execute experimental strategies to obtain new data for testing theories or evolving new theories. They sometimes invent and construct new instruments for gathering new kinds of data or more precise data. There are other things that scientists do, but this list at least illustrates the variety of activities in which they engage, any of which may produce a creative discovery.

A number of these activities, but not all, have been simulated by computer. In addition, historians of science have recounted the courses of events that led to a substantial number of important discoveries.

A computer program called BACON (Langley *et al.*, 1987), when given the data available to the scientists in historically important situations, has rediscovered Kepler's Third Law, Ohm's Law, Boyle's Law, Black's Law of Temperature Equilibrium, and many others. In the course of finding these laws, BACON has reinvented such fundamental concepts as inertial mass, atomic weight and molecular weight, and specific heat. We do not have to speculate about how discoveries of these kinds are made; we can examine the behaviour of programs like BACON, and compare them with the historical record (or with the behaviour of human subjects presented with the same problems).

The KEKADA program (Kulkarni and Simon, 1988) plans experimental strategies, responding to the information gained from each experiment to plan the next one. On the basis of its knowledge and experience, it forms expectations about the outcome of experiments, and switches to a strategy for exploiting its surprise when these expectations are not fulfilled. With the aid of these capabilities, it is able to track closely the strategy that Hans Krebs used to elucidate the synthesis of urea *in vivo*, and Faraday's strategy in investigating the production of electrical currents by the variation of magnetic fields. Here, the accuracy with which the program explained the human processes was tested by comparing its behaviour with the day-to-day course of the original research as gleaned from laboratory notebooks.

Programs like BACON and KEKADA show that scientists use essentially the same kinds of processes as those identified in more prosaic kinds of problem-solving (solving puzzles or playing chess). Very high-quality thinking is surely required for scientific work, but thinking of basically the same kinds as are used to solve more humdrum problems.

These successes in simulating scientific work put high on the agenda the simulation of other facets of science (inventing instruments, discovering appropriate problem representations) that have not yet been tackled. There is no reason to believe that they will disclose thinking processes wholly different from those that have been observed in the research I have just sketched.

AFFECT, MOTIVATION, AND AWARENESS

I have said nothing about the motivation required for successful human thinking. Motivation comes into the picture through the mechanism of attention. Motivation selects particular tasks for attention and diverts attention from others. When the other conditions for success are present, strong motivation sustained over long periods of time may secure the cognitive effort that is required to find a problem solution. In this manner, motivation and the mechanisms that strengthen and weaken it, can be brought into models of problem-solving in a quite natural manner.

Putting the matter in this over-simple way does not demean the importance of motivation in human thinking, but suggests that its impact on thought processes is rather diffuse and aggregative rather than highly specific. Moreover, if affect and cognition interact largely through the mechanisms of attention, then it is reasonable to pursue our research on these two components of mental behaviour independently. For example, in laboratory studies of problem-solving, as long as we establish conditions that assure the subjects' attention to the task, we can study the cognitive processes without simultaneously investigating just how the motivation is generated and maintained.

The theory of thinking I have been describing says very little about consciousness—except in equating ability to report information with its presence in short-term memory. Many of the symbolic processes that support thought are in conscious awareness, but others are not. The presence or absence of awareness has strong implications for the ease or difficulty of testing the details of the theory, but few other implications. I will not try to pursue this difficult topic further here.

CONCLUSION: COMPUTERS THINK—AND OFTEN THINK LIKE PEOPLE

The conclusion we can draw from the evidence I have sketched is simple: computers can be programmed, and have been programmed, to simulate at a symbolic level the processes that are used in human thinking. We need not talk about computers thinking in the future tense; they have been thinking (in smaller or bigger ways) for forty years. They have been thinking 'logically' and they have been thinking 'intuitively'—even 'creatively'.

Why has this conclusion been resisted so fiercely, even in the face of massive evidence? I would argue, first, that the dissenters have not looked very hard at the evidence, especially the evidence from the psychological laboratory. They have grasped and held onto a romantic picture of the human mind that attributes to it capabilities that it simply does not have—not even the minds of Mozart and Einstein, to say nothing of the rest of us poor mortals.

The human mind does not reach its goals mysteriously or miraculously. Even its sudden insights and 'ahas' are explainable in terms of recognition processes, well-informed search, knowledge-prepared experiences of surprise, and changes in representation motivated by shifts in attention. When we incorporate these processes into our theory, as empirical evidence says we should, the unexplainable is explained.

Perhaps there are deeper sources of resistance to the evidence. Perhaps we are reluctant to give up our claims for human uniqueness—of being the only species that can think big thoughts. Perhaps we have 'known' so long that machines can't think that only overwhelming evidence can change our belief. Whatever the reason, the evidence is now here, and it is time that we attended to it. If we hurry, we can catch up to Turing on the path he pointed out to us so many years ago.

REFERENCES

Baylor, G. W., and Simon, H. A. (1966), 'A Chess Mating Combinations Program', *1966 Spring Joint Computer Conference, AFIPS Conference Proceedings*, 28: 431–47.

Bloom, B. S. (ed.) (1985), *Developing Talent in Young People*, New York: Ballantine Books.

Chase, W. G., and Simon, H. A. (1973), 'Perception in Chess', *Cognitive Psychology*, 4: 55–81.

Clark, H. H., and Chase, W. G. (1972), 'On the Process of Comparing Sentences against Pictures', *Cognitive Psychology*, 3: 472–517.

De Groot, A. D. (1965), *Thought and Choice in Chess*, The Hague: Mouton (2nd edn., 1978).

Feigenbaum, E. A., and Simon, H. A. (1984), 'EPAM-like Models of Recognition and Learning', *Cognitive Science*, 8: 305–36.

Hayes, J. R. (1989), *The Complete Problem Solver*, Hillsdale, NJ: Erlbaum (2nd edn.).

—— and Simon, H. A. (1974), 'Understanding Written Problem Instructions', in L. W. Gregg (ed.), *Knowledge and Cognition*, Potomac, Md.: Erlbaum, 167–200.

Kaplan, C. A., and Simon, H. A. (1990), 'In Search of Insight', *Cognitive Psychology*, 22: 374–419.

Kosslyn, S. M. (1980), *Image and Mind*, Cambridge, Mass.: Harvard University Press.

Kulkarni, D., and Simon, H. A. (1988), 'The Processes of Scientific Discovery: The Strategy of Experimentation', *Cognitive Science*, 12: 139–75.

Langley, P., Simon, H. A., Bradshaw, G. L., and Zytkow, J. M. (1987), *Scientific Discovery*, Cambridge, Mass.: MIT Press.

Larkin, J. H., and Simon, H. A. (1987), 'Why a Diagram is (sometimes) Worth Ten Thousand Words', *Cognitive Science*, 11: 65–100.

Newell, A., and Simon, H. A. (1972), *Human Problem Solving*, Englewood Cliffs, NJ: Prentice-Hall.

—— —— (1976), 'Computer Science as Empirical Inquiry', *Communications of the ACM*, 19: 113–26.

Novak, G. S. (1977), 'Representation of Knowledge in a Program for Solving Physics Problems', *Proceedings of the Fifth International Joint Conference on Artificial Intelligence*. Cambridge, Mass.: IJCAI.

Paige, J. M., and Simon, H. A. (1966), 'Cognitive Processes in Solving Algebra Word Problems', in B. Kleinmuntz (ed.), *Problem Solving*, New York: Wiley, 51–119.

Richman, H. B., and Simon, H. A. (1989), 'Context Effects in Letter Perception: Comparison of Two Theories', *Psychological Review*, 96: 417–32.

Siklóssy, L. (1972), 'Natural Language Learning by Computer', in H. A. Simon and L. Siklóssy (eds.), *Representation and Meaning*, Englewood Cliffs, NJ: Prentice-Hall, 288–328.

Simon, H. A. (1976), 'The Information-Storage System Called "human memory"', in M. R. Rosenzweig and E. L. Bennett (eds.), *Neural Mechanisms of Learning and Memory*, Cambridge, Mass.: MIT Press.

—— (1981), *The Sciences of the Artificial*, Cambridge, Mass.: MIT Press.

—— and Gilmartin, K. A. (1973), 'A Simulation of Memory for Chess Positions', *Cognitive Psychology*, 5: 29–46.

Turing, A. M. (1950), 'Computing Machinery and Intelligence', *Mind*, 59: 422–60.

6

Minds, Machines, and Gödel: A Retrospect

J. R. LUCAS

I must start with an *apologia*. My original paper, 'Minds, Machines and Gödel', was written in the wake of Turing's 1950 paper in *Mind*, and was intended to show that minds were not Turing machines. Why, then, didn't I couch the argument in terms of Turing's theorem, which is easyish to prove and applies directly to Turing machines, instead of Gödel's theorem, which is horrendously difficult to prove, and doesn't so naturally or obviously apply to machines? The reason was that Gödel's theorem gave me something more: it raises questions of truth which evidently bear on the nature of mind, whereas Turing's theorem does not; it shows not only that the Gödelian well-formed formula is unprovable-in-the-system, but that it is true. It shows something about reasoning, that it is not completely rule-bound, so that we, who are rational, can transcend the rules of any particular logistic system, and construe the Gödelian well-formed formula not just as a string of symbols but as a proposition which is true. Turing's theorem might well be applied to a computer which someone claimed to represent a human mind, but it is not so obvious that what the computer could not do, the mind could. But it is very obvious that we have a concept of truth. Even if it is not the *summum bonum*, it is a *bonum*, and one it is characteristic of minds to value. A representation of the human mind which could take no account of truth would be inherently implausible. Turing's theorem, though making the same negative point as Gödel's theorem, that some things cannot be done by even idealized computers, does not make the further positive point that we, inasmuch as we are rational agents, can do that very thing that the computer cannot. I have, however, sometimes wondered whether I could not construct a parallel argument based on Turing's theorem, and have toyed with the idea of a von Neumann machine. A von Neumann machine was a black box, inside which was housed John von Neumann. But although it was reasonable, on inductive grounds, to credit a von Neumann machine with the power of solving any problem in finite time—about the time taken to get from New York to Chicago by train—it did not have the same edge as Gödel's proof of his own first incompleteness theorem. I leave it therefore to the reader to consider further how Turing's theorem bears on mechanism, and whether a Turing machine could plausibly represent a mind, and myself return to the argument I actually put forward.

I argued that Gödel's theorem enabled us to devise a schema for refuting the various different mechanist theories of the mind that might be put forward. Gödel's theorem is a sophisticated form of the Cretan paradox posed by Epimenides. Gödel showed how we could represent any reasonable mathematical theory within itself. Whereas the original Cretan paradox, 'This statement is untrue' can be brushed off on the grounds that it is viciously self-referential, and we do not know what the statement is, which is alleged to be untrue, until it has been made, and we cannot make it until we know what it is that is being alleged to be false, Gödel blocks that objection. But in order to do so, he needs not only to represent within his mathematical theory some means of *referring* to the statement, but also some means of expressing mathematically what we are saying about it. We cannot in fact do this with 'true' or 'untrue': could we do that, a direct inconsistency would ensue. What Gödel was able to do, however, was to express within his mathematical system the concept of being *provable-*, and hence also *unprovable-*, in-that-system. He produced a copper-bottomed well-formed formula which could be interpreted as saying 'This well-formed formula is unprovable-in-this-system.' It follows that it must be both unprovable-in-the-system and none the less true. For if it were provable, and provided the system is a sound one in which only well-formed formulae expressing true propositions could be proved, then it would be true, and so what it says, namely that it is unprovable-in-the-system, would hold; so that it would be *un*provable-in-the-system. So it cannot be provable-in-the-system. But if it is unprovable-in-the-system, then what it claims to be the case is the case, and so it is true. So it is true but unprovable-in-the-system. Gödel's theorem seemed to me to be not only a surprising result in mathematics, but to have a bearing on theories of the mind, and in particular on mechanism, which is as much a background assumption of our age as classical materialism was towards the end of the last century in the form expressed by Tyndale. Mechanism claims that the workings of the mind can be entirely understood in terms of the working of a definite finite system operating according to definite deterministic laws. Enthusiasts for artificial intelligence are often mechanists, and are inclined to claim that in due course they will be able to simulate all forms of intelligent behaviour by means of a sufficiently complex computer garbed in sufficiently sophisticated software. But the operations of any such computer could be represented in terms of a formal logistic calculus with a definite finite number (though enormously large) of possible well-formed formulae and a definite finite number (though presumably smaller) of axioms and rules of inference. The Gödelian formula of such a system would be one that the computer, together with its software, would be unable to prove. We, however, could. So the claim that a computer could in principle simulate all our behaviour breaks down at this one, vital point.

The argument I put forward is a two-level one. I do not offer a simple knock-down proof that minds are inherently better than machines, but a schema for constructing a *dis*proof of any plausible mechanist thesis that might be proposed. The disproof depends on the particular mechanist thesis being maintained, and does not claim to show that the mind is uniformly better than the purported mechanist representation of it, but only that it is one respect better and therefore different. That is enough to refute that particular mechanist thesis. By itself, of course, it leaves all others unrefuted, and the mechanist free to put forward some variant thesis which the counter-argument I constructed does not immediately apply to. But I claim that it can be adjusted to meet the new variant. Having once got the hang of the Gödelian argument, the mind can adapt it appropriately to meet each and every variant claim that the mind is essentially some form of Turing machine. Essentially, therefore, the two parts of my argument are first a hard negative argument, addressed to a mechanist putting forward a particular claim, and proving to him, by means he must acknowledge to be valid, that his claim is untenable; and secondly a hand-waving

positive argument, addressed to intelligent men, bystanders as
well as mechanists espousing particular versions of mechanism, to
the effect that some sort of argument on these lines can always
be found to deal with any further version of mechanism that may
be thought up.

I read the paper to the Oxford Philosophical Society in October
1959 and subsequently published it in *Philosophy*,[1] and later set
out the argument in more detail in *The Freedom of the Will*.[2] I
have been much attacked. Although I argued with what I hope
was becoming modesty and a certain degree of tentativeness, many
of the replies have been lacking in either courtesy or caution. I
must have touched a raw nerve. That, of course, does not prove
that I was right. Indeed, I should at once concede that I am very
likely not to be entirely right, and that others will be able to
articulate the arguments more clearly, and thus more cogently,
than I did. But I am increasingly persuaded that I was not entirely
wrong, by reason of the very wide disagreement among my critics
about where exactly my arguments fail. Each picks on a different
point, allowing that the points objected to by other critics, are in
fact all right, but hoping that his one point will prove fatal. None
has, so far as I can see. I used to try and answer each point fairly
and fully, but the flesh has grown weak. Often I was simply point-
ing out that the critic was not criticizing any argument I had put
forward but one which he would have liked me to put forward
even though I had been at pains to discount it. In recent years I
have been less zealous to defend myself, and often miss articles
altogether.[3] There may be some new decisive objection I have
altogether overlooked. But the objections I have come across so
far seem far from decisive.

To consider each objection individually would be too lengthy a
task to attempt here. I shall pick on five recurrent themes. Some of
the objections question the idealization implicit in the way I set up
the contest between the mind and the machine; some raise questions of modality and finitude; some turn on issues of transfinite

---

[1] J. R. Lucas (1961), 'Minds, Machines and Gödel', *Philosophy* 36: 112–27;
repr. in Kenneth M. Sayre and Frederick J. Crosson (eds.), *The Modeling of Mind*,
Notre Dame: University of Notre Dame Press (1963), 255–71; and in A. R.
Anderson, *Minds and Machines*, Englewood Cliffs: Prentice-Hall (1964), 43–59.

[2] Lucas (1970), *The Freedom of the Will*, Oxford: Oxford University Press.

[3] I give at the end a list of some of the major criticisms I have come across, and
most of the references in the following notes are to the items on that list.

arithmetic; some are concerned with the extent to which rational inferences should be formalizable; and some are about consistency. Many philosophers question the idealization implicit in the Gödelian argument. A context is envisaged between 'the mind' and 'the machine', but it is an idealized mind and an idealized machine. Actual minds are embodied in mortal clay, actual machines often malfunction or wear out. Since actual machines are not Turing machines, not having an infinite tape, that is to say an infinite memory, it may be held that they cannot be automatically subject to Gödelian limitations. But Gödel's theorem applies not only to Peano Arithmetic, with its infinitistic postulate of recursive reasoning, but to the weaker Robinson Arithmetic Q, which is only potentially, not actually infinite, and hardly extends beyond the range of plausible computer progress. In any case, limitations of finitude reduce, rather than enhance, the plausibility of some computer's being an adequate representation of a mind. Actual minds are embodied in mortal clay. In the short span of our actual lives we cannot achieve all that much, and might well have neither the time nor the cleverness to work out Gödelian formulae. Hanson points out that there could be a theorem of Elementary Number Theory that I cannot prove because a proof of it would be too long or complex for me to produce.[4] Any machine that represented a mind would be enormously complicated, and the calculation of its Gödel sentence might well be beyond the power of any human mathematician.[5] But he could be helped. Other mathematicians might come to his aid, reckoning that they also had an interest in the discomfiture of the mechanical Goliath.[6] The truth of the Gödelian sentence under its intended interpretation in ordinary informal arithmetic is a mathematical truth, which even if pointed out by other mathematicians would not depend on their testimony in the way contingent statements do. So even if aided by the hints of other mathematicians, the mind's asserting the truth of the Gödelian sentence would be a genuine ground for differentiating it from the machine.

Some critics of the Gödelian argument—Dennett, Hofstadter, and

---

[4] W. H. Hanson (1971), 12; cf. D. R. Hofstadter (1979), 475.
[5] R. Rucker (1985), 168.
[6] I owe this suggestion to M. A. E. Dummett, at the original meeting of the Oxford Philosophical Society on 30 Oct., 1959. A similar suggestion is implicit in H. Wang (1974), 316.

Kirk—complain that I am insufficiently sensitive to the sophist-
ication of modern computer technology, and that there is a fatal
ambiguity between the fundamental level of the machine's operations and the level of input and output that is supposed to represent the mind: in modern parlance, between the machine code and
the programming language, such as Prolog. But although there is
a difference of levels, it does not invalidate the argument. A compiler is entirely deterministic. Any sequence of operations specified
in machine code can be uniquely specified in the programming
language, and vice versa, hence it is quite fair to characterize the
capacity of the mechanist's machine in terms of a higher-level
language. In order to begin to be a representation of a mind it
must be able to do simple arithmetic. And then, at this level, Gödel's
theorem applies. The same counter applies to Dennett's complaint
that the comparison between men and Turing machines is highly
counter-intuitive because we are not much given to wandering round
uttering obscure truths of ordinary informal arithmetic. Few of us
are capable of asserting a Gödelian sentence, fewer still of wanting
to do so. 'Men do not sit around uttering theorems in a uniform
vocabulary. They say things in earnest and in jest, make slips of
the tongue, speak several languages, signal agreement by nodding
or otherwise acting nonverbally, and—most troublesome for this
account—utter all kinds of nonsense and contradictions, both
deliberately and inadvertently.'[7] Of course, men are unmachinelike in these ways, and many philosophers have rejected the claims
of mechanism on these grounds alone. But mechanists claim that
this is too quick. Man, they say, is a very complicated machine, so
complicated as to produce all this unmachinelike output. We may
regard their contention as highly counter-intuitive, but should not
reject it out of hand. I therefore take seriously, though only in
order to refute it, the claim that a machine could be constructed
to represent the behaviour of a man. If so, it must, among other
things, represent a man's mental behaviour. Some men, many men,
are capable of recognizing a number of basic arithmetical truths,
and, particularly when asked to (which can be viewed as a particular input) can assert them as truths. Although 'a characterization of a man as a certain sort of theorem-proving machine'[8]
would be a less than complete characterization, it would be an

---

[7] D. C. Dennett (1972), 530.   [8] Ibid., 527.

essential part of a characterization of a machine if it was really to represent a man. It would have to be able to include in its output of what could be taken as assertions the basic truths of arithmetic, and to accept as valid inferences those that are validated by first-order logic. This is a minimum. Of course it may be able to do much more—it may have in its memory a store of jokes for use in after-dinner speeches, or personal reminiscences for use on subordinates—but unless its output, for suitable questions or other input, includes a set of assertions itself including Elementary Number Theory, it is a poor representation of some human minds. If it cannot pass O-level maths, are we really going to believe a mechanist when he claims that it represents a graduate?

Actual minds are finite in what they actually achieve. Wang and Boyer see difficulties in the infinite capabilities claimed for the mind as contrasted with the actual finitude of human life. Boyer takes a post-mortem view, and points out that all of the actual output of Lucas, Astaire, or anyone else can be represented *ex post facto* by a machine.[9] Actual achievements of mortal men are finite, and so simulable. When I am dead it would be possible to program a computer with sufficient graphic capacity to show on a video screen a complete biographical film of my life. But when I am dead it will be easy to outwit me. What is in issue is whether a computer can copy a living me, when I have not as yet done all that I shall do, and can do many different things. It is a question of potentiality rather than actuality. Wang concedes this, and allows that we are inclined to say that it is logically possible to have a mind capable of recognizing any true proposition of number theory or solving a set of Turing-unsolvable problems, but life is short.[10] In a finite life-span only a finite number of the propositions can be recognized, only a finite set of problems can be solved. And a machine can be programmed to do that. Of course, we reckon that a man *can* go on to do more, but it is difficult to capture that sense of infinite potentiality. This is true. It *is* difficult to capture the sense of infinite potentiality. But infinite potentiality is an essential part of the concept of mind, and a modally 'flat' account of a mind in terms only of what it has done is as unconvincing as an account of a cause which considers only constant conjunction, and not what would have been the case had circumstances been

[9] D. L. Boyer (1983).   [10] Wang (1974), 315.

different. In order to capture this sense of potentiality, I set out
my argument in terms of a challenge which leaves it open to the
challenger to meet it in any way he likes. Two-sided, or 'dialectical', arguments often succeed in encapsulating concepts that elude
explication in purely monologous terms: the epsilon–delta exegesis
of infinitesimals is best conveyed thus, and more generally any
alternation of quantifiers, as in the EA principles suggested by
Clark Glymour for the ultimate convergence of theories on truth
(in his contribution to this volume, pp. 265–91).

Although some degree of idealization seems allowable in considering a mind untrammelled by mortality and a Turing machine
with infinite tape, doubts remain as to how far into the infinite it
is permissible to stray. Transfinite arithmetic underlies the objections of Good and Hofstadter. The problem arises from the way
the contest between the mind and the machine is set up. The object
of the contest is not to prove the mind better than the machine, but
only different from it, and this is done by the mind's Gödelizing
the machine. It is very natural for the mechanist to respond by
including the Gödelian sentence in the machine, but of course that
makes the machine a different machine with a different Gödelian
sentence all of its own, which it cannot produce as true but the
mind can. So then the mechanist tries adding a Gödelizing operator, which gives in effect a whole denumerable infinity of Gödelian
sentences. But this, too, can be trumped by the mind, who produces the Gödelian sentence of the new machine incorporating the
Gödelizing operator, and out-Gödelizes the lot. Essentially this is
the move from ω, the infinite sequence of Gödelian sentences
produced by the Gödelizing operator, to $\omega + 1$, the next transfinite
ordinal. And so it goes on. Every now and again the mechanist
loses patience, and incorporates in his machine a further operator
designed to produce in one fell swoop all the Gödelian sentences
the mentalist is trumping him with: this is in effect to produce
a new limit ordinal. But such ordinals, although they have no
predecessors, have successors just like any other ordinal, and the
mind can out-Gödel them by producing the Gödelian sentence of
the new version of the machine, and seeing it to be true, which the
machine cannot. Hofstadter thinks there is a problem for the
mentalist in view of a theorem of Church and Kleene on Formal
Definitions of Transfinite Ordinals.[11] They showed that we cannot

---

[11] Hofstadter (1979), 475.

program a machine to produce names for all the ordinal numbers. Every now and again some new, creative step is called for, when we consider all the ordinal numbers hitherto named, and we need to encompass them all in a single set, which we can use to define a new sort of ordinal, transcending all previous ones. Hofstadter thinks that, in view of the Church–Kleene theorem, the mind might run out of steam, and fail to think up new ordinals as required, and so fail in the last resort to establish the mind's difference from some machine. But this is wrong on two counts. In the first place it begs the question, and in the second it misconstrues the nature of the contest.

Hofstadter assumes that the mind is subject to the same limitations as the machine is, and that since there is no mechanical way of naming all the ordinals, the mind cannot do it either. But this is precisely the point in issue. Gödel himself rejected mechanism on account of our ability to think up fresh definitions for transfinite ordinals (and ever stronger axioms for set theory) and Wang is inclined to do so too.[12] Here, it is pertinent to note that Turing himself was, on this question, of the same mind as Gödel. He was led 'to ordinal logics as a way to "escape" Gödel's incompleteness theorems',[13] but recognized that although 'in pre-Gödel times it was thought by some that it would probably be possible to carry this programme to such a point that . . . the necessity for intuition would then be entirely eliminated', as a result of Gödel's incompleteness theorems one must instead 'turn to "non-constructive" systems of logic with which not all the steps in a proof are mechanical, some being intuitive.'[14] Turing concedes that the steps whereby we recognize formulae as ordinal formulae are intuitive, and goes on to say that we should show quite clearly when a step makes use of intuition, and when it is purely formal, and that the strain put on intuition should be a minimum. He clearly, like Gödel, allows that the mind's ability to recognize new ordinals outruns the ability of any formal algorithm to do so, though he does not draw Gödel's conclusion. It may be, indeed, that the mind's

---

[12] Wang (1974), 324–6.

[13] Solomon Feferman (1988), 'Turing in the Land of O(z)', in Rolf Herken (ed.), *The Universal Turing Machine*, Oxford: Oxford University Press, 113–47.

[14] A. M. Turing (1939), 'Systems of Logic Based on Ordinals', *Proceedings of the London Mathematical Society* 2/45: 161–228; repr. in M. Davis (ed.), *The Undecidable*, New York: Raven Press (1965), 155–222; quotations from pp. 209 and 210 (of Davis), also quoted by Feferman (1988) 'Turing in the Land of O(z)', 129.

ability to recognize new ordinals is the issue on which battle should be joined; Good claimed as much[15]—though disputes about the notation for ordinals lack the sharp edge of the Gödelian argument. But whatever the merits of different battlefields, it is clear that they are contested areas in the same conflict, and undisputed possession of the one cannot be claimed in order to assert possession of the other.

In any case Hofstadter misconstrues the nature of the contest. All the difficulties are on the side of the mechanist trying to devise a machine that cannot be out-Gödelized. It is the mechanist who resorts to limit ordinals, and who may have problems in devising new notations for them. The mind needs only to go on to the next one, which is always an easy, unproblematic step, and out-Gödelize whatever is the mechanist's latest offering. Hofstadter's argument, as often, tells against the position he is arguing for, and shows up a weakness of machines: there is no reason to suppose that it is shared by minds, and in the nature of the case it is a difficulty for those who are seeking to evade the Gödelian argument, not those who are deploying it.

Underlying Hofstadter's argument is a rhetorical question that many mechanists have raised. 'How does Lucas know that the mind can do this, that, or the other?' It is no good, they hold, that I should opine it or simply assert it; I must prove it. And if I prove it, then since the steps of my proof can be programmed into a machine, the machine can do it too. Good puts the argument explicitly:

What he must prove is that he personally can always make the improvement: it is not sufficient to *believe* it since belief is a matter of probability and Turing machines are not supposed to be capable of probability judgements. But no such proof is possible since, if it were given, it could be used for the design of a machine that could always do the improving. (Good, 'Gödel's Theorem is a Red Herring', *BJPS* 19(1969): 357)

The same point is made by Webb in his sustained and searching critique of the Gödelian argument:

[It is only because Gödel has given an effective method of constructing the Gödelian sentence that Lucas feels confident that] he can find the Achilles'

[15] I. J. Good (1969), 357-8.

heel of any machine. . . . But . . . then . . . if Lucas can effectively stump any machine, . . . there must be a machine which does this too! . . . [This] is the basic dilemma confronting anti-mechanism: just when the constructions used in its arguments become effective enough to be sure of, [the result that every humanly effective computation procedure can be simulated by a Turing machine] then implies that a machine can simulate them. In particular, it implies that our very behavior of applying Gödel's argument to arbitrary machines—in order to conclude that we cannot be modelled by a machine—can indeed be modelled by a machine. Hence any such conclusion must fail, or else we will have to conclude that certain machines cannot be modelled by any machine! In short, anti-mechanist arguments must either be ineffective, or else unable to show that their executor is not a machine.[16]

The core of this argument is an assumption that every informal argument must either be formalisable or else invalid. Such an assumption undercuts the distinction I have drawn between two senses of Gödelian argument: between a negative argument according to an exact specification, which a machine could be programmed to carry out, and on the other hand a certain style of arguing, similar to Gödel's original argument in inspiration, but not completely or precisely specified, and therefore not capable of being programmed into a machine, though capable of being understood and applied by an intelligent mind. Admittedly, we cannot *prove* to a hidebound mechanist that we can go on. But we may come to a well-grounded confidence that we can, which will give us, and the erstwhile mechanist if he is reasonable and not hide-bound, good reason for rejecting mechanism.

Against this claim of the mentalist that he has got the hang of doing something which cannot be described in terms of a mechanical program, the mechanist says 'Sez you' and will not believe him unless he produces a program showing how he would do it. It is like the argument between the realist and the phenomenalist. The realist claims that there exist entities not observed by anyone: the phenomenalist demands empirical evidence; if it is not forthcoming, he remains sceptical of the realist's claim; if it is, then the entity is not unobserved. In like manner the mechanist is sceptical of the mentalist's claim, unless he produces a specification of how he would do what a machine cannot: if such a specification is not forthcoming, he remains sceptical; if it is, it serves as a basis for programming a machine to do it after all. The mechanist position, like the phenomenalist, is invulnerable but unconvincing. I cannot prove to the mechanist that anything can be done other than what a machine can do, because he has restricted what he will accept as a proof to such an extent that only 'machine-doable' deeds will be accounted doable at all. But not all mechanists are so limited. Many mechanists and many mentalists are rational agents wondering whether, in the light of modern science and cybernetics, mechanism is, or is not, true. They have not closed their minds by so redefining proof that none but mechanist conclusions can be established. They can recognize in themselves their having 'got the hang' of something, even though no program can be written for giving a machine the hang of it. The parallel with the *sorites* argument is helpful. Arguing against a finitist, who does not accept the principle of mathematical induction, I may see at the meta-level that if he has conceded $F(o)$ and $(\forall x)(F(x) \to F(x + 1))$ then I can claim without fear of contradiction $(\forall x)F(x)$. I can be quite confident of this, although I have no finitist proof of it. All I can do, *vis-à-vis* the finitist, is to point out that *if* he were to deny my claim in any specific instance, I could refute him. True, a finitist could refute him too. But I have generalized in a way a finitist could not, so that although each particular refuting argument is finite, the claim is infinite. In a similar fashion each Gödelian argument is effective, and will convince even the mechanist that he is wrong; but the generalization from individual tactical refutations to a strategic claim does not have to be effective in the same sense, although it may be entirely rational for the mind to make the claim.

Nevertheless an air of paradox remains. The idea of a totally intuitive, unformalizable argument arouses suspicion: if it can convince, it can be conveyed, and if it can be conveyed, it can be formulated and expressed in formal terms. Let me therefore stress that I am not claiming that my, or any, argument is absolutely unformalizable. Any argument can be formalized, but, as the Tortoise proved to Achilles, the formal axiom or rule of inference invoked will be no more convincing than the original unformalized argument. I am not claiming that the Gödelian argument cannot be formalized, but that, whatever formalization we adopt, there are further arguments which are clearly valid though not captured by that formalization. Not only, again as the Tortoise proved to Achilles, must we always be ready to recognize some rules of inference as applying and some inferences as valid without more ado, but we shall be led, if we are rational, to extend our range of acknowledged valid inferences beyond any antecedently laid-down bounds. This does not preclude our subsequently formalizing them, but only our supposing that any formalization is inferentially complete.

But we always can formalize; in particular, we can formalize the argument that Gödel uses to prove that the Gödelian formula is unprovable-in-the-system but none the less true. At first sight there seems to be a paradox. Gödel's argument purports to show that the Gödelian sentence is unprovable but true. But if it shows that the Gödelian sentence is true, surely it has proved it, so that it is provable after all. The paradox in this case is resolved by distinguishing provability-in-the-formal-system from the informal provability given by Gödel's reasoning. But this reasoning can be formalized. We can go over Gödel's argument step by step, and formalize it. If we do so we find that an essential assumption for his argument that the Gödelian sentence is unprovable is that the formal system should be consistent. Else every sentence would be provable, and the Gödelian sentence, instead of being unprovable and therefore true, could be provable and false. So what we obtain, if we formalize Gödel's informal argumentation, is not a formal proof within Elementary Number Theory (ENT for short) that the Gödelian sentence, G is true, but a formal proof within Elementary Number Theory

$$\vdash \text{Cons(ENT)} \rightarrow G,$$

where Cons(ENT) is a sentence expressing the consistency of Elementary Number Theory. Only if we also had a proof in Elementary Number Theory yielding

$$\vdash \text{Cons(ENT)}$$

would we be able to infer by *modus ponens*

$$\vdash G.$$

Since we know that

$$\nvdash G,$$

we infer also that

$$\nvdash \text{Cons(ENT)}.$$

This is Gödel's second theorem. Many critics have appealed to it in order to fault the Gödelian argument. Only if the machine's formal system is consistent and we are in a position to assert its consistency, are we really able to maintain that the Gödelian sentence is true. But we have no warrant for this. For all we know, the machine we are dealing with may be inconsistent, and even if it is consistent we are not entitled to claim that it is. And in default of such entitlement, all we have succeeded in proving is

$$\vdash \text{Cons(ENT)} \to G,$$

and the machine can do that too.

These criticisms rest upon two substantial points: the consistency of the machine's system *is* assumed by the Gödelian argument and *cannot* be always established by a standard decision-procedure. The question 'By what right does the mind assume that the machine is consistent?' is therefore pertinent. But the moves made by mechanists to deny the mind that knowledge are unconvincing. Paul Benacerraf suggests that the mechanist can escape the Gödelian argument by not staking out his claim in detail.[17] The mechanist offers a 'black box' without specifying its program, and refuses to give away further details beyond the claim that the black box represents a mind. But such a position is both vacuous and untenable: vacuous because there is no content to mechanism unless some specification is given—if I am presented with a black box but 'told not to peek inside' then why should I think it contains a machine and not, say, a little black man? The mechanist's position is also untenable: for although the mechanist has refused to specify what machine it is that he claims to represent the mind, it is evident that the Gödelian argument would work for any consistent machine and that an inconsistent machine would be an implausible representation. The stratagem of playing with his cards very close to his chest in order to deny the mind the premisses it needs is a confession of defeat.

Putnam contends that there is an illegitimate inference from the true premiss

I can see that $(\text{Cons(ENT)} \to G)$

to the false conclusion

---

[17] P. Benacerraf (1967).

Cons(ENT) → I can see that (G).[18]

It is the latter that is needed to differentiate the mind from the machine, for what Gödel's theorem shows is

Cons(ENT) → ENT machine cannot see that (G),

but it is only the former, according to Putnam, that I am entitled to assert. Putnam's objection fails on account of the dialectical nature of the Gödelian argument. The mind does not go round uttering theorems in the hope of tripping up any machines that may be around. Rather, there is a claim being seriously maintained by the mechanist that the mind can be represented by some machine. Before wasting time on the mechanist's claim, it is reasonable to ask him some questions about his machine to see whether his seriously maintained claim has serious backing. It is reasonable to ask him not only what the specification of the machine is, but whether it is consistent. Unless it is consistent, the claim will not get off the ground. If it is warranted to be consistent, then that gives the mind the premiss it needs. The consistency of the machine is established not by the mathematical ability of the mind but on the word of the mechanist. The mechanist has claimed that his machine is consistent. If so, it cannot prove its Gödelian sentence, which the mind can none the less see to be true: if not, it is out of court anyhow.

Wang concedes that it is reasonable to contend that only consistent machines are serious candidates for representing the mind, but then objects it is too stringent a requirement for the mechanist to meet because there is no decision-procedure that will always tell us whether a formal system strong enough to include Elementary Number Theory is consistent or not.[19] But the fact that there is no decision-*procedure* means only that we cannot always tell, not that we can never tell. Often we can tell that a formal system is not consistent, e.g. it proves as a theorem:

$$\vdash p \ \& \ \neg \ p$$

or,

$$\vdash o = 1.$$

[18] H. Putnam (1960).   [19] Wang (1974), 317.

Also, *we* may be able to tell that a system *is* consistent. We have finitary consistency proofs for propositional calculus and first-order predicate calculus, and Gentzen's proof, involving transfinite induction, for Elementary Number Theory. We are therefore not asking the impossible of the mechanist in requiring him to do some preliminary sorting out before presenting candidates for being plausible representations of the mind. Unless they satisfy the examiner—the mechanist—in prelims on the score of consistency, they are not eligible to enter for finals, and all those that are thus qualified can be sure of failing for not being able to assert their Gödelian sentence.

The two-stage examination is thus able to sort out the inconsistent sheep who fail the qualifying examination from the consistent goats who fail their finals, and hence enables us to take on all challenges even from inconsistent machines without pretending to possess superhuman powers. Although all machines are entitled to enter for the mind-representation examination, only relatively few machines are plausible candidates for representing the mind, and there is no need to take a candidate seriously just because it is a machine. If the mechanist's claim is to be taken seriously, some recommendation will be required, and at the very least a warranty of consistency would be essential. Wang protests that this is to expect superhuman powers of him, and in a response to Benacerraf's 'God, The Devil and Gödel', I picked up his suggestion that the mechanist might be no mere man but the Prince of Darkness himself to whom the question of whether the machine was consistent or not could be addressed in expectation of an answer.[20] Rather than ask high-flown questions about the mind we can ask the mechanist the single question whether or not the machine that is proposed as a representation of the mind would affirm the Gödelian sentence of its system. If the mechanist says that his machine will affirm the Gödelian sentence, the mind then will know that it is inconsistent and will affirm anything, quite unlike the mind which is characteristically selective in its intellectual output. If the mechanist says that his machine will not affirm the Gödelian sentence, the mind then will know since there was at least one sentence it could not prove in its system it must be consistent; and

[20] Benacerraf (1967), 22–3; Lucas, (1968), 'Satan Stultified', *The Monist* 52: 145–58.

knowing that, the mind will know that the machine's Gödelian sentence is true, and thus will differ from the machine in its intellectual output. And if the mechanist is merely human, and moreover does not know what answer the machine would give to the Gödelian question, he has not done his homework properly, and should go away and try to find out before expecting us to take him seriously.

In asking the mechanist rather than the machine, we are making use of the fact that the issue is one of principle, not of practice. The mechanist is not putting forward actual machines which actually represent some human being's intellectual output, but is claiming instead that there could in principle be such a machine. He is inviting us to make an intellectual leap, extrapolating from various scientific theories and skating over many difficulties. He is quite entitled to do this. But having done this he is not entitled to be coy about his in-principle machine's intellectual capabilities or to refuse to answer embarrassing questions. The thought-experiment, once undertaken, must be thought through. And when it is thought through, it is impaled on the horns of a dilemma. Either the machine can prove in its system the Gödelian sentence or it cannot: if it can, it is inconsistent, and not equivalent to a mind; if it cannot, it is consistent, and the mind can therefore assert the Gödelian sentence to be true. Either way the machine is not equivalent to the mind, and the mechanist thesis fails.

A number of thinkers have chosen to impale themselves on the inconsistency horn of the dilemma. We are machines, they say, but very limited, fallible and inconsistent ones. In view of our many contradictions, changes of mind and failures of logic, we have no warrant for supposing the mind to be consistent, and therefore no ground for disqualifying a machine for inconsistency as a candidate for being a representation of the mind. Hofstadter thinks it would be perfectly possible to have an artificial intelligence in which propositional reasoning emerged as consequences rather than as being pre-programmed. 'And there is no particular reason to assume that the strict propositional calculus, with its rigid rules and the rather silly definition of consistency that they entail, would emerge from such a program.'[21]

None of these arguments goes any way to making an inconsistent

---

[21] Hofstadter (1979), 578; cf. C. S. Chihara (1972), 526.

machine a plausible representation of a mind. Admittedly the word 'consistent' is used in different senses, and the claim that a mind is consistent is likely to involve a different sense of consistency and to be established by different sorts of arguments from those in issue when a machine is said to be consistent. If this is enough to establish the difference between minds and machines, well and good. But many mechanists will not be so quickly persuaded and will maintain that a machine can be programmed, in some such way as Hofstadter supposes, to emit mind-like behaviour. In that case it is machine-like consistency rather than mind-like consistency that is in issue. Any machine, if it is to begin to represent the output of a mind must be able to operate with symbols that can be plausibly interpreted as negation, conjunction, implication, etc., and so must be subject to the rules of some variant of the propositional calculus. Unless something rather like the propositional calculus with some comparable requirement of consistency emerges from the program of a machine, it will not be a plausible representation of a mind, no matter how good it is as a specimen of artificial intelligence. Of course, any plausible representation of a mind would have to manifest the behaviour instanced by Wang, constantly checking whether a contradiction had been reached and attempting to revise its basic axioms when that happened. But this would have to be in accordance with certain rules. There would have to be a program giving precise instructions how the checking was to be undertaken, and in what order axioms were to be revised. Some axioms would need to be fairly immune to revision. Although some thinkers are prepared to envisage a logistic calculus in which the basic inferences of propositional calculus do not hold (e.g. from p & q to p), or the axioms of Elementary Number Theory have been rejected, any machine which resorted to such a stratagem to avoid contradiction would also lose all credence as a representation of a mind. Although we sometimes contradict ourselves and change our minds, some parts of our conceptual structure are very stable, and immune to revision. Of course it is not an absolute immunity. One can allow the Cartesian possibility of conceptual revision without being guilty, as Hutton supposes,[22] of inconsistency in claiming knowledge of his own consistency. To claim to know something is not

---

[22] A Hutton (1976).

to claim infallibility, but only to have adequate backing for what is asserted. Else all knowledge of contingent truths would be impossible. Although one cannot say 'I know it, although I *may* be wrong', it is perfectly permissible to say 'I know it, although I *might conceivably* be wrong.' So long as a man has good reasons, he can responsibly issue a warranty in the form of a statement that he knows, even though we can conceive of circumstances in which his claim would prove false and would have to be withdrawn. So it is with our claim to know the basic parts of our conceptual structure, such as the principles of reasoning embodied in the propositional calculus or the truths of ordinary informal arithmetic. We have adequate, more than adequate, reason for affirming our own consistency and the truth, and hence also the consistency, of informal arithmetic, and so can properly say that we know, and that any machine representation of the mind must manifest an output expressed by a formal (since it is a machine) system which is consistent and includes Elementary Number Theory (since it is supposed to represent the mind). But there remains the Cartesian possibility of our being wrong; and that we need now to discuss. Some mechanists have conceded that a consistent machine could be out-Gödeled by a mind, but have maintained that the machine representation of the mind is an inconsistent machine, but one whose inconsistency is so deep that it would take a long time ever to come to light. It therefore would avoid the quick death of non-selectivity. Although in principle it could be brought to affirm anything, in practice it will be selective, affirming some things and denying others. Only in the long run will it age—or mellow, as we kindly term it—and then 'crash' and cease to deny anything; and in the long run we die—usually before suffering senile dementia. Such a suggestion chimes in with a line of reasoning which has been noticeable in Western thought since the eighteenth century. Reason, it is held, suffers from certain antinomies, and by its own dialectic gives rise to internal contradictions which it is quite powerless to reconcile, and which must in the end bring the whole edifice crashing down in ruins. If the mind is really an inconsistent machine then the philosophers in the Hegelian tradition who have spoken of the self-destructiveness of reason are simply those in whom the inconsistency has surfaced relatively rapidly. They are the ones who have understood the inherent inconsistency of reason, and who, negating negation, have abandoned hope of rational discourse, and having brought mind to the end of its tether, have had on offer only counsels of despair.

Against this position the Gödelian argument can avail us nothing. Quite other arguments and other attitudes are required as antidotes to nihilism. It has long been sensed that materialism leads to nihilism, and the Gödelian argument can be seen as making this *reductio* explicit. And it is a *reductio*. For mechanism claims to be a rational position. It rests its case on the advances of science, the underlying assumptions of scientific thinking, and the actual achievements of scientific research. Although other people may be led to nihilism by feelings of *angst* or other intimations of nothingness, the mechanist must advance arguments or abandon his advocacy altogether. On the face of it we are not machines. Arguments may be adduced to show that appearances are deceptive, and that really we are machines, but arguments presuppose rationality, and if, thanks to the Gödelian argument, the only tenable form of mechanism is that we are inconsistent machines, with all minds being ultimately inconsistent, then mechanism itself is committed to the irrationality of argument, and no rational case for it can be sustained.

REFERENCES

Benacerraf, Paul (1967), 'God, the Devil and Gödel', *The Monist* 51: 9–32.

Bostock, David (1984), 'Gödel and Determinism', private communication, Nov. 1984.

Bowie, G. Lee (1982), 'Lucas' Number is Finally Up', *Journal of Philosophical Logic* 11: 279–85.

Boyer, David L. (1983), 'J. R. Lucas, Kurt Gödel, and Fred Astaire', *Philosophical Quarterly* 33: 147–59.

Chihara, Charles S. (1972), 'On Alleged Refutations of Mechanism using Gödel's Incompleteness Results', *Journal of Philosophy* 69/17: 507–26.

Coder, David (1969), 'Goedel's Theorem and Mechanism', *Philosophy* 64: 234–7, esp. 236.

Dennett, D. C. (1972), review of *The Freedom of the Will* (Lucas 1970), *Journal of Philosophy* 59: 527–31.

Fernando, Emmanuel Q. (1980), 'Mathematical and Philosophical

Implications of the Gödel Incompleteness Theorems', MA thesis, College of Arts and Sciences, University of the Philippines, Quezu City, Sept. 1980.

Glover, Jonathan (1970), *Responsibility*, London: Routledge & Kegan Paul, 31.

Good, I. J. (1967), 'Human and Machine Logic', *British Journal for the Philosophy of Science* 18: 144–7.

—— (1969), 'Gödel's Theorem is a Red Herring', *British Journal for the Philosophy of Science* 19: 357–8.

Hanson, William H. (1971), 'Mechanism and Gödel's Theorems', *British Journal for the Philosophy of Science* 22: 9–16.

Hofstadter, Douglas R. (1979), *Gödel, Escher, Bach*, New York: Basic Books, 475.

Hutton, Anthony (1976), 'This Gödel is Killing Me', *Philosophia* 6/1: 135–44.

Kenny, A. J. P. (1972), in A. J. P. Kenny, H. C. Longuet-Higgins, J. R. Lucas, and C. H. Waddington, *The Nature of Mind*, Edinburgh: Edinburgh University Press, 75–87.

Kirk, Robert (1986), 'Mental Machinery and Gödel', *Synthese* 66: 437–52.

Lewis, David (1969), 'Lucas against Mechanism', *Philosophy* 64: 231–3.

—— (1979), 'Lucas Against Mechanism II', *Canadian Journal of Philosophy* 9: 373–6.

Mackie, J. L. (1977), *Ethics: Inventing Right and Wrong*, Harmondsworth: Penguin, 219.

Putnam, Hilary (1960), 'Minds and Machines', in Sidney Hook (ed.), *Dimensions of Mind: A Symposium*, New York: New York University Press, 138–64; repr. in A. R. Anderson (ed.), *Minds and Machines*, Englewood Cliffs: Prentice-Hall (1964), 72–97.

Rucker, Rudy (1985), 'Gödel's Theorem: The Paradox at the Heart of Modern Man', *Popular Computing*, Feb. 1985, 168.

Sleazak, P. (1982), 'Gödel's Theorem and the Mind', *British Journal for the Philosophy of Science* 33: 41–52.

Smart, J. J. C. (1961), 'Gödel's Theorem, Church's Theorem, and Mechanism', *Synthese* 13, 105–110.

—— (1963), 'Man as a Physical Mechanism', ch. 6 in his *Philosophy and Scientific Realism*, London: Routledge & Kegan Paul.

Thorp, J. W. (1976), 'Free Will and Neurophysiological Determinism', Oxford D.Phil. thesis, 79.

Wang, Hao (1974), *From Mathematics to Philosophy*, London: Routledge & Kegan Paul, 319–26.

Webb, Judson C. (1980), *Mechanism, Mentalism and Metamathematics: An Essay on Finitism*, Dordrecht: D. Reidel, 230.

Whiteley, C. H. (1962), 'Minds, Machines and Gödel: A Reply to Mr Lucas', *Philosophy* 37: 61–2.

Other works are cited in J. R. Lucas (1970), *The Freedom of the Will*, Oxford· Oxford University Press, 174–6.

7

Human versus Mechanical Intelligence

ROBIN GANDY

———•———

> I believe that in about fifty years' time it will be possible
> to programme computers, with a storage capacity of about
> 10^9, to make them play the imitation game so well that an
> average interrogator will not have more than 70 per cent
> chance of making the right identification after five minutes
> of questioning.
>
> Alan Turing, 'Computing Machinery and Intelligence',
> *Mind* (1950), 442

In fact Turing believed, or at very least saw no reason not to
believe, much more than this: that there would, eventually, turn
out to be no essential difference between what could be achieved by
a human intellect in, say, mathematics, and what could be achieved
by a machine. The 1950 paper was intended not so much as a
penetrating contribution to philosophy but as propaganda. Turing
thought the time had come for philosophers and mathematicians
and scientists to take seriously the fact that computers were not
merely calculating engines but were capable of behaviour which
must be accounted as intelligent; he sought to persuade people that
this was so. He wrote this paper—unlike his mathematical papers—
quickly and with enjoyment. I can remember him reading aloud to
me some of the passages—always with a smile, sometimes with a
giggle. Some of the discussions of the paper I have read load it
with more significance than it was intended to bear. I shall discuss
it no further.

What I do want to discuss is arguments for the assertion that
human thought is *essentially* non-mechanical; that we can arrive
at true (communicable) assertions and solve problems which could
not conceivably be done by computers—however complex their
programs. At the end I shall both accept and reject these arguments.

I have in mind particular arguments given by Gödel, Lucas, and Penrose. Each of these asserts that there are certain trains of thought about abstract objects and of a mathematical kind, which are essentially non-mechanical, non-algorithmic. I shall refer to trains of thought which at least seem to be non-mechanical as showing the 'divine spark'. I think Gödel, and perhaps Lucas would accept this phrase; perhaps Penrose would prefer 'the effects of quantum gravity'. 'Intuition', though often used in similar contexts, would be wrong and misleading: I am concerned with *analysable trains* of thought.

Before I consider some examples I should like quickly to dismiss a supposedly logical point frequently expounded by John Searle: programs operate on syntactic structures, while thoughts are concerned with the underlying semantics. Of course in many contexts—expert systems, for example—the point is correct. But, like Tarski's theory of truth, it is superficial: when the going gets rough, when the problems become interesting, it contributes nothing. When I am doing arithmetic, or thinking about the theory of numbers, there is no semantics going on underneath my syntactically expressed or envisaged thoughts; and of course this is even more true of, say, an engineer who has never even considered the question 'What is the number 2?' And if the people in that Chinese room were dealing with questions about numbers they would fairly soon understand the questions and answers even if they had never seen the Chinese arithmetical ideograms before. To paraphrase Wittgenstein: 'When asked for the meaning look for the use'. For abstract objects the use is often given, though not always wholly, by syntax. Searle's point is interesting conceptually, but it is not a *logical* point.

Some examples of the divine spark. First a personal example. When I was 10, it came to me, almost in a flash, that the sum of the first so many odd numbers was a perfect square. Unlike the infant Gauss, I had not been set this as a problem; also, unlike the infant Gauss, I had no notion of proving it—or even, I think, that it required proof; I imagine I checked it out up to 25 or 27, and then *knew* that it was true. I can still recall where this happened and that I felt quite faint with pleasure; and the memory of the pleasure was so strong that I soon decided that what I wanted to be was a mathematician. I imagine that there are, or soon will be, AI programs which would discover this as a plausible rule; it would not give them pleasure, and they might not treat it as an established truth.

A slightly less trivial example. In Book IX Euclid states that given any number of primes there is a prime different from all of them. He proves it for three primes; he assumes that his reader has enough of the divine spark to *see* that the argument will work for any number. It is certainly conceivable that an AI program when provided with several examples of this proof would come up with the proof for the general case.

And now for a highly non-trivial example; one which I think exhibits one of the great discoveries in Western mathematics. To make my point clear I should remind you that at the time of Hammurabi (say 1800 BC) the Babylonians had developed a place system for numerals, were quite capable of handling large numbers with ease, and so were aware that the number series could be continued indefinitely:

$$1, 2, 3, \ldots \text{and so on.}$$

I shall call this the Babylonian view of the natural numbers.

Gödel claims (and I agree) that one of the things that distinguishes human thought from mechanical thought is our ability to work with abstract concepts. An example of this is the handling by the Greeks of the concept of the ratio of two magnitudes. For mystical and musical reasons the Pythagoreans had studied rational ratios, but they had also realized that in geometry there were irrational ratios—incommensurable magnitudes. In order to deal, for example, with the properties of similar figures it is necessary to have a general notion of ratio; one way—some scholars believe it was historically the first way—of making this notion precise is by the Euclidean algorithm—applied geometrically: the construction and relevant theorems are given at the beginning of Book X. Starting with one magnitude which I shall call r_{-1} and a shorter one r_0 one continues to subtract r_0 from r_{-1} until one is left with a remainder r_1 (possibly zero) which is less than r_0:

$$r_{-1} = n_0 \cdot r_0 + r_1,$$

now one repeats this step, starting with r_0:

$$r_0 = n_1 \cdot r_1 + r_2,$$

and so on. One can define the ratio, r_{-1}/r_0 to be this process, which Euclid calls anthyphairesis, or more exactly to be the sequence n_0, $n_1, \ldots$ The magnitudes r_{-1} and r_0 are multiples of a common unit if and only if the process terminates, the unit being the last non-zero reminder. In modern terminology $n_0, n_1, \ldots$ are the successive partial quotients in the representation of the ratio (rational or irrational) as a continued fraction.

Here is a practical example of the process. The *golden section* is the ratio $x/1$ defined by the diagram (Fig. 1), where the shaded rectangle is similar to the original one—so $x/1 = 1/(x - 1)$:

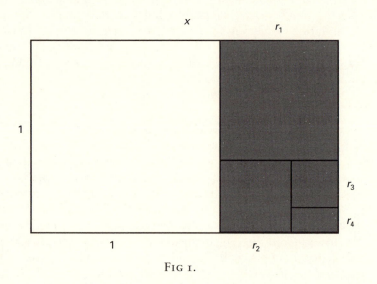

The Greeks knew how to construct such a rectangle: to divide a line in the extreme and mean ratio. We have:

$$x = 1 + r_1.$$

But by similarity we have

$$1 = r1 + r2$$
$$r1 = r2 + r3,$$

and so on; plainly the process can be continued indefinitely. The practical man, or a Babylonian (or a fifth generation AI program) would say 'Eventually we don't please to continue—the figure has got too small to consider' and he could work out an approximate value of x using the sequence $n_0 = 1$, $n_1 = 1 + n_0$, $n_2 = n_0 + n_1$ ... (though he would more likely work with the equation $x^2 - x - 1 = 0$). If all one wants is an approximate value of x, a question whether $x/1$ is rational or irrational does not arise. But for the Greeks, perhaps partly for mystical reasons, the dichotomy rational–irrational was important; so it was essential to distinguish between:

'the sequence n_0, n_1 ... and so on'

and

'the sequence n_0, n_1, ... *ad infinitum*' (of non-halting computations).

The claim, cogently argued by D. H. Fowler in his *Mathematics in Plato's Academy* (Clarendon Press, 1987), is that a number of such non-terminating geometrical constructions for particular irrationals were known before the development of the theory of irrationals given in Euclid Book V, and that in these cases the ratio (a single conceptual object) *was seen as, could be identified with, the actually infinite process of the Euclidean algorithm*. This really is a divine spark. I cannot see any way in which a machine, however intelligent, could pass from the 'Babylonian' to the 'Greek' view. And although Chinese mathematics—in particular arithmetic and algebra—prior to the time of the Renaissance was much more sophisticated than Greek and Western mathematics, the Chinese mathematicians did not, as far as I have been able to make out, pass from the Babylonian to the Greek view.

Several comments are in order:

(1) The anthyphairetic version of ratio does not occur explicitly in Euclid (or Archimedes), and so was not available to the founders of European mathematics. But both it, and more plainly the Greek '*ad infinitum*', are implicit in Euclid X 2 waiting (as deep insights often do) to be fully understood. Euclid's algorithm (in the form of a continued fraction) was used in the eighteenth century to prove the irrationality of e and π.

(2) It can be argued that the Greek view is also implied in the discussion by Aristotle and others of Zeno's paradoxes. I do not know if this should be taken seriously, but the concept of tending

to a limit (as opposed to the existence of a limit) as it occurs in Greek mathematics can be understood and expressed in terms of the Babylonian view. What, for example, Archimedes proved was that the area of a circle differs from πr^2 by *as little as one pleases.*

(3) Euclid X 2 can be expressed, in a very un-Greek way, as follows:

$$r_{-1}/r_0 \text{ is rational iff } \exists n \ (r_n = 0)$$
$$\text{is irrational iff } \forall n \ (r_n \neq 0).$$

These *general* assertions require the use of a quantifier—whereas assertions made on the Babylonian view can always be expressed in a suitable free-variable calculus. Further the dichotomy 'r_{-1}/r_0 is rational or it is irrational' requires the use of classical logic at least for single quantifier formulae. The Greeks accepted the dichotomy; Brouwer denied it.

(4) To sum up:

(A) The transition from the Babylonian to the Greek view is a paradigm of the divine spark.

(B) It is implicit in Euclid X 2.

(C) Most of Western mathematics, in particular our notions of limit and continuity, depend on the transition.

Now I turn to an instance of the divine spark which is central to the arguments of both Lucas and Penrose; namely our ability to see that the unprovable Gödelian sentence is true. In my view neither author examines closely enough exactly what the spark *is*—how it is that we see the sentence is true.

We are supposing that the arithmetic statements produced by a machine are all theorems of some formal system S for number theory (I shall discuss this supposition later). Instead of Gödel's first theorem I shall use his second theorem. This does not affect the *validity* of what I am saying, but it makes it easier to see *what* I am saying.

Let $OK_s(n)$ stand for 'n does not code a proof in S of $0 \neq 0$'. I assume that $OK(n)$ can be (easily) decided. Gödel's Theorem asserts:

$$\text{If } S \text{ is consistent then } \nvdash_s \forall x OK_s(x). \tag{1}$$

The proof of this theorem requires that certain constraints (the derivability conditions) be placed on the formal expression of provability; they are satisfied by any natural coding of proofs and need not concern us.

What does the antecedent of (1) mean? It means:

$$OK_s(0) \text{ and } OK_s(1) \text{ and} \ldots \qquad (2)$$

Let us fix S to be a particular formal system, e.g. Peano arithmetic or some fragment of it. The divine spark tells us that $\forall x OK_s(x)$ is true; how does it do this—how do we *know* that it is true? Our knowledge comes in two steps: we recognize.

(A) $OK_s(0)$ and $OK_s(1)$ and ...
(B) If a property P holds for all numbers then $\forall x P x$ is true.

(A) indeed represents an instance of the divine spark—a triumph of the human intellect. Mathematicians realized the truth of (A) long before they had any idea as to how to give a precise proof of it. I think the way this comes about is something like the following.

(1) We picture the number series
   0, 1, 2, ... *ad infinitum.*
   This picture tell us that Peano's 3rd and 4th axioms are satisfied (no looping back).

(2) We see that if a formula $\phi(x)$ holds for $x = 0$ and is inductive then it must hold for $x = 1$, and then it must hold for $x = 2$ and so on. Thus the formulae which one proved in S will be true in the picture, and so S is consistent.

As for (B), although it is true that the formal expression of (B) is unprovable in S, it is provable in a quite mechanically obtained extension of S (it is interesting to note that Post, in a clearly stated version of Lucas's argument—written in 1941, based on notes of his work in the early 1920s—makes this same point).[1] Nevertheless I think that the judgement (B) is not, in general, a mechanical matter: like (A) it comes from our *picture* of the number series and should be counted as an instance of the divine spark.

A rather more sophisticated illustration of the divine spark is provided by Gödel's proof of the consistency of arithmetic by the so-called 'Dialectica' interpretation. Gödel himself saw this as a good example of the way in which our 'use of abstract objects on the basis of their meaning' transcends mechanical or purely formal

---

[1] Emil L. Post, 'Absolutely Unsolvable Problems and Relatively Undecidable Propositions—Account of an Anticipation', in Martin Davis (ed.), *The Undecidable* (New York: Raven Press, 1965), pp. 340–433, esp. pp. 417–24.

methods. The abstract objects in question are the primitive recursive functionals at all finite types. We start with processes (that is functional programs together with the means of implementing them) corresponding to the familiar primitive recursive functions. Now we consider processes of the second kind; such a process takes a process of the first kind, P say, considered as a whole—i.e. not just particular outputs of P—and gives out another process of the first kind. For example P applied to f might give out the n-th iterate of f, where n is, say, $f(0)$; another example is provided by the operation that takes one from each column of the Ackermann function to the next. Then we proceed to operations of the third kind and so on. It is not hard to set down analogues of the familiar recursive schemes for primitive recursive functions for these higher-type objects. But for Gödel's proof one has to recognize that there *are* objects which satisfy these schemes; what Gödel claims is that this recognition depends on seeing what the objects mean, what they are. In fact I think that what the reader does is this: he considers examples at types two and three, and perhaps at type four, and then says 'I see how it goes.' Anyone who has worked in type theory knows that, with a struggle, one gets a firm grasp on what is going on at low types, and then just accepts that things will be the same higher up.

All the examples of the divine spark I have given so far have the same form. One has a vague picture of an infinite sequence; one investigates in detail a rather small number of instances of some proposition or construction and then one says

'I SEE HOW IT GOES.'

Presumably before long there will be (perhaps there already are) AI programs which will formulate plausible rules for infinite sequences based on a finite number of examples. What is 'divine', apparently non-mechanical, in my examples is that when we say 'I see how it goes' we do not think that we are making a plausible conjecture; we *know* that it does go like that.

There are of course other ways in which the divine spark works in mathematics. I mention two:

(A) 'WOULDN'T IT BE NICE IF . . . '

Two examples: (*a*) The Riemann Hypothesis and (*b*) Unique factorization in principal ideal rings.

(B) 'THIS LOOKS RATHER LIKE (or reminds me of) THAT.'

Perhaps this is the most important slogan in the development of mathematics (and in science). But I have nothing interesting—non-platitudinous—to say about it. I should, though, mention that Category theory was developed largely to analyse in-depth situations where 'this' did look like 'that', and is very successful in doing so.

It is now necessary to think about the ways in which there could be a mechanical not a divine spark. We have to consider how, say, a tenth-generation computer might be organized. There may be readers who have thought long and hard about this, and I apologize to them for making only rather naïve remarks. On the other hand the anti-mechanists, in particular Lucas and Penrose have not, I think, thought hard enough about it.

First of all, at the highest level, there must be a master control program which never changes. There will be inputs corresponding to instructions and (external) experience. At the lowest level there will be basic processors (chips) of the known kind. In between there will be a hierarchy of levels of program manipulators (controllers). Among other activities these will judge between programs at a lower level, and alter them, perhaps by random mutations; they may also experiment between different forms of representation. Then, after various checks for correctness, they will pass on working programs to the basic processors.

Because of the external inputs and of the incorporation of random devices it looks, at first sight, as if the work of such a machine cannot be represented by a formal system. However, I think in fact Lucas and Penrose are right to deny this:

(a) One can suppose that the teaching input comes to an end (when, say, the machine has obtained a doctorate).

(b) If one supposes that the machine is concerned with problems in number theory, or pure algebra, then one can also suppose that the 'experience' and the problems are provided by another part of the machine.

(c) I do not think (and certainly Turing did not think) that it would make any difference if the random choices were in fact made by using a mechanical random-number generator.

So it is not unreasonable to assume: *An n-th generation machine has a fixed program and so its action can be represented within a formal system.* BUT IT IS A TOTAL *NON SEQUITUR* TO CONCLUDE FROM THIS THAT, BY GÖDEL'S THEOREM, THERE ARE TRUE SENTENCES WHICH THE MACHINE WILL NOT PRODUCE.

What the formal system corresponding to the machine proves is simply a set of strings of symbols which code the successive states (and outputs) of the machine. One can set up this formal system, like a Chomsky grammar, so that the actual theorems of the system (terminal expressions) contain neither variables nor quantifiers.

Of course what we are interested in is not the outputs as strings of symbols, but those output strings which are, or encode, formulae of, say, first-order arithmetic. It is true that from the formal system for the machine we can derive a formal system S such that the formulae given out by the machine are all theorems of S; but we *cannot* infer from the consistency of the formal system which describes the machine that S will consistent. (The machine might output, for example, the string '0 ≠ 0'.) This, I believe, is what lay behind Turing's insistence that an intelligent machine might make mistakes *as do human beings.*

It is a fact that highly gifted mathematicians (Frege, Quine, and Martin-Löf for example) have produced inconsistent systems. Mathematicians might point out that it is only logicians who do this. But of course straight mathematicians (Euler is a classic example) 'prove' false theorems and use inconsistent methods to get valid results. I believe that they, *and* the *n*-th-generation machines, will continue to do this.

And yet, and yet? Inconsistencies do get removed, false 'theorems' do get corrected or abandoned. How? It used to be thought that set theory provided *the* foundation for mathematics, despite the obvious fact that many mathematical concepts had to be grotesquely deformed before they could be made to fit within it. But what axiomatic set theory does provide is a rather straightforward though highly artificial method of checking for inconsistencies and *non sequiturs.* The consistency of the set theory—for most purposes quite small fragments of ZF suffice—is justified by the divine spark; the *n*-th-generation machines will have to be taught some formal set-theoretic system by which they can check their results. Besides direct appeals to intuition, another thing which mathematicians do is to turn an incorrectly proved or unproved assertion which they hope or believe to be true into a hypothesis or conjecture. I have already suggested that machines will construct plausible rules from examples. It seems to me quite likely that, in the future, machines and the mathematicians who use them will not distinguish as sharply as we do at present between true and conjectured assertions.

Let me sum up the argument so far. Human mathematicians do, from time to time, arrive at true results using methods which appear to us to be unmechanizable. But, if we admit that machines, like humans, can be fallible, then we cannot *prove* unmechanizability.

How could one prove unmechanizability? Gödel and Penrose suggest two different though not totally disconnected approaches. Gödel suggests that there may eventually emerge a coherent and compelling theory of rational thought, and that the mind's ability to solve mechanically unsolvable problems would be a consequence of this theory. (Unlike Penrose Gödel believed that the mind is not tied to the brain.) Such a theory would not of course be formal or even mathematical—though it might include ideas drawn from, say, category theory. It would look more like a metaphysical system; and indeed such theories of mind were included in the metaphysical systems of Kant, Hegel, and others. Results from cognitive psychology—and even AI—may be lightly suggestive, but they are far indeed from providing a basis on which such a theory could be built. I remark that René Thom—whose writings I find difficult—has thought hard about this problem. And there may well be others of whom I am ignorant. It seems to me there are two great difficulties: first, where to start? and secondly, how to avoid being side-tracked into 'psychologism' either by introspection or by studying psychology.

Penrose, on the other hand, is concerned with the brain: his two books[2] both discuss what he calls 'The Physics of Mind'. He anticipates that, perhaps quite soon, there will arise a theory of quantum gravity which, although in a fairly straightforward sense deterministic, yet will have non-computable observable consequences. Now crystals have been grown that have pentagonal symmetry. If this is not just a chance effect then what happens at one point of crystal growth must be determined by the whole of the rest of the already formed crystal—a global not a local determination. Penrose hopes that the new theory will cover this phenomenon; and suggests that it could then apply to the formation of synapses in the brain. In contrast, the determination of what

---

[2] *The Emperor's New Mind* (New York: OUP, 1989) and *Shadows of the Mind* (Oxford: OUP, 1994).

happens next in a Turing machine or a polycellular automation has a strictly local character.

Now it is time for me to come down off the fence—on both sides.

1. I think it conceivable that in fifty or a hundred years time there will be machines of the tenth or twentieth generation which in some areas of mathematics will be regarded by first-rate mathematicians as valuable *colleagues* (not merely assistants). The machines will write papers, argue back when criticized, and will take part in discussion on how best to tackle a new problem. This is an updated version of the Turing Test. The conception raises an important point. In his book Penrose asserts forcefully that consciousness is essential to rational thought; I do not quite understand what he means by consciousness. But machines of the kind I am imagining would display the effects of consciousness—the ability to concentrate attention on a particular part or aspect of their input, the ability to reflect on and to alter the behaviour of subsystems in their hierarchic structure, the ability to produce a range of alternatives, and even, in a very restricted way, an ability to adapt their social behaviour.

I remember a long time ago asking Donald MacKay what sort of evidence or knowledge he thought would be required to attribute consciousness to a computer; he replied that it would not primarily be a matter of using evidence and knowledge, but a matter of having the nerve. If my fantasy becomes fact, people will have the nerve.

2. Now for the other side of the fence. Even if machines of that kind are built, discussions about them, explanations of their working, proposals for their improvement will (when not concerned only with the lowest levels of this hierarchical structure) be carried on not in terms of algorithms but in the same sort of terms as we use—as I used—in discussing human intelligence and rational thought. At a sophisticated level it is not practical, nor useful, nor sensible to discuss intelligent behaviour solely in terms of algorithms or machine programs; and this would remain true even if there were some master program producing the behaviour.

8

The Church–Turing Thesis:
Its Nature and Status

ANTONY GALTON

1. The Church–Turing thesis (CT), as it is usually understood, asserts the identity of two classes of functions, the *effectively computable* functions on the one hand, and the *recursive* (or *Turing-machine computable*) functions on the other. In support of this thesis, it is customary to cite the circumstance that all serious attempts to characterize the notion of an effectively computable function in precise mathematical terms have ended up by defining the same class of functions, albeit in quite different ways. Thus CT is supported by a series of *theorems* to the effect that these various characterizations of effective computability (viz. Turing-machine computability, general recursiveness, λ-definability, Markov algorithm computability, and the rest) are extensionally equivalent.

Open any text on the theory of computing at the point where CT is discussed. You will find there a statement to the effect that CT is not a theorem, and thus cannot be proved, because one of the terms it contains, namely 'effectively computable', cannot be defined precisely, but rather refers to our vague, intuitive idea of what constitutes computability. This special character of CT as not susceptible to formal verification was already recognized by Church and Turing.[1] Thus Church (1936), in defining the notion

---

[1] Even before Church and Turing, Gödel had considered what may be thought of as a precursor to CT, that the class of functions computable by means of a finite procedure was coextensive with the class of recursive functions, where however Gödel does not (in contradistinction to Church) provide a precise definition of the latter class. Most pertinent for our present concern is Gödel's remark that this thesis 'cannot be proved, since the notion of finite computation is not defined, but it serves as a heuristic principle' (Gödel, 1934: p. 44).

of an *effectively calculable* function of positive integers, remarks that

> This definition is thought to be justified by the considerations which follow, so far as positive justification can ever be obtained for the selection of a formal definition to correspond to an intuitive notion.

Turing (1936), similarly, notes that

> [a]ll arguments which can be given [for CT] are bound to be, fundamentally, appeals to intuition, and for this reason rather unsatisfactory mathematically. (p. 249)

Despite this, it is almost universally admitted that the equivalence theorems mentioned above, together with various other considerations such as Turing's own account of his motivation for the detailed definition of his machines, constitutes *evidence* for CT. The suppositions that (*a*) CT does not admit rigorous proof, and (*b*) there exists evidence to support it, suggest that CT is more like a proposition of natural science than of mathematics, and thus properly to be regarded as an empirical hypothesis, even though its *subject-matter* appears to be mathematical in character.

2. Let us examine more closely the idea that certain considerations, both formal and informal, constitute evidence for CT. Evidence for a thesis means evidence that the thesis is true; so if it is to be meaningful to adduce evidence for CT, it must at least have a chance of being true. But has it? Doubt has been cast on this by Wang (1974):

> One often hears that in mathematical logic a sharp concept has been developed which corresponds exactly to our vague intuitive notion of computability. But how could a sharp notion correspond exactly to a vague notion?

Wang's own solution to this difficulty is to say that

> [a] closer look reveals that the sharp notion ... is actually not as sharp as it appears at first sight. (p. 83)

In Wang's view, then, it would appear that the CT really asserts the identity not of a sharp notion with a vague one, but of two vague ones. This will hardly do, though, because, even if Wang is correct in saying that the formal notion is not as sharp as one would like, there can surely be no denying that it is *very much sharper* than our 'vague, intuitive' notion. And this leaves us with the problem of how two notions of very different degrees of imprecision can actually *be* equivalent.

If, as these last remarks suggest, CT is not even something that could possibly be true, then either we must modify it so that it no longer suffers from this defect, or we must revise our views as to its status.

3. Let us take it that the form of CT is *aRb*, where *a* is the vague, intuitive term ('effective computability'), *b* is the precise mathematical term (recursiveness, Turing-machine computability, or what have you), and *R* expresses the relation that is said to hold between them. In what I shall call the *classical formulation* of CT, *a* and *b* denote *classes*—the class of effectively computable partial functions from the natural numbers to the natural numbers, and the class of general recursive functions, respectively—and *R* is the identity relation. The thesis, on this interpretation, thus asserts that two classes of functions are identical. The unease we noted above arose from the fact that *a* is not well-defined, whereas *b* is, or at least much more nearly so, and hence cannot be meaningfully equated to *a*.

One obvious way in which we might try to alleviate this uneasiness is by redefining the role of the relational term *R*. Instead of regarding CT as an assertion *that* two classes are identical, we might regard it as having a *stipulative* force, in effect *defining* 'effective computability' to be the same as recursiveness.

This way of looking at the matter is suggested by some formulations of the thesis that one finds in the literature. Hermes (1965), for example, speaks of suggestions to 'make precise' the concept of algorithm and related concepts (including, by implication, effective computability),[2] while Minsky (1967) speaks of 'the thesis that Turing's notion of computability is an acceptable technical counterpart of our intuitive notion of effective computability'. This stipulative understanding of CT is also compatible with Church's original formulation, which uses the idea of 'correspondence'.

---

[2] Note, incidentally, that Hermes later on comes closer to what I called the classical formulation, when he speaks of the 'identification of the originally intuitively given concept of algorithm with a certain, exactly defined concept'. Likewise, Kleene (1952) explicitly countenances both interpretations when he says that CT 'may be considered a hypothesis about the intuitive notion of effective calculability or a mathematical definition of effective calculability' (pp. 318 f.).

Turing's formulation, on the other hand, is less readily interpretable in this way. His claim is that

the [Turing machine] computable numbers *include* all numbers which
could naturally be regarded as computable.[3] (p. 249)

The fact that Turing is here concerned with the computability of
numbers rather than of functions need not worry us in this context: in Turing's treatment, a real number is in any case identified with the function which maps each positive integer n onto the
nth place in the decimal expansion of that number. If we assume
that Turing would have regarded all Turing-machine computable
numbers (or functions) as computable in the intuitive ('natural')
sense, it is hard to avoid reading Turing here as asserting the
identity of two classes, in other words as stating the classical
formulation of CT.

4. If we do opt for the weaker, stipulative interpretation, according to which recursiveness or an equivalent is proposed as a replacement for our ill-defined intuitive notion of computability, what
follows? In effect, CT sets bounds on what we can reasonably set
out to achieve computationally. It tells us not to waste our time
looking for general solutions to the halting problem and other
recursively unsolvable problems.

Now the trouble with taking CT purely stipulatively like this is
that it does not supply us with a reason *why* we should regard
certain prima-facie computable problems as off limits. The classical
formulation of CT yields the same advice, and at the same time it
gives us a reason for following that advice, namely it is a waste of
time looking for general solutions to recursively unsolvable problems precisely *because no solutions exist*. This last move can only
be made on the classical formulation, because only the classical
formulation takes seriously the idea that there is such a thing as
the class of all effectively computable functions, even if we cannot
characterize it precisely independently of CT itself.

I take it that these considerations imply that the stipulative
interpretation of CT, however attractive it may seem at first sight,
cannot be seriously upheld. At best, it is arbitrary, and at worst
incoherent. Let us then assume that the classical formulation is

---

[3] Turing (1936), my italics.

correct in so far as it asserts an identity between two classes of functions. By 'correct' here I mean that if there is to be a coherent statement of CT at all then it must be along these lines, however much modified in detail from the classical version. This still leaves us with the tension we noted earlier, arising from the impossibility we thought we discerned in the idea of equating a vague notion with a precise one.

The obvious remedy, if only it could be achieved, would be to try to sharpen the vague term (*a*) in the identity. But *this* seems impossible to do without begging the question: after all, as already remarked, every serious attempt to give a precise characterization of *a* has resulted in a *formal* notion of computability that is provably equivalent to recursiveness, the various proofs of equivalence being precisely what is held up as the main supporting evidence for the thesis. We thus seem to have the curious circumstance of a corpus of exact mathematical results being held up as evidence for a thesis which it is impossible to state clearly while maintaining its distinctness from those results.[4]

In the next two sections I consider what happens if we try to sharpen the intuitive notion *a* in the thesis *without* going so far as to define something that is already provably equivalent to the sharp term *b*. Note that there is an air of paradox about this plan: I am deliberately setting out to produce a formulation of CT that stands a chance of being true but which cannot be proved. The unprovability is necessary here, for an attempted formulation which *could* be proved would no longer be CT, but a piece of evidence for the 'real' CT—if such a thing exists. So my aim here is to see whether or not CT *can* be coherently formulated at all.

5. Gandy (1988) has argued that, contrary to received opinion, CT *is* a theorem, which he states in the following form:

Turing's Theorem: Any function which is effectively calculable by an abstract human being following a fixed routine is effectively calculable by a Turing machine . . . and conversely. (p. 83)

---

[4] Kalmár (1959: 79) regards this as a reason for rejecting CT: 'There are pre-mathematical concepts which must remain pre-mathematical ones, for they cannot permit any restriction imposed by an exact mathematical definition. Among these belong . . . such concepts as that of effective calculability, or of solvability, or of provability by arbitrary correct means, the extension of which cannot cease to change during the development of Mathematics.'

But in order for this to be a theorem in the mathematical sense, a determinate proposition capable of being definitively proved, the terms occurring in it must all be definable in a precise way; in particular we need a precise definition of the term 'abstract human being'. If this is defined by means of a purely mathematical construction, the question arises how the computational power of this construction is related to that of real human beings, or real computing machines: in effect the core issue addressed by CT is pushed back, with Gandy's *a* term ('abstract human-being computability') becoming the new *b* term, the new *a* term reverting once more to the original imprecisely formulated notion of effective computability.

If, on the other hand, the notion of an abstract human being is not defined in such a way as to allow 'Turing's theorem', as stated by Gandy, to be proved, then it does not seem correct to call this formulation a theorem. If an abstract human being is obtained from a real human being by abstracting away 'the—very important—practical limitations on time and space' (Gandy, 1988: 83), then Gandy's version of CT begins to look very much like an empirical hypothesis about the computational powers of human beings. More often, though, CT has been understood as making a broader claim, about what *any* entity, real or abstract, can compute, not specifically about human beings. Thus while Gandy's formulation, in which the *a* term is made more precise without however becoming provably equivalent to the *b* term, is a step in the direction we have set ourselves to explore, it is arguably not general enough to play the role traditionally assigned to CT, that of defining the limits to computation *in general*.

If now we consider the various formal notions that have been used as the second, precise term of CT, i.e. recursiveness, Turing-machine computability, λ-definability, etc., we note that each of them gives us a *computationally specific* way of defining functions. By this I mean that each of them characterizes a class of computable functions by giving us a framework within which we can actually compute them. The Turing machine model of computability, for example, provides a precise specification of the class of all Turing machines. Each Turing machine does the job of computing the values for a particular function. Likewise, the scheme of primitive recursion plus the μ-operator shows us how to construct individual function definitions which we can use to compute values of the functions thereby defined.

My point here is that each of the formal notions provides a *realization* or *implementation* of the general notion of a computable function. Now the complement, as it were, of implementation is *specification*. A specification is precise about *what* is wanted but is silent on *how* it is to be achieved; an implementation does not in itself tell us *what* it gives us, but it is explicit about *how* it does it. And the relation between specification and implementation is, ideally, that a specification is *correctly realized* by an implementation.

If, then, we regard the specific models of computation which belong on the right-hand side of CT as implementations, then what goes on the left-hand side must be a specification. But so far, it is only a vague specification—that is the root of our problem. What we need to do is to put down the specification precisely: after all, a specification ought to be no less precise, in its own way, than an implementation, the difference being that, as already indicated, what they are precise about are quite different things.

Our task, then, is to find a precise term which can stand in relation to recursiveness and its formal equivalents as specification to implementation. We require a notion of computation which is precise as to what sort of thing results from a computation but is vague as to how it is achieved. To this end I propose to examine the following notion of *black-box computability*:

A partial function *f* from the natural numbers to the natural numbers is *black-box computable* if there could exist a black box with input and output ports and a representation scheme for natural numbers, such that for each natural number *n*, when the representation of *n* is fed into the input port of the black-box then, if *f(n)* is defined, its representation will eventually emerge from the output port, whereas if *f(n)* is not defined, either nothing will ever emerge, or what emerges is not the representation of a natural number using the specified scheme.

This definition says nothing at all about the nature of the mechanisms inside the black box: anything will do, so long as the outward behaviour of the box is as specified. Thus black-box computability is defined in a very different way from Turing-machine computability, for which the details of the mechanism are crucial (even though to some extent arbitrary in the sense that they can be changed without affecting the notion of computability thereby defined).

6. The 'black-box formulation' of CT is that the class of black-box computable functions is equal to the class of recursive functions. In effect, this version of the thesis states that whatever mechanism a particular black box contains, it can be replaced by a Turing machine without altering its functional specification.

Is the black-box formulation of CT precise enough to avoid the incoherence we imputed to the classical formulation? It is surely not yet *perfectly* precise. A conspicuous source of vagueness lies in the use of the words 'there could exist'. In order to make precise what is meant here, we should need to specify exactly what space of possibilities is intended.

To appreciate the problems involved in doing this, consider the following black box. It is simply a form of universal Turing machine. But it has a special property: in any computation that it performs, the first step takes one second, and each subsequent step takes half the time of the one that precedes it. When a numerical encoding of any given Turing-machine/tape pair (M, T) is presented to the input port of the black box, the black box immediately proceeds to simulate the computation that would occur if the Turing machine M were to be activated with initial tape-configuration T. If the simulation reaches a 'halt' state after a finite number of steps, the black box halts and delivers the output 1 (meaning that the computation specified by the input terminates). But if after two seconds the simulated computation has not reached a 'halt' state, then the black box halts and delivers the output 0 (meaning that the computation specified by the input does not terminate).

Clearly, this black box solves the halting problem for Turing machines. Does this mean that the halting problem (or rather, the corresponding numerical function) is black-box computable? It all depends on the space of possibilities underlying the requirement that an appropriate black box 'could exist'. The black box I have described could not exist in physical form in our universe, although one can, perhaps, conceive of alternative possible universes in which it could: it is, after all, mathematically consistent. When we describe an abstract model of computation, it is customary to insist that it produce its result after only finitely many steps, because only in this case can the abstract process be realized physically: ultimately what interests us is the actual physical computations.

It therefore seems reasonable to introduce constraints into our understanding of what is possible so that the black boxes referred to in the definition of black-box computability could exist physically. If we do this, though, do we have any reason to suppose that there will be *any* correspondence between black-box computability and Turing-machine computability? For on the one hand, to quote Deutsch (1985: 101), 'there is no *a priori* reason why physical laws should respect the limitations of the mathematical processes we call "algorithms"', which suggests that the introduction of physical considerations, so far from being a *limitation*, might allow us to go beyond the bounds of Turing-machine computability. And on the other hand, to quote Deutsch again,

[n]or, conversely, is it obvious *a priori* that any of the familiar recursive functions is in physical reality computable. The reason why we find it possible to construct, say, electronic calculators, and indeed why we can perform mental arithmetic, cannot be found in mathematics or logic. *The reason is that the laws of physics 'happen to' permit the existence of physical models for the operations of arithmetic* such as addition, subtraction and multiplication. If they did not, these familiar operations would be non-computable functions. We might still know *of* them and invoke them in mathematical proofs (which would presumably be called 'non-constructive') but we could not perform them. (p. 101)

Even if we suppose that there is sufficient harmony between the physical world and the abstract world of mathematical logic for arbitrary Turing machines or their equivalents to be constructible in principle, it will still be the case that many, indeed most, Turing-machine computable functions will fail to be black-box computable, because the resources they require exceed the capacity of the physical world to supply them. After all, even so simple a function as addition can only be computed physically for arguments up to a certain size, and there must certainly exist infinitely many Turing-machine computable functions for which the computation for *any argument(s)*, using Turing machines or their equivalent, exceeds the resource bounds imposed by the physical world. If CT is right, these functions cannot be computed by any physical means at all.

Unfortunately, it seems impossible to specify the physical constraints on our black box in a non-arbitrary way. What we say here must clearly be influenced by the current state of our knowledge of the extent of the physical world, both in the large and in the small, and also by our current technological capacities. As Enderton (1977) puts it,

A person with a digital computing machine may regard a function f as being computable only when $f(x)$ is computable on his machine in a reasonable length of time. Of course, the matter of what is reasonable may change from day to day. And next year he hopes to get a faster machine with more memory space and tape drives. At that time, his idea of what is computable in a practical sense will be extended considerably.

The class of effectively computable functions is obtained in the ideal case where all of the practical restrictions on running time and memory space are removed. Thus the class is a theoretical upper bound on what can ever in any century be considered computable. (pp. 529 f.)

Enderton here endorses the traditional view that purely physical considerations are not generally considered to be a part of the theory of computability.

But this has the result that CT, as ordinarily formulated, tends to be seen as irrelevant to the issue of defining what can or cannot be computed in practice. To quote von Neumann (1961),

Throughout all modern logic, the only thing that is important is whether a result can be achieved in a finite number of elementary steps or not. The size of the number of steps which are required, on the other hand, is hardly ever a concern of formal logic. Any finite sequence of correct steps is, as a matter of principle, as good as any other. . . . In dealing with automata, this statement must be significantly modified. In the case of an automaton the thing which matters is not only whether it can reach a certain result in a finite number of steps at all but also how many such steps are needed. (p. 303)

We thus find, in conventional computability theory, on the one hand the requirement that a computation be completed in finitely many steps, and on the other hand the lack of any constraint on the complexity of a computation. The justification for the former requirement is that infinite computations cannot actually be implemented physically; the justification for the latter non-requirement is that our theory of computation is purely abstract and hence should not be constrained by physically motivated considerations. There is a tension here which needs to be resolved if CT is to be seen as having direct relevence to practical computational issues. What is required here is an answer to what is perhaps the central question in all this, namely: when is a computation procedure *effective*?

Even if we do not insist that the black box should be able to exist and perform its computations physically, one might suppose, *pace* Deutsch, that this condition should be sufficient in the sense that the possibility of physical realization should qualify a black box for the role required of it in the black-box formulation of CT. But as J. R. Lucas pointed out in discussion (see this volume, p. 104), there would be no reason, on this supposition, to disqualify a black-box which contained a human being who is responsible for deciding what output to give in response to each input. If we accept this (in effect allowing that the black box might *be* a person), then the black-box formulation of CT becomes identical with the ('strong AI') thesis that people too are subject to all the limitations of Turing machines, a position which Lucas himself has consistently argued against.

A more modest formulation of black-box computability seems to be in order. What further constraints should we add? One possibility is to insist that we can, in principle, *construct* the black box. This amounts to a substantial limitation inasmuch as we have no idea how to set about constructing a black box that is in any relevant sense equivalent to a person. But in 'we can construct' there appears once again a 'can', and we have to ask more closely just what sort of possibility or potentiality we require here.

One obvious answer is that there should be an effective procedure for constructing the black box. But if we insist on this then the black-box formulation of CT becomes circular: a function is effectively computable if and only if there is an effective procedure for constructing a black box which will compute it (cf. Péter's argument against the classical formulation of CT, discussed below). In order to break out of the circle we need to define what we mean by *effective*, and this is just what we were originally trying to use CT to tell us.

Suppose now we try to pin down what we mean by calling a black box effectively constructible by specifying what sorts of operations are to be allowed in the construction of it. At this point we would be well on the way to converting what we intended as a completely general specification of a computational model into a specific implementation. In short, we are following the same path as Turing when he originally invented Turing machines.

We thus find that while there is something very attractive about the notion of a black box standing in relation to a class of

particular models of computation as specification to implementations, it is extremely hard to make the specification precise without converting it into one of those implementations. This is a
situation curiously reminiscent of that prevailing in artificial
intelligence (AI). It has often been claimed that the classical
'specify-and-verify' methodology advocated in software engineering is inappropriate to AI precisely because it is not possible in AI
to specify in advance the behaviour (essentially some aspect(s) of
human behaviour) that one is attempting to realize computationally.
Instead, proponents of AI tend to favour a methodology of
'exploratory programming', in which the programming process is
guided by the programmers' confidence that although they cannot
specify in advance the behaviour they are aiming for, they will at
any rate recognize it when they see it. In a similar way, one might
say of CT that even though one cannot give a general characterization of what sort of thing is to count as a computation, one
might be able to recognize, informally, that such-and-such a specific formal model of computation succeeds in capturing that notion
precisely.

7. In order to clarify the status of CT, a good plan would be
to consider in what ways the thesis might come to be discredited.
We may discount here the remote possibility that the proofs of
equivalence for the various formal notions of computability might
turn out to be flawed, thereby undermining the chief mathematical grounds for accepting CT. If this were to happen, CT would
in effect be broken up into a collection of *rival* theses, each stating that a function is computable if and only if it has a certain
formal property, viz. Turing-machine computability, recursiveness,
computability by a normal Markov algorithm, and so on. The big
question then would be which, if any, of these rival theses was
correct.

We assume in what follows that we do have a robust formal
notion of computability, and the question at issue concerns the
relationship between this formal notion and our intuitive notion
of computability. Here we are primarily concerned with the possibility that CT may come to require *revision*. We can envisage
two kinds of revision, which differ according to whether it is the
'*a*' term in the '*aRb*' presentation of the thesis that is changed, or
the '*b*' term. Revision of the former kind amounts to *conceptual*

revision, because it involves a shift in what we want to understand by the notion of effective computability. To advocate conceptual revision of CT is not necessarily to stigmatize the older version of the thesis as false, but only to recommend the replacement as in some way more appropriate or relevant to one's needs. Revisions of the second kind, however, are *substantial*, since they do directly contradict the version that is replaced: whereas the older version identifies the effectively computable functions with the recursive functions, the replacement identifies the same set of effectively computable functions with some other class.

We can also classify possible revisions of CT according to whether they postulate that the class of computable functions is more or less inclusive than in the classical version. We may speak of *upward* and *downward* revisions respectively.

8. Substantial revision of CT would be necessitated if someone were either to discover an effective method for computing some function that is demonstrably not recursive (upward substantial revision), or if it were to be shown that not all recursive functions were effectively computable after all (downward substantial revision).

Downward substantial revision hardly seems possible, since we already know how to specify a black box to compute any given recursive function: it is called a Turing machine. We must not be too hasty, however. To be sure, if we *construct* a Turing machine, then it is reasonable to claim that the function it computes is effectively computable. To extrapolate from this observation to the notion that an arbitrary function can be regarded as effectively computable if and only if there exists a Turing machine which can compute it, however, is not necessarily legitimate. The problem, as was pointed out by Péter (1959), is that the notion of existence represented by the phrase 'there is' has to be defined constructively in order for it to play the role required of it in this formulation of CT: we need to insist, in other words, that we can effectively construct a Turing machine to do the job. But we cannot insist on this without circularity, since the whole purpose of CT is to provide a *definition* of the notion of effectiveness.

In order to avoid this circularity, the best we can do is to restrict our notion of effective computability to cover those classes of functions for whose Turing machines we have up to now discovered effective constructions. But to do this is, in effect, to propose a substantial downward revision of CT, albeit one for which no universality can be claimed, since it is not possible to predict what advances may be made in our ability to specify effective methods for constructing Turing machines.

If we reject this argument (and it is surely not totally compelling), then the only other way in which downward revision of CT could occur would be if we were to argue that some Turing-machine computations, for example those which require exponential time, do not really count as computations. But this would be a conceptual revision of CT, not a substantial one. We shall consider this case in its proper place.

Upward revision of the thesis, on the other hand, could be genuinely substantial, involving the discovery of a new technique. Of course, we cannot say what such a technique would be, though we might suspect that the appropriate direction to look would be in the area of either analogue computation or connectionism. We do not yet know enough about the formal relations between these two kinds of computation and ordinary digital computation for us to be able to rule such a discovery out of court. A few general observations are possible, however.

Suppose someone presents us with a black box which he claims can solve the halting problem for Turing machines. If this claim is true, then the black box can compute a function which no Turing machine can, a non-recursive function. But if the black box can compute it, then it must be computable, in our informal intuitive sense. Hence CT is false.

That is the claim made by the person who made the box. But why should we accept it? How do we *know* that the black box really does solve the halting problem? We might try it out on a large number of examples for which we already know the answer, and find that in every case the correct result appears. But this does not *prove* that the machine has the capacity claimed for it. For what is claimed is that the black box will correctly determine termination or non-termination for *every possible* machine/tape pair. Nothing short of this will do: after all, we already have respectable recursive techniques for testing large classes of *algorithms* for termination, and there is no reason to suppose that such techniques could not be adapted to Turing machines instead. What we lack, and this black box purports to provide, is a *general* technique.

How could the owner of the black box convince us that it does what he claims it does? Only by revealing to us its *mechanism*. Unless he can prove that what goes on inside the box is always such as to lead from an input machine/tape pair to a correct determination of whether or not the corresponding computation terminates, we have no reason whatever for accepting his claim.

In saying this, I am in no way prejudging the issue as to what kind of thing is going on inside the box. However, since both the input and output are in discrete, digital form, it is natural to expect that the inner workings of the box will have this form too. In that case what goes on in the box must be a sequence of operations (or perhaps a set of such sequences in parallel). This sequence can, presumably, be broken down into a set of primitive operations together with a set of controlling principles which govern the way in which the primitive operations are combined to yield the completed sequence. Some of these operations and controlling principles will doubtless be things that can be performed by a Turing machine, but *at least one* of them must be beyond the capability of such a machine.

Now one is inclined to think that a primitive operation must be rather simple. Turing's original construction of his machine was motivated by a close analysis of all the possible processes which might form part of any computational technique. Here we are postulating the existence of some simple operation that Turing missed; something sufficiently unobvious for all subsequent researchers to have missed too. It does not seem very likely, but on the other hand we cannot entirely rule out the possibility. In this connection, Webb (1983, p. 337) has pointed out that the only plausible candidate for an effective operation that might be expected to take us beyond the realm of the recursive, namely diagonalization, actually fails to do so, inasmuch as the class of general recursive functions is closed under this operation.

But perhaps we are begging the question in assuming that the mechanism inside the box has to be analysable into a sequence of discrete steps. Perhaps it is an essentially continuous process which cannot be redescribed in discrete terms, even though its input and output are both discrete. We enter here the realm of speculation and it is very difficult at this stage to say much about what may or may not be possible.

But *if* such a discovery were to be made, there would be a need for us, as upholders of CT, to respond in some way to it. The more conservative approach would be to insist that the new discovery just doesn't count as a case of black-box computability, for example because the relevant internal mechanism of the box is not discrete. This would amount to a conceptual revision of CT, and properly belongs in the next section. It would enable us to retain our faith in CT, but is somewhat desperate, and tantamount to a rejection of the black-box formulation of the thesis, since it replaces black-box computability by *discrete* black-box computability.

A more radical response would be to try to revise CT to accommodate the new technique. This would require us to try to extend the formal term, i.e. to look for a new formal account of computation which coincides in extension with the enhanced notion of computability provided by the new computation techniques. Once again, it is impossible for us to say, at our present state of knowledge, what such a formal account would look like.

9. We now turn to conceptual revisions of CT. As I remarked in the previous section, downward conceptual revision of CT would occur if, as is perfectly possible, we came to embrace a notion of effective procedure that incorporated a resource bound, such as polynomial time, as an intrinsic part.

To some extent, this has already happened, in that it is common to regard as *feasible* only those computations which can be performed in polynomial time. So an exponential algorithm, on this view, is not an effective procedure. We could justify adopting this line on the grounds that feasibility, as here defined, is, like recursiveness, a *robust* notion, that is, it remains constant over a wide range of possible modifications of technique and representation (cf. Harel, 1987).

Suppose then that computer scientists very generally came to accept that a function is effectively computable if and only if it can be computed by a black box in polynomial time. Let us call this *polynomial black-box computability*. If we simply substitute polynomial black-box computability for black-box computability *tout court* in our black-box formulation of CT, we would obtain the thesis that polynomial black-box computability is equivalent to Turing-machine computability. But this is highly implausible: it amounts to the claim that any Turing machine, even if its computations exceed polynomial time, is equivalent to a black box whose computations only require polynomial time.

For that reason, the natural response to the feasibility requirement is to revise CT downwards so that it equates effective computability with polynomial Turing-machine computability. But the black-box formulation of this revised CT comes out looking suspiciously like a special case of the original: it says that polynomial black-box computability equals polynomial Turing-machine computability. In view of the invariance of the major complexity classes across different models of computation, this formulation of CT does not look all that different from the original black-box formulation. And as I shall indicate, the new formulation gives rise to a problem that we do not find in the original.

For on the one hand it is quite easy to design a standard language for the description of Turing machines, in such a way that there is an effective decision procedure for determining whether an expression in this language is the description of a Turing machine or not. Similar remarks apply to recursive function expressions, λ-expressions, normal Markov algorithms, and so on. In other words, the class of entities which CT, in any of its original forms, associates with the intuitive notion of effective computability, is itself effectively computable.

On the other hand, by contrast, there does not appear to be *any* effective way of identifying those Turing machines which perform all their non-terminating computations in polynomial time. In other words, the formal term in the correspondence posited by the downward-revised CT is itself not amenable to effective determination. This makes things very awkward from the point of view of *applying* the thesis. Currently, if one holds the original form of the thesis, it is enough to find a Turing machine which computes a given function for one to be satisfied that that function is computable; there need never be any doubt that what is offered *is* a Turing machine, though admittedly proving that it does what is claimed for it can be tricky, and is in general recursively unsolvable. But with the downward-revised version of the thesis, things are much worse, for now it is, in general, impossible to be sure whether what is offered is a polynomial-time Turing machine, let alone that it computes the function in question.

Because of this difficulty, the downward-revised CT which identifies effective computability with computability by Turing machine in polynomial time has much less to commend it than the original. The original CT, if we accept it, in effect succeeds in identifying an effective implementation of black-box computability. The revised version, on the other hand, does not. Instead, it merely replaces one specification with another: for it insists that a Turing machine have polynomial complexity, without providing any implementational details as to how this can be achieved.

For the downward-revised CT to have more 'punch', it would be necessary that we discover some *new* construction, which can be specified and recognized effectively, and which is either exactly equivalent to the polynomial-time Turing machine, or sufficiently nearly so to be a satisfactory replacement for it in the revised CT: at all events, we require some implementational schema which is guaranteed to produce polynomial computations. As far as I am aware, no such construction has ever been found, nor is it at all clear how one might set about looking for one (cf. Gurevich, 1988). As Minsky (1967, §8.5) says,

Those who object that Church's (or Turing's) thesis . . . allows too much, usually do so on the grounds that the Turing machine formulation of computability allows computations whose lengths cannot be bounded in advance in any reasonable way. The impossibility of computing bounds . . . is one of the obstacles that seems to stand in the way of finding a formulation of computability which is weaker yet not completely trivial. (p. 153)[5]

An alternative here would be to shift the focus from computational *mechanisms* to computational *problems*. Our concern, after all, is to characterize what is or is not computable; traditionally, we have done this by defining an abstract model of computation and then saying that a function is computable if and only if it can be computed using that model. This is fine so long as we are not interested in resource bounds; but as we have seen, it is very difficult to modify a given abstract computational model in such a way that the computations it defines have some complexity bounds specifiable in advance.

The work reported in Stewart (1996) gives ground for hope that the problem-oriented approach suggested here might meet with more success than the traditional, mechanism-oriented approach. This work shows that one can characterize the complexity of problems

[5] Cf. Rogers (1967, §1.1).

in terms of the logical resources needed to specify them. A given logic $\mathscr{L}$ might correspond to a complexity class of computational problems $\mathscr{C}$ in the sense that a problem belongs to $\mathscr{C}$ if and only if it can be specified using the logic $\mathscr{L}$. A resource-bounded formulation of CT might then run something like this: A function is effectively computable if and only if it can be defined in the logic $\mathscr{L}$ (where the particular logic $\mathscr{L}$ chosen will depend on what complexity of computations one is prepared to countenance as effective).

10. What about upward conceptual revision? An argument of Kalmár (1959) appears to fit into this category. Kalmár considers functions of the form

$$\psi(x) \equiv \begin{cases} y & \text{if } y \text{ is the least natural number such that } \phi(x, y) = 0 \\ 0 & \text{if } \phi(x, y) \neq 0 \text{ for every natural number } y, \end{cases}$$

where ϕ is general recursive. Kalmár claims that any function of this form is effectively computable by means of the following procedure:

Calculate in succession the values $\phi(p, 0)$, $\phi(p, 1)$, $\phi(p, 2)$, ... and simultaneously try to prove by all correct means that none of them equals 0, until we find either a (least) natural number q for which $\phi(p, q) = 0$ or a proof of the proposition stating that no natural number y with $\phi(p, y) = 0$ exists; and consider in the first case q, in the second case 0 as result of the calculation.

Yet Kleene (1936) had shown that some functions ψ of this form are not general recursive. It follows that, if CT is correct, then for suitable ϕ and p, none of the numbers $\phi(p, 0)$, $\phi(p, 1)$, $\phi(p, 2)$, ... is zero and yet this fact cannot be proved by any correct means. Rather than accept this 'very strange consequence', Kalmár concludes that the totality of 'correct means' of proof goes beyond the realm of the general recursive, thus falsifying CT.

Kalmár is not here postulating the existence of some specific technique for computing non-general-recursive functions. Rather, by allowing 'any correct means' of proof, he would appear to be expressing the belief that no particular collection of techniques can ever be regarded as exhaustive. Only by laying down in advance what techniques of proof and calculation are allowable does it appear plausible that the realm of the effectively calculable is limited to the general recursive functions. There is no reason to suppose that, if arbitrary computational procedures are allowed, this limitation cannot be transcended.

There is certainly something quite attractive about Kálmar's view, but it has not been widely adopted. It is, in some ways, the opposite of the position held by Péter, which we discussed above. Péter felt that the notion of 'arbitrary recursive function' was too general, and that for the computation of a function to be effective in a way that does not simply beg the question (because of circularity) it must involve some more specific form of recursion; Kalmár, on the other hand, wants to allow 'arbitrary correct means' of computation, which he believes can take us beyond the realm of the general recursive.

Another kind of upward conceptual revision might occur if it could be shown that the notion of black-box computability we have been using is too narrow to characterize everything that we should be prepared to count as a computation. For according to this notion, a computation takes a single input and delivers a single output, and moreover, both the space of possible inputs and the space of possible outputs must be discrete. Only if these conditions are met can we legitimately think of a computation as computing a function from the natural numbers to the natural numbers.

Now there are at least two ways in which these conditions might be regarded as inadequate. On the one hand, one might seek to relax the requirement that what is computed is a relation between an initially given input and a final output. On the other hand, one might want to consider 'computations' in which the input space or output space (or both) is continuous rather than discrete. And of course, one may well wish to make both of these moves at the same time. In the next section we will consider the implications for CT of the first possibility, and in the section after that we shall consider the implications of the second.

11. Pnueli (1985) distinguishes two views of computational systems:

The first view regards programs as *functions* from an initial state to a final state . . . This view is particularly appropriate for programs that accept all of their inputs at the beginning of their operation and yield their outputs at termination. We call such programs *transformational* . . . On the other hand, there are systems that cannot be covered by the transformational view. Some systems, such as operating systems, process control programs, seat reservation systems, etc., ideally never terminate. Moreover, the purpose for which they are run is not to obtain a final result, but rather to maintain some interaction with their environment. We refer to such systems as *reactive systems*. (pp. 510f.)

Pnueli indicates that the techniques used for reasoning about transformational programs, e.g. to prove their correctness relative to some specification, cannot be applied to reactive programs, and goes on to advocate temporal logic as a suitable tool for reasoning about the more complex correctness requirements of the latter class.

From our point of view, it is necessary to determine whether reactive programs involve a notion of computation that goes beyond the kind of computation considered in CT, the kind of computation which, according to CT, can always be performed on a Turing machine. To this end, let us define a *reactive black box*. This does not simply accept an input and, after executing some processes hidden from our view, deliver an output; instead, it generates a (possibly infinite) output stream $O_1 O_2 O_3 \ldots$ in response to a (possibly infinite) input stream $I_1 I_2 I_3 \ldots$, with no requirement that the input be completed before the output begins.

Can we replace a reactive black box by an ordinary (transformational) black box with the same computational characteristics? In fact, we can do so quite easily. What we need to do is to see the reactive black box as computing a function from natural numbers to natural numbers. Now the class of all possible infinite input streams is non-denumerable and hence such streams cannot be replaced by natural numbers in a one-to-one fashion. Instead we exploit the following *monotonicity* property of reactive systems: if the finite input stream I yields the finite output stream O, then any extension of I must yield an extension of O. This property is a necessary consequence of the reactive nature of the system, which cannot know, once it has received input stream I, whether or not further inputs will arrive, and hence its response must be such as to be appropriate in either case.

Hence if input stream $I_1 I_2 I_3 \ldots$ yields output stream $O_1 O_2 O_3 \ldots$ then the finite input streams $I_1,\ I_1 I_2,\ I_1 I_2 I_3, \ldots$ must yield the finite output streams $O_1,\ O_1 O_2,\ O_1 O_2 O_3, \ldots$, respectively, and moreover, this denumerably infinite set of finite input–output pairs uniquely determines the single infinite input–output pair we began with. Moreover, the set of *all* finite input–output pairs for the system is denumerable and yet uniquely determines the non-denumerable set of all infinite input–output pairs. It follows that the complete behaviour of a reactive system can be specified by a denumerable set of input–output pairs, and hence can be regarded as computing a function from the natural numbers to the natural numbers.

A natural objection to this analysis is that a reactive system will not always respond identically to identical inputs, and hence the system cannot be considered to be computing a function. Thus in a certain well-known operating system the output corresponding to the input 'ls' will differ according to the contents of the current directory. But this is to miss the point. Let us call the state of the system when it is first installed, before it has performed any computations at all, the 'zero state'. The argument above, which showed that the reactive black box could be replaced by an equivalent transformational one, must be taken as referring to the zero state of the system. After performing some computations, the reactive system will, in general, be in a different state from the zero state. There will, correspondingly, be a different transformational black box corresponding to the system in this state. That is why identical inputs received by a reactive system at different times may yield different outputs: the equivalent transformational systems at the two times may be different. But this in no way lessens the force of the original argument.

To conclude this section then, it seems clear that, while reactive systems are such that they require very different techniques from a practical point of view, from the point of view of computability theory they still fall within the terms of reference of what I have called black-box computability, and hence CT, if it is true, must apply to reactive systems just as much as to transformational ones.

12. The second extension to the notion of computability that we envisaged was to allow the input and output spaces to be continuous. A possible motivation for this would be that such an extension might allow us to regard many physical processes as computations which would otherwise be hard to describe in this way.

A major problem facing any attempt to define computations over continuous spaces arises from the finiteness requirement discussed in section 6. An effective computation must be completable in a finite amount of time. We must include in this the time taken to enter the input into the black box and to retrieve the output. If the input and output spaces are to be truly continuous, it is not possible for the data to be presented digitally, i.e. as strings of symbols taken from a finite alphabet, for the only way a truly continuous space can be represented in this way is for us to allow expressions containing an infinite number of digits (cf. the real numbers).

But if the data are not presented digitally, they must be presented in an 'analogue' way, i.e. by means of some continuously variable physical quantity. The process of retrieving the output then becomes one of *measurement*, and the limitations of this kind of computation can only be determined by a close consideration of the physical nature of measurement. Fields (1989, and see p. 168 below) argues that if we accept the nonclassical (quantum mechanical) conception of measurement then even continuous systems cannot compute anything that a Turing machine cannot. This suggests that inclusion of continuous input and output spaces does not, in fact, take us beyond the class of Turing-machine computable functions. This conclusion is not contradicted by that of Deutsch (1985), who claims that his Universal Quantum Computer has 'remarkable powers not reproducible by any Turing machine'—which do not, however, include the computation of non-recursive functions.

But even apart from this issue, there are reasons to treat cautiously any proposal to extend the notion of computation to cover continuous processes. It seems plausible that *any* physical system can be regarded in indefinitely many different ways as a black box which takes input from a continuous space of possibilities and delivers output from a continuous space of possibilities. On the other hand, to extend our notion of computation so that anything that happens is a computation reduces the whole enterprise to absurdity. It is therefore necessary, if we are to extend CT so as to encompass computations with continuous input and output, to find a way of specifying what properties a process must have in order to count as a computation in this sense. A preliminary attempt to do this (Sloman, 1988, and see also his paper in this volume, pp. 179–219) suggests that when we start looking at things in this way, what we will find is not just a single replacement of CT but a whole battery of replacements, corresponding to different views, all equally legitimate, of what constitutes the essence of computationality.

13. I conclude with some remarks concerning the relevance of CT to artificial intelligence. In view of the difficulty of finding a satisfactory formulation of CT that encompasses systems whose input and output form continuous spaces, I shall restrict the discussion to the discrete input–output case. This is not a restriction from the point of view of conventional AI, since the tool of this trade is the digital computer, which does indeed satisfy the discreteness condition. Some, but possibly not all, forms of connectionism can probably be accommodated under this rubric too. So our terms of reference are certainly broad enough to be getting along with, even if we should eventually want to broaden them.

Depending on one's viewpoint, CT might be used either in support of the thesis that all human cognitive processes can be simulated on a machine, or to argue against it. The two arguments, both of which are valid, run as follows:

1. A function is black-box computable iff it is Turing-machine computable.
   A human being is a black box.
   Therefore, a human being is equivalent to a Turing machine.

2. A function is black-box computable iff it is Turing-machine computable.
   A human being is not a black box.
   Therefore, a human being is not equivalent to a Turing machine.

In both cases, the claim rests on two premisses. The first premiss in each case is simply CT. The second premiss is, in the first case, that human beings can be regarded as black boxes in the sense required by CT; and in the second case, that they cannot. The crucial question is therefore whether or not we can legitimately regard a human being as a black box in the sense required by the black-box formulation of CT.

It need not matter here that human cognition appears to be separable into a collection of processes each enjoying a certain autonomy. This does not mean that we cannot consider the aggregate of such functions as a single superprocess representing the total cognitive activity of a human individual. A collection of black boxes packed into one big black box can itself be regarded as a black box. The input to the big black box is in turn fed into one or more of the internal black boxes; the eventual output is determined in some way, either systematic or random, from the output(s) produced by the internal black boxes.

Nor, as we have seen, is it a serious consideration that people resemble reactive systems rather than transformational ones.

The crucial issue has rather to do with the functionality of a human being *qua* black box. For CT to get any purchase, we must be dealing with inputs and outputs taken from some denumerable space of possibilities. Now it is not entirely clear that, for the human, this is the case. *Sensory* input, to be sure, may well be in the last analysis digital, since it is limited by thresholds as regards both the extent of its range and its resolution power. But cognition is not a function of sensory input alone. One's thinking is deeply affected by one moods and feelings, and these depend, in part, on the state of one's body chemistry, e.g. the concentrations of various chemicals in the bloodstream, which in turn are influenced by external non-sensory inputs such as food and air.

A computing mechanism is not specified until its behaviour over the whole range of predetermined possible inputs is specified. Now, for a human, *what counts as an input, and what counts as an output?* Is the cheese sandwich I had for lunch an input? I don't just mean the taste and feel of the sandwich: being sensory these are inputs in the relevant sense, sure enough; I mean the sandwich itself. It went into my stomach, some of its molecules are by now doubtless coursing through my brain: so the food I eat cannot be wholly separated from my cognitive activities. As Dennett (1978, ch. 13) puts it,

we have to decide which of the impingements on the animal count as input and which as interference, and it is not at all clear what criteria we should use in deciding this. (p. 260)

Later, Dennett draws the even more despairing conclusion that

By suitable gerrymandering . . . it ought to be possible to interpret any man as any Turing machine—indeed as all Turing machines at the same time. (p. 262)

which recalls my earlier worries about the infinity of ways of describing a given physical system as a continuous black box.

Now it *may* be that these factors can be dismissed as irrelevant. One might, for example, adopt the stance that human cognitive behaviour as we actually observe it must be conceived as a *performance* which only imperfectly realizes an underlying cognitive *competence*, and that it is the latter which is the true object of study in AI.[6] The imperfect transition from competence to performance can be explained, on this view, as arising from just such messy biochemical considerations as we have already considered. The cheese sandwich (as opposed to its sensory qualities) is not a cognitively relevant input, since its effect on my cognitive performance is incidental, accomplished through biochemical pathways that are quite disjoint from the mechanisms of cognitive competence.

The opposing view would be that it simply is not possible to make a clean separation between cognitive and non-cognitive aspects of human behaviour; this is argued for fairly persuasively by French (1990). It would appear to follow from this (though French himself does not so argue) that the attempt to account for human cognition in terms that allow CT to be applied is fundamentally misconceived. Thus viewed, human behaviour is simply the wrong kind of thing to be regarded as computational, not because it lacks a physical basis, but because its physical basis resists description in the discrete terms required of CT.

This would be the case if, for example, Deutsch's notion (mentioned above in section 6) that there need be no exact correspondence between what is computable in the mathematical sense and what is computable in the physical sense, were correct. In that case, the physical nature of human behaviour and cognition would tell *against* the possibility of simulating it on a machine whose design is guided by the mathematical notion of computation; but it would still leave open the possibility of simulating human behaviour on a radically different kind of machine, for example a neural network, or the Universal Quantum Computer discussed by Deutsch.

All this is relevant to the 'strong' AI thesis that the human brain is a computer, and human cognitive processes are its computations. It is not very relevant to the business of a more modest brand of AI, which merely seeks computational ways of performing certain tasks or solving certain problems which humans are rather good at but which machines, so far, have done rather badly, if at all. No

---

[6] For the distinction between competence and performance, originally introduced in relation to linguistic behaviour, see Chomsky, 1965.

doubt it is the former variety of AI, rather than the latter, that is more in harmony with Turing's own convictions.

REFERENCES

Chomsky, N. (1965), *Aspects of the Theory of Syntax*, Cambridge, Mass.: MIT Press.

Church, A. (1936), 'An Unsolvable Problem of Elementary Number Theory', *American Journal of Mathematics*, 58: 345–63.

Dennett, D. C. (1978), *Brainstorms: Philosophical Essays on Mind and Psychology*, Hassocks: Harvester Press.

Deutsch, D. (1985), 'Quantum Theory, the Church-Turing Principle and the Universal Quantum Computer', *Proceedings of the Royal Society, London A*, 400: 97–117.

Enderton, H. B. (1977), 'Elements of Recursion Theory', in J. Barwise (ed.), *Handbook of Mathematical Logic*, Amsterdam: North-Holland, 527–66.

Fields, C. (1989), 'Consequences of Nonclassical Measurement for the Algorithmic Description of Continuous Dynamical Systems', *Journal of Experimental and Theoretical AI*, 1: 171–8.

French, R. M. (1990), 'Subcognition and the Limits of the Turing Test', *Mind*, 99: 53–65, and this volume, pp. 11–26.

Gandy, R. (1988), 'The Confluence of Ideas in 1936', in R. Herken (ed.), *The Universal Turing Machine*, Oxford: Oxford University Press, 55–111.

Gödel, K. (1934), 'On Undecidable Propositions of Formal Mathematical Systems', in M. Davis (ed.), *The Undecidable*, New York: Raven Press, 1965: 41–74.

Gurevich, Y. (1988), 'Algorithms in the world of bounded resources', in R. Herken (ed.), *The Universal Turing Machine*, Oxford: Oxford University Press, 407–16.

Harel, D. (1987), *Algorithmics: the Spirit of Computing*, Reading, Mass.: Addison-Wesley.

Hermes, H. (1965), *Enumerability, Decidability, Computability*, Berlin: Springer Verlay.

Kalmár, L. (1959), 'An Argument against the Plausibility of Church's Thesis', in A. Heyting (ed.), *Constructivity in Mathematics*, Amsterdam: North-Holland, 72–80.

Kleene, S. C. (1936), 'General Recursive Functions of Natural Numbers', *Mathematische Annalen*, 112: 727–42.

—— (1952), *Introduction to Metamathematics*, Amsterdam: North-Holland.

—— (1967), *Mathematical Logic*, New York: Wiley.

Minsky, M. L. (1967), *Computation: Finite and Infinite Machines*, Englewood Cliffs, NJ: Prentice-Hall.

Péter, R. (1959), 'Rekursivität und Konstruktivität', in A. Heyting (ed.), *Constructivity in Mathematics*, Amsterdam: North-Holland, 226–33.

Pnueli, A. (1985), 'Applications of Temporal Logic to the Specification and Verification of Reactive Systems: A Survey of Current Trends', in J. W. de Bakker, W.-P. de Roever, and G. Rozenberg (eds.), *Current Trends in Concurrency*, Springer: Lecture Notes in Computer Science 224.

Rogers, H. (1967), *Theory of Recursive Functions and Effective Computability*, New York: McGraw-Hill.

Sloman, A. (1988), 'What isn't Computation?', in *Proceedings of the 8th European Conference on Artificial Intelligence*, 728–30.

Stewart, I. (1996), 'The Demise of the Turing Machine in Complexity Theory', this volume, pp. 221–32.

Turing, A. (1936), 'On Computable Numbers, with an Application to the Entscheidungs-problem', *Proceedings of the London Mathematical Society*, Series 2, 42: 230–65.

von Neumann, J. (1948), 'General and Logical Theory of Automata', in *Cerebral Mechanisms in Behaviour—the Hixon Symposium*, New York: John Wiley.

Wang, H. (1974), *From Mathematics to Philosophy*, London: Routledge & Kegan Paul.

Webb, J. C. (1983), 'Gödel's Theorem and Church's Thesis: A Prologue to Mechanism', in R. S. Cohen and M. W. Wartofsky (eds.), *Language, Logic, and Method*, Dordrecht: Reidel, 309–53.

9
Measurement and Computational Description

CHRIS FIELDS

INTRODUCTION

The mathematical theory of computation does not directly address the questions of whether, and if so, how physical processes might be characterized as computations, or physical systems characterized as computers. These questions lie at the heart, however, of the technology of computer design, and of empirical investigations in cognitive science, computational neuroscience, and other sciences concerned with the processing of information. Addressing these questions requires a theory not of computation *per se*, but of the computational description of physical systems. My purposes in the present paper are, first, to outline a theory of computational description that is based explicitly on the theory of physical measurement, and, second, to examine some consequences of this theory for some questions in the philosophy of computer science and artificial intelligence.

The ubiquity and utility of abstract computational descriptions in cognitive science have been pointed out by a number of authors, writing from a number of theoretical perspectives (e.g. Fodor, 1974; Marr, 1982; Cummins, 1983; Pylyshyn, 1984; Ullman, 1986; Sejnowski *et al.*, 1988). The notion of a virtual machine developed in computer science (e.g. Tanenbaum, 1976, ch. 1) typically serves as the starting-point for accounts of computational description as it is applied to natural systems. Marr (1982, ch. 1),

I thank Eric Dietrich, Stephanie Forrest, and Aaron Sloman for comments on an earlier draft of this paper. This work was partially supported by NASA Innovative Research Program grant NAGW-1592 to the author and J. Barnden.

for example, argued that computational theories of the behaviour of naturally occurring information-processing systems must, to be complete, describe such systems at three distinct levels: (i) that of the processes in the system's hardware that are viewed as implementations of algorithms and data structures, (ii) that of the algorithms and data structures themselves, viewed as abstractions, and (iii) that of the computations realized by the algorithms being executed, viewed as transformations of inputs to outputs. These levels may be mapped directly onto the conventional levels of description of artificial computing systems: (i) that of physical processes in the hardware, (ii) that of the virtual machine defined by a set of processes of interest, and (iii) that of the computational behaviour of this virtual machine, viewed abstractly. Marr also argues, however, that the three levels of description are 'only rather loosely related' (p. 25), and that many natural systems might in practice only be described at one or two of the three levels. This argument is based on the observations that a given computation may be realized by many different algorithms, that a given algorithm may be implemented by many different physical processes, that input–output experiments alone cannot distinguish between different algorithms or implementations (cf. Ashby, 1956; Moore, 1956), and hence that one can specify the computation being executed by a system without thereby specifying either the algorithm or its implementation.

The description of computational behaviour in abstraction from the physical mechanisms underlying it permits, and indeed encourages, a conceptual break between the physics of a system and its computational properties. While this break is convenient for programmers, and often for theorists, it obscures the key role played by measurement—a physical process—in the construction of computational descriptions of both natural and artificial systems. Neglecting the role of measurement in computational description has led, I believe, to the generation of a number of conceptual problems, which are revealed as incoherent when the role of measurement is considered explicitly. I begin, therefore, by reconsidering the role of physical measurement of a system's behaviour as the first step in constructing a computational description of the system. I argue that computational descriptions of a system at different levels can be viewed as resulting from different measurements of the physical state transitions occurring in the system. Complex computational behaviour thus 'emerges' from physical dynamics when those dynamics are measured in particular ways. I then consider the model-theoretic assignment of semantic contents to the states of a system. This process, which is an essential component of computational description, is identical in the cases of natural and artificial systems, but the practice of abstract description often obscures this, and encourages unwarranted conclusions about the nature of semantics. I conclude by questioning the utility of the differences in perspective commonly taken toward natural and artificial systems in both AI research and computational neuroscience.

MEASUREMENT

Let S be a physical system that is identified informally as the system of interest. The only restrictions placed on S are that it be localizable with some finite precision in space, and identifiable over time as an entity distinct from its surroundings. We are interested in the behaviour of S with respect to some parameter that is regarded as an independent variable; typically this is time t, which is measured by an operation represented by an operator, T. The state of S at time t_k is represented (in Dirac's notation) by $\mid t_k >$. S changes state via the action of a Hamiltonian, or time-propagation operator H, which may itself be time-dependent, i.e. $H(t_k) \mid t_k > = \mid t_{k+1} >$. These state changes can be represented by diagrams:

$$
\begin{array}{ccccccc}
 & t_k & & & t_{k+1} & & \\
H(t_{k-1}) & T\uparrow & H(t_k) & & T\uparrow & H(t_{k+1}) & \\
\cdots \quad \rightarrow & \mid t_k > & \rightarrow & & \mid t_{k+1} > & \rightarrow & \cdots
\end{array}
$$

The physical dynamics represented by $H(t)$ are only observable via a physical measurement process. If the scale at which measurements are made is sufficiently large, the measurements may be regarded as classical, as is done, e.g. by Ashby (1956). If the scale is small, the measurements must be treated quantum mechanically. The theory of measurement is an integral part of quantum mechanics (e.g. Jauch, 1968, ch. 11); von Neumann (1932) was an early contributor to the theory. The two cases are treated together here.

If behaviour in time is what is of interest, then time is the first parameter that must be measured. The time that S remains in a particular state can only be measured with finite precision; values of t therefore represent discrete intervals with a finite width Δt. This is true independently of whether the dynamics being measured are themselves discrete or continuous. In practice, the finite resolution of time measurements is a consequence of the finite resolution of practical clocks; in principle, it follows from quantum mechanical considerations. Time cannot be measured with infinite precision—Δt cannot be zero—without sacrificing all knowledge of the system's energy, and thus allowing arbitrary violations of either the localization or identifiability requirements. This limitation on the resolution of time measurement has the consequence that the *observable* behaviour of any informally localizable and identifiable system, regardless of its underlying dynamics, consists of a discrete sequence of state transitions, each of which has a temporal width of at least the Δt of the associated time measurements. The observable behaviour of any system of computational interest can, therefore, in principle be simulated on a discrete machine, such as a Turing machine. The Church–Turing thesis— that any computable function can be computed by a universal Turing machine—thus has an analog for computational description: that any observable behaviour can be simulated on a universal Turing machine (Fields, 1989).

The states $\mid t_k >$ of S are measured by interacting with S, at each t_k, via an operation that can be represented as an operator M mapping states of S to values of a state variable m, which may be multi-dimensional:

$$
\begin{array}{ccccccc}
 & & t_k & & & t_{k+1} & \\
H(t_{k-1}) & & T \uparrow & H(t_k) & & T \uparrow & H(t_{k+1}) \\
\cdots & \rightarrow & \mid t_k > & \rightarrow & \mid t_{k+1} > & \rightarrow & \cdots \\
 & & M \downarrow & & M \downarrow & & \\
 & & m(t_k) & & m(t_{k+1}) & &
\end{array}
$$

If measurement via M is treated quantum mechanically, exact simultaneity of measurements of m and t requires that the operators M and T commute, i.e. that $MT \mid t_k > \, = TM \mid t_k >$. This condition in turn implies that the measurement operator M will not commute with the Hamiltonian, because T does not commute with the Hamiltonian. Lack of commutivity between M and H has two related consequences: the state variable m cannot be a constant of the motion driven by H, and measurements of m will perturb the dynamics. The first of these consequences is intuitively clear for all systems, whether treated quantum mechanically or classically: in order for a measurement operator M to be useful for picking out state transitions, it must measure a non-constant of the motion. The second consequence can be neglected at large scales, but becomes significant as Δt becomes small. In quantum or classical chaotic systems, in particular, small perturbations of a state induced by an interaction with a measuring apparatus may be amplified into large changes in subsequent behaviour. In such cases, only the behaviour of the system *as perturbed* by the presence of the measuring apparatus is observable.

A description of a system is an interpretation of the available measurements. A dynamic description of the behaviour of a system S can be specified as a function $f(s)$ of a parameter s, such that there are s_k for which $f(s_k) = m(t_k)$, for the t_k of interest in the description. In practice, s is typically assumed to be a continuous variable, and $f(s)$ is required to be smooth, and to behave as simply as possible between the values of s—the s_k—identified with measured values of t. The behaviour of S can be simulated by executing an algorithm for $f(s)$, with a simulation time step equal to the Δt of the original measurements of S. The states of the virtual machine defined by the algorithm—which can be represented by the relevant values of $f(s)$—can then be mapped homomorphically, by an interpretation function I, to the measured states of S:

$$
\begin{array}{ccccccc}
& & t_k & & & t_{k+1} & \\
H(t_{k-1}) & & T\uparrow & H(t_k) & & T\uparrow & H(t_{k+1}) \\
\cdots \;\; \rightarrow & & |t_k> & \rightarrow & & |t_{k+1}> & \rightarrow \;\; \cdots \\
& & M\downarrow & & & M\downarrow & \\
& & m(t_k) & & & m(t_{k+1}) & \\
& & I\uparrow & & & I\uparrow & \\
\cdots \;\; \rightarrow & & f(s_k) & \rightarrow & & f(s_{k+1}) & \rightarrow \;\; \cdots
\end{array}
$$

Descriptions of systems in physics, and other sciences that typically treat processes as continuous in time, have this form. Such descriptions involve no specific claim about the type of behaviour S displays, other than that it can be modelled by f. A dynamic physical model of fluid flow, for example, is regarded as *describing* fluid flow, but not as *being* fluid flow.

A computational description of S differs from a dynamic description by interpreting S itself as a computer, and hence interpreting the behaviour displayed by S as computation. Such a description is constructed by mapping the state transitions of S to the steps of an algorithm A, via an interpretation I that maps the states of S to a sequence of abstract states (a), where a_k is obtained by applying the first k steps of A to a suitable input:

$$
\begin{array}{ccccccc}
& & t_k & & t_{k+1} & & \\
H(t_{k-1}) & & T\uparrow & H(t_k) & T\uparrow & H(t_{k+1}) & \\
\cdots & \rightarrow & |t_k> & \rightarrow & |t_{k+1}> & \rightarrow & \cdots \\
& & M\downarrow & & M\downarrow & & \\
& & m(t_k) & & m(t_{k+1}) & & \\
& & I\downarrow & & I\downarrow & & \\
\cdots & \rightarrow & a_k & \rightarrow & a_{k+1} & \rightarrow & \cdots \\
A(k-1) & & & A(k) & & A(k+1) &
\end{array}
$$

The mapping of state transitions in S to steps of A is accomplished by requiring that this diagram algebraically commutes. Dietrich (1989) has pointed out that such an interpretation can only be constructed if S is antecedently, and informally, viewed as instantiating a function that can be computed by the algorithm A, and if the steps $A(k)$ of A are recognized as computations of antecedently understood subfunctions.

A single episode in the behaviour of a system can be interpreted as an instance of the execution of an algorithm A on some input a_i, provided only that the number of observed states of S is sufficient to map onto the computational states traversed by A when it is applied to a_i. A system S can be interpreted coherently as a virtual machine for A only if the behaviour of S from an initial state interpretable as an input to A is always interpretable as an execution of A for that input. Artificial computers are designed, at the hardware level, to make this the case for the algorithms of interest—in the case of general-purpose computers, all algorithms —up to memory limitations and unpredictable problems such as hardware failures. A general-purpose computer, in other words, is a physical system of sufficient behavioural complexity that, for any algorithm A and input a_i, there is a sequence of measurable state transitions that is interpretable as an execution of A on a_i.

Two conclusions, which illustrate the relation between natural and artificial computing systems, follow from this account of the roles of measurement and interpretation in computational description. The first is that any system that can be interpreted as simulating a virtual machine for some function *f* is a virtual machine for *f*. Similarly, any system that can be interpreted as simulating a universal computer is a universal computer. This feature of computation—that *simulating computing is computing*—is what sets it apart from uninterpreted dynamic processes such as fluid flow. This feature is often overlooked in discussions of the role of computational description in cognitive science. Searle (1980), for example, fails to understand the 'systems reply' to the Chinese Room example —the claim that simulating understanding is understanding— because he misses this point (cf. Harnad, 1989, who also appears to miss it).

The second conclusion is that a single physical system can often be interpreted as different virtual machines on the basis of different sets of measurements, by interpreting the values of different sets of variables as indicative of the state of the system. This is perhaps clearest in the case of artificial neural networks. Consider a conventional feed-forward network with several hidden layers and all units initially at zero excitation, the input units of which are clamped in some state of non-zero excitation at time t_o. If the excitations of all of the units in the network are measured at time-steps much smaller than the time required for the network to reach a new quasi-stable state, it is very natural to describe the behaviour of the network in terms of computations of the individual node functions, e.g. by an equation such as:

$$dx_i/dt = I_i - x_i + \sigma(\Sigma_j w_{ij} x_j),$$

where x_k and I_k are the excitation and external input, respectively, of the kth unit, w_{ij} is a constant coefficient representing the *i-j* connection strength, and $\sigma(z)$ is a sigmoidal transfer function (e.g. Grossberg, 1988). However, if only the excitations of the input and output units are measured, and measurements are made at a temporal interval long with respect to the equilibration time, the network may be described as, e.g. computing some complicated pattern-recognition function mapping input-excitation vectors to output-excitation vectors. Such a function may, in cases in which the output vectors can be regarded as binary-valued, be most naturally described in terms of rules or schema (e.g. Rumelhart *et al.*, 1986; Gorman and Sejnowski, 1988). This 'high-level' computational behaviour emerges as a result of the spatially and temporally limited measurements.

The same thinking can be applied to general-purpose computers. Running a high-level application program on such a machine involves placing the machine in a state that can be interpreted as an initial state for the algorithm implemented by the program, allowing the machine to behave until a new quasi-stable state is reached, and interpreting the results of measurements made during the behaviour as steps in the execution of the algorithm. Artificial computers are designed to make specific sets of variables measurable during specific operations simply by pressing keys and observing the screen. Typically the variables associated with only one or two specified, high-level virtual machines—e.g. an application program and its associated compiler—are measurable in this way. Alternative computational behaviours can be observed, however, through the use of other measuring devices, e.g. another terminal or an oscilloscope. The conventional language of computer science, by employing multiple layers of names and the program–data distinction, allows users to view a general-purpose computer solely as a particular high-level virtual machine, and to ignore all of the other possibilities for measuring and interpreting its behaviour. Hence users typically do not have to know the initial states into which the hardware must be placed in order to realize particular virtual machines, or the types of measurements that are necessary to make a particular virtual machine's behaviour emerge from the physical dynamics. Such knowledge was necessary, however, for users of early, single-level computers that were programmed and provided with data by manually rearranging wiring or flipping switches.

Not all machines can be measured and interpreted at all dynamically significant levels. An extreme example is provided by quantum ballistic-computing models of the Feynman type, in which the Hamiltonian of the system is specified in the definition of the model. The configuration of the components of such a machine is, therefore, mixed and inaccessible to measurement at all times except the asymptotic beginning and end of the computation (Feynman, 1985; Benioff, 1986). Only the input and output states of this machine can be directly interpreted; the intermediate states cannot be interpreted because they cannot be measured. The algorithm that such a machine executes cannot, therefore, be determined; indeed, such a machine executes a mixture of algorithms. While Feynman has shown that quantum mechanics imposes no restrictions on the ability of physical systems to compute, the non-commutivity of the state variables does, in cases such as this, restrict our ability to construct interpretations of quantum systems as computers.

The discovery of sets of variables that support coherent computational interpretations is often the major difficulty facing computational analyses of natural systems. Any collection of variables that change in value during a behaviour can potentially be interpreted as specifying a virtual machine, but the machines that most collections of variables specify are either too simple or too complicated to be of use in understanding the behaviour. The goal of high-level computational modelling of such systems is often to assist in the variable-discovery process by generating descriptions of target virtual machines (e.g. Sejnowski *et al.*, 1988); measurement procedures can then be designed to search for variables that display appropriate behaviour.

SEMANTICS

The notion of interpretation as homomorphic mapping employed in the above discussion is that of model-theoretic and denotational semantics (e.g. DeLong, 1970; Stoy, 1977). Such a semantics is entirely stipulative; set homomorphism, and for interpretations of processes, algebraic commutivity, are the only requirements placed on the interpretation mapping. In practice, the stipulative nature of the semantics entails, for example, that any function $f(s)$ that satisfies the requirement that $f(s_k) = m(t_k)$ for all relevant values of t is an equally good simulation of a dynamic system traversing states characterized by the m_k. Further choices between simulations must be based on pragmatic or aesthetic criteria, such as parsimony. Similarly, a system can be interpreted as an implementation of any virtual machine with which its measured state transitions are isomorphic. Choices between competing interpretations must again be made using nonsemantic—e.g. pragmatic—criteria.

In the context of a specified interpretation mapping, the states and transitions of a system may be said to represent the states of the data structures and steps of the algorithm that the system is interpreted as executing (Cummins, 1983). This is the case independently of whether the system is natural or an artefact. This sense of 'representation' based on stipulative semantic interpretation is distinct from the equally common sense of 'representation' that is based on causal interaction, i.e. on the physical dynamics of the system and its environment. The latter sense is the sense in which a state of a system S may be said to represent either a previous state of S, or a state of an external system with which S has previously interacted. Activity patterns in the visual cortex, for example, may be taken to represent, in this second sense, visually perceived objects. The two senses of representation are entirely independent: a cortical activity pattern that represents, in the second sense, an object in the present visual field might be interpreted as representing, in the first sense, something entirely different— e.g. a vector of real numbers—in the context of a computational description of the behaviour of the cortex. This point carries over exactly to artificial systems. A state of a virtual machine implemented on a general-purpose computer may represent, in the dynamic sense, keystrokes from the user, and may itself be represented at a later time by the printing of characters on the screen. The same physical states and events may represent, in the context of a user's interpretation of the behaviour of the system, the input, processing, and output of words in English.

These two senses of representation are often conflated in the context of the 'symbol-grounding problem', the purported impossibility of computational models explaining the 'intentionality' of the internal representing states—e.g. states of perceiving an object—of natural systems (e.g. Sayre, 1986; Reeke and Edelman, 1988; Harnad, 1989). It is commonly claimed that such states intrinsically, and independently of observation by other agents, represent objects in the world, while states of a computer only represent the world through a process of stipulative interpretation by external agents. This argument overlooks both the stipulative nature of computational descriptions of natural systems, and the possibility—indeed inevitability—of dynamic representations in artificial systems. Dynamic representations, whether in natural or artificial systems, are *always* grounded; dynamic representation is a feature of the physics of the system-environment interaction. Model-theoretic representations, in systems of either type, are *never* grounded. Thus a state of the visual cortex of a cat may dynamically represent a mouse, and the state of a flip-flop in a computer may dynamically represent an 'a' keystroke, but the interpretation of either of these states as an input, and hence as a 'perceptual representation', is entirely stipulative. In the absence of an interpreting observer, both are simply physical states of the system. The semantic equivalence of natural and artificial systems becomes clear when the latter break down. The process of tracing a computer hardware failure with a probe and an oscilloscope, for example, is strikingly similar to the process of tracing neuronal connections with the same equipment.

Arguments that the semantics of states in organisms and machines are qualitatively different, such as those surrounding the symbol-grounding problem, appear to be based on a quite powerful intuition that evolved organisms cannot be described adequately as mechanisms. This latter-day form of vitalism often appears correlated, interestingly, with the essentially non-mechanistic, homuncular view of computation expressed by Fodor (1968): the view that computers literally read—and understand—data and instructions, and literally decide what to do with them (cf. the critique of this view in Cummins, 1983, ch. II). In both cases, it is an unwillingness to view 'information-processing' as one possible interpretation of the observed behaviour of a dynamic physical system that leads to paradox.

CONCLUSION

Hopcroft and Ullman (1979) characterize computer science as embracing two tasks: the theoretical characterization of algorithms, and the design of machines—typically virtual machines—that implement specific algorithms (p. 8). Computer science can, however, be viewed considerably more broadly: it is the experimental and theoretical study of the computational behaviour of physical systems. This endeavour involves measurement, and interpretation according to certain standards of coherence. Computer science, on this view, is similar in methods and scope to physics; the principal distinctions between them are the former's focus on dynamically non-conserved variables, and on its use of algorithms to define coherent interpretations. If computer science is viewed from this broader, more empirical perspective, its relation to the theory of computation becomes similar to the relation between physics and mathematics: in either case, the latter, completely abstract discipline provides the formal tools that enable the former, empirical discipline to construct its descriptions of the natural world.

The above characterization of computer science systematically ignores the distinction between artefacts and natural systems. This distinction is, however, purely a social construct. If humans are viewed as physical systems, then their design and construction of artefacts is a physical process like any other, and the physical results of this process are as natural as the humans that constructed them. Computational behaviour emerges when systems of either sort are measured in particular ways. The scientific study of the dynamic and algorithmic similarities in the behaviour of humans and some of their constructions need not take this socially motivated distinction into account.

REFERENCES

Ashby, W. R. (1956), *An Introduction to Cybernetics*, London: Chapman & Hall.

Benioff, P. (1986), 'Quantum Mechanical Hamiltonian Models of Computers', *Annals of the New York Academy of Science*, 480: 475–86.

Cummins, R. (1983), *The Nature of Psychological Explanation*, Cambridge, Mass.: MIT/Bradford.

DeLong, H. (1970), *A Profile of Mathematical Logic*, Reading, Mass.: Addison-Wesley.

Dietrich, E. (1989), 'Semantics and the Computational Paradigm in Cognitive Psychology', *Synthese*, 79: 119–41.

Feynman, R. (1985), 'Quantum Mechanical Computers', *Optics News*, 11: 11–20; also *Foundations of Physics*, 16: 507–31.

Fields, C. (1989), 'Consequences of Nonclassical Measurement for the Algorithmic Description of Continuous Dynamical Systems', *Journal of Experimental and Theoretical Artificial Intelligence*, 1: 171–78.

Fodor, J. A. (1968), 'The Appeal to Tacit Knowledge in Psychological Explanation', *Journal of Philosophy*, 65: 627–40.

—— (1974), 'Special Sciences', *Synthese*, 28: 97–115.

Gorman, R. P., and Sejnowski, T. J. (1988), 'Analysis of Hidden Units in a Layered Network Trained to Classify Sonar Targets', *Neural Networks*, 1: 75–89.

Grossberg, S. (1988), 'Nonlinear Neural Networks: Principles, Mechanisms, and Architectures', *Neural Networks*, 1: 17–61.

Harnad, S. (1989), 'Minds, Machines, and Searle', *Journal of Experimental and Theoretical Artificial Intelligence*, 1: 5–25.

Hopcroft, J., and Ullman, J. (1979), *Introduction to Automata Theory, Languages, and Computation*, Reading, Mass.: Addison-Wesley.

Jauch, J. M. (1968), *Foundations of Quantum Mechanics*, Reading Mass.: Addison-Wesley.

Marr, D. (1982), *Vision*, San Francisco: W. H. Freeman.

Moore, E. F. (1956), Gedanken-Experiments on Sequential Machines, in C. E. Shannon and J. McCarthy (eds.), *Automata Studies*, Princeton: Princeton University Press, 129–53.

Pylyshyn, Z. W. (1984), *Computation and Cognition: Toward a Foundation for Cognitive Science*, Cambridge, Mass.: MIT/Bradford.

Reeke, G. N., and Edelman, G. M. (1988), 'Real Brains and Artificial Intelligence', *Daedalus*, 117: 143–73.

Rumelhart, D. E., Smolensky, P., McClelland, J. L., and Hinton, G. E. (1986), 'Schemata and Sequential Thought Processes in PDP Models', in J. L. McClelland and D. E. Rumelhart (eds.), *Parallel Distributed Processing: Explorations in the Microstructure of Cognition*, ii, Cambridge, Mass.: MIT/Bradford, 7–57.

Sayre, K. M. (1986), 'Intentionality and Information Processing: An Alternative Model for Cognitive Science', *Behavioral and Brain Sciences*, 9: 121–65.

Searle, J. R. (1980), 'Minds, Brains, and Programs', *Behavioral and Brain Sciences*, 3: 417–24.

Sejnowski, T. J., Koch, C., and Churchland, P. S. (1988), 'Computational Neuroscience', *Science*, 241: 1299–306.

Stoy, J. E. (1977), *Denotational Semantics: The Scott-Strachey Approach to Programming Language Theory*, Cambridge, Mass.: MIT.

Tanenbaum, A. S. (1976), *Structured Computer Organization*, Englewood Cliffs, NJ: Prentice-Hall.

Ullman, S. (1986), 'Artificial Intelligence and the Brain: Computational Studies of the Visual System', *Annual Review of Neuroscience*, 9: 1–26.

von Neumann, J. (1932), *Mathematical Foundations of Quantum Mechanics*, Berlin: Springer Verlag.

IO

Beyond Turing Equivalence

AARON SLOMAN

—————•—————

1. THE PROBLEM

Artificial intelligence has revolutionized the study of mind by introducing computational theories of mental processes. Many people believe that computational concepts and theories suffice to explain the nature of perception, learning, creativity, motivation, emotions, feelings, consciousness, etc. because all these are thought to be computational states, events, or processes. Indeed, I once put forward such a view (Sloman, 1978). But this presupposes that we know what computations are. Do we? Do analog computers do computations? The concept has become less clear with the growth of interest in 'neural computations'. I shall try to show that we have the following options:

(*a*) Define 'computation' in the logico-mathematical sense (Turing equivalence), but accept that in this sense computational mechanisms are not central to explaining intelligence.

(*b*) Extend the definition to include all the kinds of processes that play a role in intelligence. It is then hard to draw a line between computational and non-computational processes, without falling into either circularity (computational processes are the ones needed for intelligence) or triviality (all processes are computational).

(*c*) Abandon the idea that any precisely defined concept of computation can be the *key* notion underlying intelligence, and instead study different kinds of architectures and mechanisms to learn what kinds of roles different sorts of machines can play in the design or explanation of intelligent systems.

In support of (*c*) I'll explain why most attempts to define 'computation' either fail to define a concept adequate to explain intelligence, or else fall into circularity or triviality. I'll then expand further on option (*c*) and end with a discussion of how to give semantic capabilities to computational and non-computational machines. All this is not an attack on AI, but a recipe for progress.

2. THE FORMAL CONCEPT OF COMPUTATION

The mathematical concept of 'computation' is the only well-defined concept of computation. It is concerned with purely formal structures. This point can be obscured by the process–product ambiguity. A process of computation may produce a *trace*, for example a long division presented on paper. Both the process and its enduring trace can be called computations, but in different senses. The formal concept of computation involves no notion of process, causation, or time, and is concerned only with the structural properties of such traces, no matter how they are produced. (Similar process–product ambiguities are associated with: 'proof', 'derivation', 'calculation', 'analysis', 'design', 'construction'.)

Formally a computation is a discrete sequence of structures satisfying certain conditions, i.e. every item in the sequence is either part of an initially given set of structures or derivable from earlier items according to fixed rules. The structures may be machine states, expressions in a logical language, or other configurations. Whether the sequence is physically embodied or merely an abstract structure is irrelevant, as is any question of what sort of mechanism, if any, produced it. In this sense leaves blown about on the forest floor could form a computation, e.g. solving an equation, as long as there is a description of the patterns formed by the leaves under which they conform to appropriate rules.

Not even physical embodiment is required. Using the unique factorization of integers as powers of primes, Gödel showed how formulas of arbitrary complexity can be systematically encoded in integers (see Nagel and Newman, 1958 for more details). A complete (finite) computation, no matter how complex, corresponds to a sequence of Gödel numbers, which itself can be expressed as one large Gödel number. Thus a number can satisfy the formal conditions for being a computation. An infinite computation, e.g.

producing the decimal expansion of π, would correspond to an infinite sequence of Gödel numbers.

This formal notion of computation, equally applicable to physical processes and non-physical mathematical structures, does not on its own enable us to build useful engines or explain human or animal behaviour. An abstract instance of computation (e.g. a huge Gödel number) cannot make anything happen. This shows that being a computation in the formal sense is not a *sufficient* condition for being an intelligent *behaving* system, even though the formal theory provides a useful conceptual framework for categorizing some behaving systems. For instance, it establishes limits to what is possible and provides a framewok for studying space–time complexity requirements and trade-offs. For the purposes of construction and explanation of intelligent systems, we need to combine computational ideas with the idea of a machine with causal powers. Smith (1988) argues, mistakenly I believe, that 'causation' is already part of the concept of computation. I have shown (Sloman, 1986, 1992b) that confusion on this point leads to systematic ambiguity in the 'Strong AI' thesis, and in criticisms of it by Searle (1980) and others.

3. IS THE STANDARD CONCEPT OF COMPUTATION BROAD ENOUGH?

The class of finitely specifiable sequences of structures turns out to be the class of sequences that can be generated by a universal Turing machine. There are at least three types of processes that might be involved in human brains that would not necessarily map onto a single Turing machine: (*a*) asynchronous parallel processes with independently varying speeds, (*b*) continuous, or at least non-discrete processes, and (*c*) physical processes that are not known to fit (or not to fit) the computational model, e.g. chemical processes in the brain. I don't know whether (*c*) is subsumed by (*a*) and (*b*) or whether other classes of exceptions to Turing equivalence exist.

Any collection of *synchronized* parallel computers can be mapped onto a Turing machine by interleaving their execution. However, for *un*synchronized variable speed parallel machines, this mapping cannot always be specified. The system does not have well-defined global states and well-defined state transformations, as a Turing machine does. Similarly if a system goes through non-discrete changes it cannot be modelled on a Turing machine, whose states form a discrete sequence. A non-discrete set (like the rational numbers) may be merely *dense* rather than *continuous*, if between any two different states there is always another. Continuity requires more than this, e.g. the existence of limits of bounded monotonic sequences. Non-discrete processes, whether merely dense or continuous, cannot be modelled on a Turing machine, for it cannot have a succession of states such that between any two states there occurs a third. A Turing machine can specify all the rationals, but cannot generate them in their natural order (as Zeno's paradoxes show). Of course, quantization allows any bounded non-discrete process to be simulated to any required degree of accuracy on a Turing machine, with a speed cost that depends on the accuracy. Chaotic processes may be an exception.

Not all processes that are used to solve problems make predictions, draw inferences, simulate something, *necessarily* involve discrete determinate processes. Both the non-discrete variation of analog computers (or slide-rules) and the random properties of quantum effects might be able to play a useful role in some kinds of calculations and simulations. Should we rule out such non-Turing processes from playing an important role in intelligence?

An example relevant to some kinds of image-processing and physical problem-solving is continuous rotation of an image. We often find it useful to rotate or slide sheets of paper and transparencies continuously relative to each other, e.g. in planning or problem solving. Digitized approximations to such continuous change are now commonplace in computer graphics, and have been used internally in AI programs (Funt, 1980). But they are only approximations. In this case it is not clear that fully continuous processes would add anything, though some non-discrete processes when embedded in physical mechanisms of an appropriate kind can go much faster than a simulation on a discrete computer, which is why analog computers are sometimes used for speed.

It is an open question whether animal intelligence depends (in part) on brain processes using non-discrete variation, such as states of neurons. Chemical soups (e.g. drugs and hormones) can alter the character of mental processes. Are these all to be called 'computational'? Why stop there? Why not include digestion, the growth of a tree, or even the processes in a thundercloud?

It may be that all physical processes are discrete at some level. Any set of measurements made over a finite time will be discrete (Fields, 1996). But for many purposes, like predicting the motion of planets, it is useful to conceive of them as non-discrete, e.g. so that differential equations can be used in making predictions. Is there any reason to rule this out in mechanisms underlying natural or artificial intelligences? Defining computation in terms of discreteness or Turing equivalence (Pylyshyn, 1986; Haugeland, 1985) excludes these things. But is this just an arbitrary restriction of mechanisms to be used in AI (for engineering purposes, or for explanatory purposes)? We could broaden the definition of 'computation' so as to include, for instance, devices for solving problems using non-discrete processes, like slide-rules and analog computers, or soap bubbles stretched on frames to work out minimum stress designs. That would increase the range of tools available within the framework of a computational approach.

It may turn out that systems that appear to be varying non-discretely are actually discrete at some lower, subatomic, level, but if so that is an empirical fact: there is no *conceptual* reason to rule out essentially continuous mechanisms from playing a useful role in human-like mental processes. However, if we allow 'computation' to include possibly non-discrete brain processes, slide-rules, and soap bubbles then it is hard to see how we can draw a boundary between computations and non-computations. Why should we bother?

Even if all processes in intelligent machines are exactly mathematically equivalent to Turing computations, it remains possible that some processes cannot be simulated on a Turing equivalent machine except too slowly for practical use. Even if all can, there may be some important differences. For example, three synchronized machines doing the same task in parallel are mathematically equivalent to one machine, yet the difference in reliability is significant to an engineer.

So, if real intelligent agents require some processes that cannot be produced by a single physically embodied Turing equivalent computer *within required constraints* (of time, cost, bulk, energy consumption, reliability, etc.) then the mere theoretical possibility of close digital approximation would be irrelevant to explaining how *actual* systems work.

A possible counter-argument is that *all* processes are computational. In (Sloman, 1978) I speculated, half-seriously, that all physical processes might turn out to be computational. Fields (1996) attempts to prove that *measurable states* of any observable physical process can be interpreted as the execution of an algorithm that could be run on a universal Turing machine. His proof assumes both quantum physics and the existence of a well-defined mapping from events to times. These assumptions need not hold in all logically possible universes. Morever, if it were true that all physical processes were computational, then it would be trivially true, and therefore uninteresting, that intelligent systems are computational, though it would remain an interesting task to try to demarcate the special types of computations required for intelligent systems.

However, if, as physicists tell us (*a*) no physical system has a totally determinate observable state, and (*b*) transitions from one state to another are probabilistic rather than deterministic, then even physical objects in themselves, as opposed to our measurements of their behaviour, cannot be treated as Turing equivalent computers, since (*a*) and (*b*) contradict requirements for Turing machines. Actual computers are built so as to minimize the large-scale effects of (*a*) and (*b*). Failure to do this completely leads to malfunctions, though mechanisms such as self-correcting memory devices reduce their impact.

We can sum up so far as follows: (i) The only precisely defined concept of 'computation' is the mathematical concept. This is a purely structural concept. (ii) This concept is in some ways too general and in other ways too narrow to provide a general framework for studying all possible mechanisms underlying intelligence. (iii) It is not clear, however, that we can find an alternative useful general definition that covers all the interesting cases and avoids the twin traps of circularity (because it presupposes some aspect of intelligence) and triviality (because it implies that all processes are computations).

Let us look at a few alternative attempts at defining 'computation': as a functional concept, as symbol manipulation, and as rule-governed processing.

3.1. *Computation as a functional concept*

Clark (1988) proposes that instead of defining computers on the basis of their intrinsic properties we should do so on the basis of their origin and use: if a mechanism was designed or used for a particular sort of purpose or if it evolved biologically to serve certain needs of organisms then it might be computational, otherwise not, i.e. 'computation' is a functional concept like 'table'. In order to be a table something has to be used as one or intended for use as one: a rock in the wilderness with a table-like structure would not be a table unless used as such. Similarly any physical process has the potential to be a computation in the functional sense, e.g. if used (like a wind-tunnel) to solve a problem such as modelling some other object, to explain or predict its behaviour.

We would still, however, have to specify exactly what functions are *characteristically* served by computations. Digestive mechanisms that discriminate and analyse chemical substances evolved to serve animal needs. Are they computational? Visual perception involves intelligence, but is the eyeball a computer, or part of one? Is it correct to say that the retina performs computations but not the lens? It is not clear that the functional analysis helps us answer such questions.

In the context of trying to explain intelligence as computational, it would be circular to define computers as those things that evolved, or were designed, for use by intelligent agents in processes like calculating, sorting, searching, perceiving, remembering, deciding. We need a characterization of computational processes that enables us to use them to explain how intelligence is possible, not one that *presupposes* the existence of intelligent systems.

3.2. *Computation as symbol manipulation*

Some people think of computation as *symbol* manipulation, where 'symbol' implies having a meaning. This also risks circularity; it is circular to assume that there are meaningful symbols to be manipulated, if we are trying to explain how meaning arises. In this context we must reject any definition of 'computation' in terms of manipulation of meaningful structures, and definitions in terms of making inferences or drawing conclusions.

3.3. *Computation as rule-governed processing*

We could drop the reference to symbols, and simply define computations as 'rule-governed' processes. But this still risks circularity, if being *governed* by rules involves *understanding* the rules.

Understanding is part of what we wish to explain: we must not assume it as a primitive. Can we avoid circularity by using a notion of being 'governed' that does not presuppose understanding, but might provide a basis for it? Computational processes would then be processes controlled by rules.

But if the rules are not understood, i.e. meanings play no role in the control, then the words 'rule' and 'governed' are misleading, and we are simply left with the notion of processes that are controlled by something. What, then, is control? Various forms of control—mechanical, hydraulic, electronic, chemical, etc.—have been studied under the heading 'control theory'. It seems acceptable to say that all computations are controlled processes, but are all controlled processes computational? Is the control of a spinning stone by its distribution of mass a computation?

Control is just a special case of the notion of causation: one thing controls another if there is some sort of causal relation between the controller and the controlled. (If it is a two-way relation, then the control includes feedback.) Analysing the concept of 'cause' is one of the hardest problems in philosophy (cf. Taylor, 1992), but I shall, for the purposes of this paper, assume we all understand it.

We now seem to be moving towards a definition of 'computation' that is so general (e.g. computations are processes controlled or partially controlled by structures) that it includes everything, trivializing the claim that mental states are computational. We could try to avoid the triviality by limiting computation to cases where the kinds of controlling structures are more like computer programs. Unfortunately, as previously indicated, that would rule out too many candidates for inclusion as computations, for instance neural computations. Moreover, the notion of 'control by program' has difficulties, as I'll now show.

4. DO COMPUTER PROGRAMS CONTROL PROCESSING?

There are several different kinds of control relation between a computer program and the behaviour it produces, some tighter than others. In particular, programs need not *totally* control the behaviour, since programs often run under operating systems that limit what they can do. On a time-shared computer each process is frequently interrupted by the operating system and suspended while another program runs. If a program attempts to access certain parts of memory or certain devices this causes it to be interrupted or aborted. Programs can have time bounds and space bounds. The 'permissions' and 'privileges' handled by modern operating systems impose various limitations of control by individual programs. So each program typically has only 'bounded control' over the processes it generates (cf. Sloman, 1992*b*).

Many programs written by human programmers are not even partially in control of the processes they generate, at least not as a driver is in control of a car. Some programs are compiled to a different, machine-code program, and after compilation the *original* program is not in control: no change in the original will affect the execution in the way that turning a steering-wheel affects the motion of a car. Control by such programs is 'ballistic', not 'online'.

A program has more direct 'online' control if it is not compiled but stored in the machine and 'interpreted'. But what is in control depends on a point of view. The program can be construed as actively controlling the process, or as a passive structure, used by the controlling interpreter. Even a compiled machine-code program can be viewed as a passive structure used by the CPU to generate behaviour.

The 'ballistic' vs. 'online' distinction is not the same as the familiar distinction between 'open-loop' and 'closed-loop' control. A machine-code program's control is online, but whether it is open-loop or closed-loop depends on whether its behaviour depends on results of preceding behaviour, i.e. whether it uses feedback, in which case the control uses a closed loop. The loop may include the external environment (accessed through sensors and motors) or just internal states. A program with no conditional instructions and no parameters set at run time via sensors would be open-loop. A program that does not use any feedback is open-loop. It may nevertheless be online if it is in direct control of behaviour.

So the attempt to define a non-circular, yet sufficiently general, notion of computation in terms of control by structures requires clarification of the amount and kind of control required, as well as what sort of entity may be in control. We can't require a separable stored program using an explicit programming language, if we wish to include neural computations—unless we stretch the notions of program and language to encompass the topology of neural interconnections and connection weights. If we are prepared to say that a neural net constitutes a program, then what isn't a program? Why not include *every* physical or chemical structure that controls the behaviour of something?

5. CONTROL BY VIRTUAL MACHINES

Another problem with compiled programs is that their instructions specify quite different actions from those referred to in the original high-level programming language: there is a *semantic mismatch*. Programs written by human programmers usually refer to 'virtual' structures and operations on them, e.g. arrays, lists, records trees, graphs, data-streams, or numbers, whereas the machine code instructions will generally refer only to operations on bit patterns and locations in a linear array of bit patterns.

Can instructions of the latter kind control processes of the former kind? Could we be mistaken in describing computers as manipulating arrays, lists, and other abstract data-structures? Do they really only manipulate bit patterns? Bit patterns themselves, however, are also virtual structures: what the *physical* machine contains is not bit patterns but wires, switches, voltages, currents, etc. Even these can be thought of as virtual mechanisms implemented in still lower-level quantum physical processes.

The word 'virtual' as used here (as in computer science) does not contrast with 'real'. (The word 'abstract' might be more appropriate.) Neither does it have anything to do with so-called 'virtual reality' systems, which are convincing simulations of physical processes. Virtual processes in virtual machines really exist and can have causal consequences. They are virtual in the sense that their contents are high-level abstractions which are *implemented* in a 'lower-level' machine. It could be argued that the kinds of physical mechanisms we normally talk about, e.g. lawnmowers, printers, are virtual machines in this sense, i.e. implemented upon lower-level machines that only physicists know about. Whether there is a 'bottom layer' is an old metaphysical question, to which I offer no answer here.

Some readers may be inclined to argue that there is only one 'ultimate' level of reality and only at that level can processes be controlled. This requires drastic rejection of most common-sense concepts of causation and control. Moreover, Taylor (1992) produces arguments for liberal applicability of the concept of 'cause' to any type of domain. I shall continue to talk as if structures in a virtual machine can control processes in a virtual machine, i.e. virtual machine states and processes can have causal powers.

Most useful computations are not spatially located physical processes, but virtual processes in virtual machines, e.g. alphabetically sorting a list of words, which rearranges pointers but does not physically move anything. Such processes can have causal roles, e.g. reordering a list of words can change the order in which external actions are performed. Similarly a virtual machine event, like adding a word to a sentence in a word-processor can cause other virtual machine events, like rearranging page boundaries. These are causal relations between states and events in virtual, not physical, machines, though their implementation depends on physical causation. So do social, political, and economic causation. In all cases, there are true counterfactual conditionals of the form: *if X had not occurred Y would not have occurred*, and *as long as X occurred, Y would have occurred even if Z had also occurred*. This justifies attributions of causality whether in physical machines, socio-economic systems, the human mind, or software systems.

Some people find it hard to accept that processes in virtual machines can have real causal powers, because they think there is a 'bottom'-level physical reality which is the only realm in which causes can operate, for which I know no good argument. If true, that would imply that most of the things that we regard as causes are not real causes. That would be disastrous for normal human planning, the operation of the law courts, software engineering, and so on (Sloman, 1994*c*).

So, when a compiled, machine-code program is controlling behaviour at the bit level, there is also usually another virtual program controlling behaviour of a higher-level virtual machine at a level of abstraction closer to the original source code. (Such a program can change itself at run time so that it no longer corresponds to the original.) When a compiler performs optimizing transformations it may not be clear exactly *which* virtual machine is implemented in the resulting code. But that does not mean there isn't one. Sometimes there are several layers of virtual machines: implementation is often multi-level. So we may have to allow our intelligent system to include some high-level virtual machines.

6. WE NEED A BETTER SET OF CONCEPTS

We have many ill-defined concepts that evolved for purposes of everyday life, but do not suffice for more sophisticated purposes. When we try to apply these concepts in new situations to make fine, previously unnoticed, distinctions we discover that they are unsuited for the job. This often happens in the development of science or a culture, leading to significant conceptual change. A striking example is the way concepts of kinds of matter developed under the influence of atomic theory, through the periodic table and theories of chemical composition. We need a similar revolution in concepts of mind and control.

The concept of computation played a useful catalytic role in extending our understanding of some intelligent processes (e.g. proving theorems, planning, parsing sentences), and has opened our minds to much wider classes of (virtual) mechanisms than were previously dreamed of. Nevertheless, for reasons given above, we do not yet have a notion of computation adequate to provide a non-circular, explanatory foundation for AI and cognitive science: (*a*) because the formal concept needs to be combined with some sort of notion of causation, control, or machine, and (*b*) because the forms of processing in intelligent systems may go beyond computations that fit the Turing equivalent model.

There is no sensible place to make a sharp boundary between computational and non-computational mechanisms, except by using one of the standard formal definitions that are all mathematically equivalent to the definition of 'computation' as what a Turing machine can do. This definition is inadequate for the purpose of identifying the central feature of intelligence, because satisfying it is neither sufficient nor necessary for a mechanism to be intelligent.

(*a*) It is not sufficient because the mere fact that something is implemented on or is equivalent to a Turing machine does not make it intelligent, does not give it beliefs, desires, percepts, etc. Moreover, a computation in this sense can be a purely static, formal structure, which does nothing.

(*b*) Turing-machine power is not necessary for such aspects of intelligence as the ability to perceive, act, learn, make plans, have desires, feel pain, or communicate, because there is no evidence that animals that have these abilities also have Turing equivalent computational abilities: human beings, for example, appear to be limited in the depth of recursion that they can use in understanding sentences. Moreover, with or without external memory aids in their calculations, they often make mistakes that no Turing machine would make.

As argued above, there is no a priori reason to rule out the possibility that non-Turing equivalent processes play a useful role in human brains. In any case, I argue (Sloman, 1992*b*, 1993, 1994*c*) that *architecture dominates mechanism*. The particular mechanisms used are not as important as the global organization of subsystems with different functions. This is what determines the main capabilities of the system. By comparison, varying the mechanisms, for instance, switching between neural and symbolic mechanisms, or introducing non-computational mechanisms will have a marginal impact on the main capabilities of the system.

Because the relevance of computation to intelligence is so problematic, I suggest that we should keep an open mind and examine the potential uses of all potentially relevant mechanisms, whether computational in any sense or not. Then the task of a theory of mechanisms for intelligence is to analyse similarities and differences between mechanisms of all kinds and their implications for both explaining and replicating animal and human capabilities. Computational mechanisms may turn out to be relevant only to a subset of human capabilities (Sloman, 1994*a*, 1995*a* describe a process of exploring mappings between 'design space' and 'niche space'.) All this is not an attack on AI, but an attempt to generalize it, and to defuse attacks on AI which claim that computation will not suffice for intelligence. We can respond by asking 'Show us the mechanisms that do suffice, and we'll add them to the AI tool kit.'

7. THE VARIETY OF 'COMPUTATION-LIKE' PROCESSES

There is a wide variety of machines whose internal and external behaviour is controlled by internal structures. We can call a machine (or its behaviour) more or less 'computation-like' according to how close it is to implementing Turing equivalent powers. This is not meant to be a precise measure.

A special case is a conventional computer 'obeying' a machine-code program expressed as bit-patterns. This provides bit-manipulations in a virtual machine controlled by a structure in the same virtual machine. The controlling structure is a set of bit-patterns interpreted as instructions, addresses, and 'data' bits. The computer has a primitive grasp of the semantics of its machine language because of combined effects of (i) structural properties (e.g. relationships between bit-patterns and an ordered set of locations) and (ii) the underlying design which provides causal links between bit-patterns and such things as internal actions, locations in the machine, and counting operations (Sloman, 1985*b*). The combination of structural and causal links provides a foundation for meaning. This is a recurring pattern.

The machine *understands*, in a limited fashion, instructions and addresses composed of bit patterns. While obeying instructions, it manipulates other bit-patterns that it need not understand at all, although it can compare them, copy them, change their components, etc. This limited, primitive understanding provides a basis on which to implement more complex and indirect semantic capabilities, including much of AI (Sloman, 1985*b*, 1987*a*).

AI need not restrict itself to processes running on conventional computers. Biologists talk of development of an embryo as a computation (with DNA as program); and it is now commonplace to regard networks of neuron-like mechanisms, as performing computations. We can also think of the biosphere and natural selection as performing computation-like processes that produce new genes and gene combinations. These all illustrate the admittedly vague concept 'computation-like' which subsumes normal computer processes but is not committed to Turing equivalence, as long as processes are controlled by some structure.

If embryo development, neural processes, biological evolution, and conventional computer processes are all computation-like, is there any process that is *not* computation-like? This request for a well-defined boundary should be resisted. In deep science *good* definitions arise from good theories, which we still lack. We should study the variety of cases, their similarities and their differences. Trying to understand many small but real boundaries and their implications is more fruitful than arbitrarily imposing binary divisions.

When you push the corner of a table, all the atoms communicate with their neighbours, adjusting their own motions and mutual relationships as needed to fit in with what the neighbours are doing. The processes are at least partly under the control of the structure of the table. Is that structure a sort of program? Is the applied force a sort of input to the program? Is the process computation-like? The best answer may be that it is a special case—just as a circle is a special case of an ellipse, lacking some properties of other ellipses. Once this is clear, any debate about whether a circle is or is not an ellipse loses interest: in the mathematical sense it is an ellipse, whereas in a colloquial sense it is not. We can then ask exactly how this special case differs from others. Similarly with special cases of computation-like processes.

What other computation-like processes are there? How are the more interesting varieties different from motion of a table? One important difference concerns structural variability, which includes changes in complexity as opposed to quantitative changes in a fixed set of dimensions. Another involves differences of functional roles within a larger architecture. I'll try to explain both.

8. STEPS TOWARDS A CLASSIFICATION OF BEHAVING SYSTEMS

8.1. *Variability of states*

One reason why computers are so useful is that their digital memory structure supports enormous variability of substates: there are astronomically large numbers of significantly different internal states between which the machine can change. In computers and brains this is achieved by having large numbers of independently switchable elements. N switches each with K possible states permit K to the power N possible total states. If N is large, even small values of K (e.g. 2) produce unimaginably large sets of possible states. The possible sequences of such states form even larger sets, supporting enormous diversity of behaviour. If the elements can vary non-discretely an even larger set of significantly different states can exist, with non-discrete transitions (though it is not clear whether this is important for intelligence). However, continuously varying systems may not be able to control themselves reliably over diverse trajectories in state space. Continuous variation makes it harder for control mechanisms to discriminate their own states reliably. Thus, even if continuous variation plays a role, it may be a restricted role.

8.2. *Redundant state transitions in serial systems*

A difference between a brain and a simple computer is that in the latter a single processor has to change all the units. Whether it changes 16 or 32 or 64 bits at a time, certain state changes cannot be done in one step, but have to go through intermediate states, whereas a parallel network of processors can all change at once. Whether the need to traverse useless intermediate states is a serious limitation will depend on such things as the speed of the processor, ways in which intermediate states can cause errors, and so on. Contrary to current philosophical fashions I do not believe that the differences between a neural net and a computer are deeply significant from the point of view of designing an intelligent system, though they may affect engineering requirements like speed and robustness: useless and potentially undesirable intermediate states occur in one but not the other.

8.3. *The importance of 'structural' variability*

Many physical systems, and their variation, are usefully represented in terms of a point moving in a high-dimensional vector space. Richer kinds of variation, allowing changing complexity, are required for biological and intelligent systems. For example, biological growth is not merely a process of changing measurements: it can produce an entirely new structure, such as an eye or wing, or a new relationship such as connection via a nerve fibre. Many kinds of human learning, e.g. learning a new language or learning algebra, seem to require structural variability, unlike, for example, the fine-tuning of a pre-existing motor skill by practice.

Similarly, states of understanding different sentences cannot easily be represented by changing values in fixed dimensional vectors of measurements, because of the potentially unbounded complexity of sentences in natural languages. There are limits to our ability to handle unbounded depth of nesting in sentence structures, but we can cope with long rambling sentences with variable numbers of significant substructures. (Compare the children's song: 'This is the house that Jack built.')

Although the retina does not change in complexity as different scenes are viewed, visual percepts do vary in structure. The differences between seeing a ballet, seeing an Indian temple, and seeing a printed poem are *differences in the numbers and kinds of objects and relationships perceived*, not just *differences in values of a fixed-size vector*. Different scenes need descriptions with quite different structures, and there does not seem to be any upper bound to the complexity of what might be seen: a square can have sides made of smaller squares, whose sides are made of smaller squares, whose sides . . . and so on.

State changes in biological and cognitive processes therefore involve creation, deletion, or rearrangement of substructures. This *structural* variation is different from either continuous or discrete variation along a one-dimensional scale, or simultaneous variation in N different dimensions in a uniform multi-dimensional space. Structural variation can involve increasing or decreasing complexity. So, for a mechanism with structural variability, the space of possible states is not homogeneous: there are different kinds of neighbourhoods at different locations.

The amount and kind of structural variability in a system limits the kinds of interactions it can have with the rest of the world. A system that can have only N distinct states cannot distinguish N + 1 kinds of environmental situations. However, the environment can be counted as part of the state, like the trail blazed by a forest-dweller (Sloman, 1978, ch. 6.)

8.4. *Structural variability in virtual machines*

Computer science and AI have shown how we can use a machine whose states are fixed-dimensional binary vectors to implement many new 'virtual' machines with very different kinds of substates and causal interactions. (Crucial to this is the use of 'pointers'— bit-patterns interpreted as referring to memory locations.) A virtual machine with great *structural variability* can be implemented in a fixed dimensional *structurally invariant* lower-level machine. Similarly, a fixed-structure neural net can implement a virtual machine providing structural variability, though usually at a great cost in speed.

AI has shown how computational systems can be connected to an environment via sensory transducers which trigger complex structural changes in internal substates, e.g. produced by changes in the environment or changes in the viewpoint. The internal substates so produced can in turn control behaviour in complex ways. Slight environmental differences can produce elaborate differences in behaviour. (Compare hearing 'Your mother is well' and 'Your mother is ill.')

Sensitivity to the environment is a feature of many life forms, including growing plants. Not all organisms support rapid internal state changes. Not all support great structural variability. Not all can build a representation of the *structure* of an object or situation, as opposed to a collection of *measures* like temperature or chemical gradients. These are some of the important 'discontinuities in design space' that will have to be understood if we are to understand the evolution of human mental capabilities.

Discrete variability, including creation of new substructures and new connections between old structures, seems to be required for some aspects of human intelligence, mainly because discreteness can support long-term stability (e.g. stored plans, or grammatical knowledge). But that does not rule out other kinds of mechanisms, including some with non-discrete variability.

8.5. *Independently variable, causally interacting, functionally differentiated substates*

A finite state machine, like the 'engine' of a Turing machine, has only one unanalysable global state at a time. Other systems, like a Turing machine together with its tape, or a thermostat, have a collection of coexisting substates that can change independently and interact causally with one another. A collection of coexisting interacting substates defines an architecture. A special type of architecture is one in which behaviour is controlled by information (Sloman, 1993, 1994c). In such a system there will be mechanisms for taking in information, for interpreting information, for transforming information, for transmitting information, and for storing information (over varying time-periods). The type and variety of information, and the kinds of uses to which it can be put, will depend on the architecture and the environment.

We have seen that substates may have fixed or changing structure, they may be physical or virtual, and causation (control) may be direct or indirect, bounded or total, online or ballistic, open-loop or closed-loop, ongoing or momentary, mediated by an 'interpreter', or physically direct. All these differences determine the kinds of functional roles available within the architecture. In some cases even the architecture can change. While a program is running in a computer the number of causally significant substructures (e.g. parse trees, or items in a database, or incrementally created subprograms) can change drastically. So the number and variety of functionally distinct substates can vary. The same seems to be true of brains, even if the underlying sub-mechanisms are very different. The virtual machine architecture of an individual's mind can develop over time.

By contrast, chairs, tables, slide-rules, amplifiers, and steam-engines, have nothing like the variety of causal interactions between different substates to be found in brains or the simplest modern computers. They lack the functional differentiation, the variety of causally distinct substates, and the ability to remove old or add new substates. This renders most physical objects unsuitable as major components in an intelligent system (though they may be used for restricted purposes as part of a more general system). A related criticism can be made of the once fashionable analogy between a brain and a telephone exchange. It is not just a matter of *degree* of complexity: a storm cloud has hugely varying internal states with intricate and changing patterns of causal interaction, but lacks the functional differentiation between states needed for intelligence.

It is not worth arguing over which mechanisms 'really' are computation-like, nor which are 'really' intelligent. We should instead ask which mechanisms are useful, or even necessary, for different kinds of intelligence. We should not expect that human intelligence requires exactly the same kinds of mechanisms as the capabilities of ants or mice or squirrels, though there is likely to be some overlap. For instance, both need the environment sometimes to control behaviour fairly directly, and sometimes indirectly.

To summarize so far: important differences between mechanisms are concerned with the number and kinds of independently variable substates that can coexist at one time, the kinds of variation of the substates, the kinds of interactions between substates, whether the number of substates is fixed or can change, and so on. These

are all *architectural* issues, concerned with functional differentiation within a global design. Different sorts of sub-mechanisms
might be used to implement the same architecture for a higher
level virtual machine, just as different electronic components can
implement the same amplifier circuit.

8.6. *Functional differentiation of mind-like substates*

In an intelligent agent, different substates have different causal
roles in the total system. For example, we can distinguish 'belief-
like' and 'desire-like' states if the system can apply a 'correspondence' test comparing substates with the environment, and failed
correspondences generate different compensatory actions for different classes of substates. If S is a belief-like substate, failure of correspondence tends to cause the S state to be changed until the test
succeeds, whereas if S is a desire-like substate, the same correspondence failure initiates processes that tend to change *the environment*
until the test succeeds. Note that for some systems the environment
will be partly internal. In more complex systems, there will be far
more than two types of controlling substates (Sloman, 1993). For
example, planning will require 'supposition-like' control states.

8.7. *Semantic correspondence without isomorphism*

It should not be assumed that the 'correspondence' mentioned
above is anything like isomorphism. Neither sentences nor most
pictures are isomorphic with what they say, describe, or depict.
All that is required is some systematic way of checking a substate
S against a perceived (internal or external) environment such that
two outcomes are possible. One of them can be given a special
status and called 'truth'. States for which the check gives that
special result are said to 'correspond' with the environment. In
that sense numerals, '1', '2', '3', etc. can be checked against groups
of objects by using a counting procedure. But there is no sense in
which the numeral '10' is *isomorphic* with the groups that correspond to it. Requiring isomorphism between representing states
and what they represent would require animals and robots to
build internal replicas of the environment, with internal eyes to
perceive the replicas, leading to an infinite regress.

9. BEHAVIOUR IS NOT ENOUGH: OBJECTIONS TO TURING TESTS

A question that causes deep philosophical disagreement is whether internal mechanisms are relevant to whether a behaving entity is intelligent or conscious or has certain mental states. One view is that since all we have to go on in judging other people to be intelligent is behaviour, nothing more should be required of machines than that they provide appropriate behaviour. This presupposes that our beliefs about other minds are based entirely on inference from evidence. I suspect this is a myth, and that evolution has imbued us with deep assumptions about the nature of agents and objects in the environment. What perceived behaviour does is merely determine details of *what* we believe about other minds, not *whether* we believe.

Evidence could never suffice, for any behaviour observed over a finite time could in principle be produced by indefinitely many very different mechanisms, including possibly a giant precomputed look-up table which would not have any intelligence: only its designer would. Even Turing-equivalent systems, i.e. systems that map the same inputs to the same outputs, may differ significantly in how they do it.

We thus have two views: (*a*) intelligence is merely a matter of *what* a system *does*, and (*b*) intelligence depends not only on *what* is done, but also on *how* it is done. It is foolish to take sides in this debate, since the relevant concepts (e.g. 'intelligence', 'mind') are too ill-defined, as Turing saw clearly (Turing, 1950). Instead what we should do is analyse exactly the space of possible designs to understand the implications of various differences in architecture or underlying mechanisms.

10. TOWARDS A CLASSIFICATION OF BEHAVING SYSTEMS

Having abandoned the precise, formal idea of computation as the central key concept, and replaced it with the more general notions of architecture and mechanism, we can now start trying to classify behaving systems according to how they work, e.g. (*a*) how many different kinds of substates they can simultaneously support, (*b*) what kind of variability those states can have, (*c*) what their causal interactions are, and (*d*) how much internal functional differentiation they have, and so on. The following questions can be asked about each design:

1. *How many independently variable (physical or virtual) coexisting substates can the machine support?*

1(*a*) Is the machine able to extend the number or is it permanently fixed? (For some machines, answers to these questions will depend on the level of analysis in the implementation hierarchy.)

2. *What forms of variation do the substates admit?*

2(*a*) Do they vary discretely, non-discretely, continuously, smoothly?

2(*b*) Do different substates have different kinds of variability?

2(*c*) Do the mechanisms support *structural* variation?

2(*d*) Do the underlying mechanisms provide the kind of variability required for logical or propositional representations (fixed function symbols with changing arguments and vice versa, with hierarchical composition)?

2(*e*) Can one substate be 'stored' in another and then later 'retrieved' on the basis of a partial match? (i.e. is there a flexible content-addressable memory?)

2(*f*) Do the mechanisms allow new associations to be created? (An association between X and Y requires a mechanism that when presented with X produces Y.)

2(*g*) Do they allow arbitrary tangled networks of associations, or only linear chains, or trees? For example, does the mechanism allow the items linked by associations themselves to be associations, like a tree of trees? Does it allow the links to have structure, e.g. with complex labels?

2(*h*) Do the mechanisms permit *implicit* substates, like the theorems implicitly stored in a logical database, or information stored in a sparse array? (Some of the virtual structures may have more components than the physical structures that implement them, making it futile to seek correlations between information states and physiology.)

3. *What kinds of causal interactions and functional differentiation does the machine support?*

3(*a*) Which changes in states can cause other changes in states? That is, which substates are causally linked?

3(*b*) Does it allow internal variation of one substate to be finely controlled 'online' by another complex substate (like a stored program controlling execution)?

3(*c*) Does it allow the addition of a new substate S to trigger further substates, and so on? (Compare production systems, forward-chaining predicate logic systems, etc.)

3(*d*) Are most of the changes controlled or initiated by the environment or is the majority of processing 'internally' generated? (In humans, mental states are continually changing, with or without external influence.)

3(*e*) What kinds of internal feedback loops does it support? (Structural variability makes possible more than just positive and negative feedback.)

3(*f*) Does it allow internal structures to be built that store information about other internal structures, or describe relations between them, for use by the machine? That is, are there belief-like states concerning the machine's own internal state?

3(*g*) Are all changes synchronized or can substates change at different independently varying speeds, i.e. asynchronously?

3(*h*) Can some states be belief-like, i.e. largely under the control of the environment, and others desire-like, i.e. able to generate actions when the environment does not 'fit' them. (See definition in section 9.3.)

3(*i*) Does the mechanism allow internal records of internal processes to be constructed for future use (in recollections, thoughts, etc.)?

(This is just a small sample of a wide variety of causal abilities and functional relationships to be investigated.)

4. *How fast can states change and causes propagate, relative to the kinds of changes that can occur in the environment?*

Speed limits can have profound design implications, e.g. I've argued elsewhere (1987*b*, 1992*a*) that certain emotional states arise out of mechanisms connected with resource limits.

5. *What is the global (high-level) architecture of the system?*

5(*a*) Are there separable, but interacting, subsystems each performing some complex function within the larger whole? What sorts of functions?

5(*b*) Are the architecture and the collection of functions fixed, or can the architecture change through pre-programmed development or learning (as seems to be the case with human children when they learn new forms of self-control, or new forms

of learning, or new reflective capabilities, or new sets of
concepts)?

5(c) Does the architecture support *semantic* capabilities, e.g.
does it allow the machine to use some substructures to refer
to others? (Discussed below.)

5(d) Does the architecture allow different sorts of mechanisms
to be used for different purposes, e.g. neural nets, production
systems, etc.? (Hybrid systems may allow sub-mechanisms to
be optimized for different tasks.)

6. *Are the different substates spatially separable*, i.e. embedded
in different substructures (like computer data-structures) or superimposed in a distributed form (like superimposed wave forms or
distributed neural states)?

7. *Is there always 'cross-talk' between the different substates*,
so that changing one always has some effect on others, or can they
be causally isolated?

8. *What kinds of internal and external self-monitoring can the
system support, how reliable is it, and what can it be used for?*

9. *How much of the internal state is displayed externally, vol-
untarily or involuntarily?*

These are only some of the kinds of questions that can be asked
about different sorts of architectures and mechanisms potentially
relevant to designing or explaining intelligent systems. The answers
will identify different classes of systems.

Some of the questions need to be made more precise, in particular the analysis of the causal roles characteristic of belief-like and
desire-like states. That requires an exercise in the global design of
intelligent systems (cf. Sloman, 1987*b*, 1992*a*, 1993). The rest of
this paper concentrates on the question how a system with independently variable substates can interpret some of its own states as
having a meaning. No completely definite answer is to be expected
because the question is inherently vague and ambiguous owing to
the indeterminacy of our ordinary concepts.

11. THE ROOTS OF SEMANTICS

If a mechanism can store and retrieve substates then people can use
it as an information store, like a filing cabinet. But a filing cabinet

does not understand anything. How can a machine treat some of its own internal substructures as referring to anything, i.e. as having a semantics for *the machine*, and not just for us? (This is the question that Haugeland 1985 posed in terms of a distinction between 'derivative meaning' and 'original meaning', which was later labelled by Harnad as the 'symbol-grounding' problem.) Does a machine with 'original meaning', i.e. a machine for which certain symbols have a meaning independently of whether they have a meaning for anyone else, have to be a computational machine, i.e. capable of being completely replicated on a Turing machine? Could a purely computational machine support 'original meaning'?

I have argued (Sloman, 1985*b*, 1987*a*) that there is no sharp distinction between systems that do and systems that don't understand the structures they manipulate. Rather there is a whole *cluster* of prototypical semantic capabilities in human beings, and different subsets of capabilities may be instantiated in different mechanisms— natural and artificial. Simple concepts from ordinary language, like 'understand', need to be replaced by a richer family of far more precisely defined concepts, related to underlying mechanisms, just as our concepts of kind of stuff evolved with advances in physics. 'Intelligent' is another such concept full of muddles: which is why I make no attempt to define it here. 'Consciousness' is an even worse swamp of confusions camouflaged by misplaced confidence that we know what we are talking about.

Some of the requirements for human-like semantic capabilities are structural (i.e. mechanisms are needed with certain capabilities), some functional (i.e. the mechanisms need to be used with certain roles within the whole system). AI work on understanding language or images hitherto has been more concerned with the structural than with the functional conditions: little or no attention has been paid to issues concerned with motivation, for instance.

I have shown (1985*b*) how some semantic capabilities can be found even in the way a digital computer uses its machine language. It uses some substructures (i.e. bit-patterns) to refer to locations in its (virtual) memory, some to possible internal actions (in a virtual machine), some to numbers, when counting, and so on. Of course the uses of semantic relations made by a simple computer are far more limited than the uses we make: for instance there is not yet motivation in the computer. Nevertheless, even now, it is the computer, not a person, that (*a*) uses the bit-pattern

in an address register to determine which location is to be inter-
rogated or changed, and (*b*) uses the bit-pattern in another register
to determine which action to perform. Filing cabinets were never
like this.

Giving a machine a larger collection of semantic capabilities,
with semantic competence closer to human abilities, requires both
(i) a richer formalism than most machine languages (i.e. substates
with richer kinds of variability) and (ii) a richer architecture, including both belief-like and desire-like roles (explained below). Such a
virtual machine could be implemented in a much simpler physical
machine.

The full story of the kind of architecture that not only begins
to allow symbols to be related to the world by the machine, but
also allows the meanings they express really to *matter* to the
machine (as the news 'Your mother is ill' would matter to you),
is very complex. It requires a theory of how different motivational
processes work, on which more below (see also Sloman, 1987*b*
and 1993).

12. COMBINING TARSKIAN SEMANTICS WITH CAUSAL LINKS

There does not have to be any direct and simple mapping between
representing structures and what they represent, as should be
obvious from the fact that there are sentences containing disjunctions, negations, and quantifiers, and pictures that have both a
smaller dimensionality than the scences they depict and often also
a different topology: a typical 2-D picture of a 3-D wire-frame cube
has more junctions than the cube has vertices, whereas a picture
of an opaque cube has fewer.

Tarski (1956) showed precisely how a set M of real or possible
objects can form a model for a set S of logical axioms, without
M and S being isomorphic, e.g. a small finite set S, like Peano's
axioms for arithmetic, may have an infinite model M. However,
if M′ is isomorphic with M, then M′ is also a model for S, whatever M′ may be. Thus Tarskian semantics can never determine a
unique referent. (In general, not all models of a given set of axioms
will be isomorphic with one another.)

If a mechanism has substates whose structural variability matches

requirements for a logical formalism, with transformations corresponding to valid rules of inference, then Tarskian semantics
will allocate an indefinitely large set of possible models to the substructures in the machine. These models may be either abstract
mathematical structures or objects and relations in the world (e.g.
a social system may model some set-theoretic axioms).

The set of possible models for S can be reduced by adding
constraints in the form of new independent axioms, but this never
suffices to pin down the model to a particular bit of the physical
world; for there is always the possibility that some other exactly
similar world, or portion of the world, provides as good a model
as the intended one. Pure syntactic structure, however intricate,
can never guarantee semantic definiteness (though uniqueness at a
certain level of description may occur).

Semantic ambiguity can be further partly constrained if some
of the substructures are causally linked with bits of the world.
For example, electronic mechanisms ensure that bit-patterns in a
computer are causally related to locations in its own memory
rather than locations in another machine, despite having the same
structural relations to both. Less direct causal links via the Internet can connect a more complex bit-pattern (or symbolic address
in a virtual machine) with a computer, or even a user, in a remote
part of the world. In software engineering, unique semantic links
of many kinds are set up by means of a judicious blend of structural mapping and causal linkage: without this mixture, electronic
information services could not work. The use of structural mapping allows the causal links to be very loose (e.g. Internet con-
nectivity is constantly changing). The existence of causal links
removes, or reduces, the ambiguity inherent in the purely structural
semantics.

Similarly, in AI systems, or animal brains, perceptual mechanisms and motors controlled by the internal substructures can set up
causal links in both directions between internal substructures and
aspects of the external environment. These links reduce the possible
Tarskian interpretations of internal 'axioms', 'predicates', 'individual constants', etc. But they never totally eliminate semantic
indeterminacy: in a rich and complex world we can always be sur-
prised by unexpected ambiguities in our words and phrases.

Much work in epistemology and the philosophy of science
has attempted to satisfy philosophical sceptics by eliminating such

semantic ambiguity, but I see no reason to require guaranteed uniqueness of reference, as long as the mechanisms *usually* function adequately for the organism or agent concerned. In any case, I don't believe such guarantees can be achieved. Some philosophers will be unhappy about this, but neither human designers nor evolution need adopt unsatisfiable requirements!

Can we extend Tarski's ideas beyond the case where the representing formalism is a logical (Fregean) notation (Sloman, 1971, 1985a, 1995c)? We also need to allow different kinds of meaning that don't easily fit into Tarski's framework, e.g. emotive meaning.

A more general theory will allow a wider variety of structures, including non-discretely variable substates, to have semantics, while extending the kinds of semantic indeterminacy that can occur. Work on computer vision shows how the structural notion of semantics can be extended beyond logical representations. Here disambiguation by causal linkage is fairly direct, though semantic relations involving intermediate and high-level interpretations (e.g. 'X looks happy') are complex and subtle (Ballard & Brown, 1982; Sloman, 1989).

Human and animal visual systems and robots using TV cameras all seem to provide existence proofs that analogical representations (e.g. pictures or diagrams), and perhaps some non-discretely variable substructures, can have a useful semantics. Can we explain how? We can extend the notion of a portion of the world being a model for some representing structure in a machine by relating machine substates to the *roles* that they can play in a behaving system, and the ways in which these roles interact with the environment, via causal loops. Examples would be the different functional roles of bit-patterns and analog sensors in a robot. However, at present I can offer only an incomplete sketch of 'loop-closing' semantics.

13. TOWARDS 'LOOP-CLOSING' SEMANTICS

Let's start with a thermostat and gradually add design complications. A thermostat connected to a room heater has a (primitive) belief-like substate that represents current temperature of the room, for example, the curvature of a bimetallic strip. The thermostat also has a (primitive) desire-like substate corresponding to the required temperature setting. For each desire-like state D there is a range R of belief-like states such that if D and R coexist the thermostat will make no attempt to change the environment. Otherwise it will turn the heater on or off. For each belief-like state B there is a set of possible states of the environment that will tend to produce B (when the sensors are working normally) and will tend to be produced by the corresponding desire-like state D(B) (when the heater is working normally).

For every sensor–controller pair there is an aspect of the environment whose variability matches the variability of the relevant internal substates. The match may be approximate. For example, temperature settings may be discrete while the range of possible environmental temperatures is non-discrete (the reverse might be true in some machines, e.g. an analog representation of the number of objects in a container). Also the correspondence may not be one-to-one because of noise, lack of resolution, time-delays, projection from 3-D to 2-D, or other aspects of the measuring device or controller.

A thermostat whose behaviour depended on who was in the house, where they were, and how they felt, would require a far more complex set of internal states with more varied causal links. If the sensor produced not just a measurement but a structural description in a logical language then the causal links between the external and internal states could be very complex and indirect (e.g. going via a parser), and the sensing process could discard some incoming information (e.g. fine detail) and add other information (e.g. inferences about unobserved surfaces or likely behaviour of perceived objects).

13.1 *Loosening the links with belief-like states*

Now consider a more complex controller that can separately measure and control a range of properties $P_1, P_2, \ldots P_n$, of a machine or plant, but can only work on one of them at a time. For each such property P_i it has

(a) some kind of sensor S_i that will produce or change the corresponding belief-like substate B_i,

(b) a settable control knob (or set of keys, etc.) C_i that modifies the corresponding desire-like substate D_i, and

(c) an output-channel O_i that controls the relevant property P_i.

Suppose also that the machine can have only one such output channel turned on at a time, and has a selector that can switch between the different environmental properties to determine which is controlled.

For such a machine, substates still correspond to possible environments, except that it is no longer true *all the time* that each desire-like substate tends to change the environment to correspond to it. However, at any time when the i-th controller is disabled we can talk about the effect the i-th desire-like state Di *would have* in that context (including the belief-like state Bi) *if* the output channel Oi were selected. Similarly, if there are more possible desire-like states than output channels, then only a subset of the Di can be having an effect on the environment at any one time. This is clearly true of human beings: our legs, hands, mouths, etc. can be used to achieve different purposes at different times, but not all of them at once.

Likewise, if the different *sensors* can be temporarily disconnected, this suppresses the environment's tendency to influence belief-like substates, yet we can ask what the causal correspondence would be IF the particular sensor or controller were connected, and working normally. (The causal link is dispositional.)

Let us further loosen the connection between sensors and belief-like substates. There might be N different sensors, and K different belief-like states all derived (possibly via a neural net) from different combinations of the sensor readings, where K varies over time. So some of the substates are 'computed' on the basis of the signals received from several sensors, perhaps also using background information. An example could be a visual system building a 3-D scene description from a 2-D array of retinal information. If the process uses prior knowledge of the world, then that weakens the causal link between environment and belief-like states, e.g. when prior information is used to resolve ambiguities and reject some evidence (e.g. not seeing mistakes when proofreading).

Some of the belief-like substates thus produced may be stored for future use, instead of being 'overwritten' as new information comes via the sensors. Then some effects of the environment would be long delayed. Similarly if desires lead to plans for future execution.

Causal links between the environment and the current set of belief-like states can be far more complex and indirect than in a thermostat, where the environment has direct online control of the belief-like state. The more complex and indirect the process that creates internal structures from sensory input, the more scope there is for internal malfunction and context-sensitive effects. Then the set of counterfactual conditionals linking the internal states to the environment becomes even more complex, and the correspondence depends less and less on direct causal links and more and more on structural properties of the internal states that constrain possible interpretations. This helps to explain the possibility of false beliefs, which cannot normally occur in a thermostat.

13.2. *Loosening links with desire-like states*

Now, instead of a fixed set of desire-like states Di permanently connected to corresponding controllers or even a changing subset of Di directly connected to output channels, consider a high-level virtual machine containing a *variable-sized* store of desire-like states, created by 'motive-generator' rules, with context-sensitive 'motive-comparator' rules and decision-making rules for determining relative priorities of desire-like states, selecting a subset for action, retrieving or creating plans, and executing plans, possibly over an extended period with different plans interleaved if necessary. As with belief-like states, this extra complexity of processing (sketched in Sloman, 1987*b*, 1992*a*, 1993; Beaudoin 1994) reduces the directness of the causal links between desire-like states and states in the environment. Instead of a simple discrepancy measure sufficing to turn control signals on and off (as in the thermostat) it may require quite complex internal processing of the relationship between belief-like and desire-like states, checking whether a desire-like state is 'satisfied', or not. Moreover, where a desire is not satisfied, complex planning and reasoning, making use of belief-like states, may be needed to produce appropriate control signals. Causation is often roundabout.

There is clearly a huge variety of possible designs for mechanisms, some whose internal belief-like and desire-like substates are directly linked to the environment, and some where the links are very indirect, with varying numbers of intermediate stages in input channels or output channels and changing allocation of input channels and output channels to particular belief-like and desire-like states. Perhaps this provides one way of categorizing the control systems of biological organisms.

13.3 *Loose causal links, and semantics*

These complex designs undermine the notion that causal connections account for semantic relations. The loose and indirect causal links do not support fine detail of semantic relations. In thermostats where the belief-like states have dedicated input channels and the desire-like states have dedicated output channels, the semantic properties of different belief-like and desire-like states are determined almost entirely by their causal links. As we move away from such simplistic designs we encounter systems with more complex, loose, and indirect causal links. Increasingly, semantic significance of their states will depend on *structural* as opposed to causal properties, i.e. we get closer to the Tarskian kind of semantics. However, we also find more and more scope for indeterminacy in the semantics, because of the weak and indirect causal links, and inability of structure to determine reference uniquely.

The more indirect and abstract semantics, together with generative capabilities in the mechanisms, can also explain the use of substates that refer to things remote in space and time or even to possibilities that are never realized (e.g. a bit-pattern addressing a non-existent location). This is an essential requirement for intelligent planning. The ability to give an internal substate a 'supposition-like' instead of a 'belief-like' role depends on the causal links with the environment being far less direct than in the thermostat.

I conjecture that biological evolution includes developments along the directions indicated here, with decreasing causal coupling of internal and external states going hand in hand with increasing structural complexity and functional differentiation of internal virtual substates, and longer-term storage replacing online control. If these 'design-space' ideas can be used to distinguish different possible kinds of machines, perhaps they are also important for understanding different kinds of nervous systems?

14. LOOP-CLOSING MODELS

Can we combine structural and causal ideas and specify a general semantic relation between substates in a behaving system and what they refer to? Consider an environment E containing an agent A, whose functional architecture supports belief-like and desire-like substates. Suppose A uses similar substructures for both, just as a machine can use bit-patterns both for addresses and for instructions. Then we can define the class of possible 'loop-closing' models for a set of structures S by considering a set of possible environments E satisfying certain conditions, when the action-producing mechanisms, the sensors, and the correspondence tests (section 8.6, above) are working normally:

(a) States in E will *tend* to select certain instances of S for A's belief-like substates.

(b) If Si is part of a desire-like state of A and E is in state Ei, and A's correspondence tests show a discrepancy between Ei and Si, then (unless A's other belief-like and desire-like states interfere) A will *tend* to produce some environmental state Ej in E which *tends* to pass A's 'correspondence' test for Si.

(c) If that happens Ej will tend to produce a new belief-like state in A.

So there are dispositional causal loops through which A's desire-like states tend to influence the environment, and the environment tends to influence A's belief-like states.

I repeatedly say 'tend to' to indicate that there are many additional factors that can interfere with the tendency, such as conflicts of desires, perceptual defects, accidents, wishful thinking, bad planning, and other common human failings. So these are very loose regularities, and cannot be taken to define internal states in any precise way. None of this presupposes that A is rational. It merely constitutes a partial specification of what 'belief-like' and 'desire-like' mean. However, a full specification will be relative to an architecture, within which functional roles can be defined more precisely.

More complex causal loops involving the environment will be involved in the way A's desire-like states are changed. This can involve internal-motive generators, urgency, importance, and relative priorities (Beaudoin, 1994; Beaudoin and Sloman, 1993). In simple designs, output is directly and continuously controlled by a discrepancy between desire-like and belief-like state, whereas in more complex cases the desire-like and belief-like states, together produce *chains* of actions, often specified in advance as part of the process of selection. In other words, advance planning is sometimes used. But not all architectures can support this. In those that do, the causal loops between states are more indirect.

14.1. *Causal loops and limited rationality*

If A were completely rational and always had consistent motives and beliefs, then the tendencies mentioned above would be strict, whereas in real agents conflicts and errors occur, and more or less irrational behaviour is possible. In extreme cases people have to be forcibly restrained from harming themselves. Even when interactions between sensory input, belief-like and desire-like states, and motor output are not rationally comprehensible, this does not mean that internal states have no semantics.

For these reasons I think that any attempt to *define* mental states or processes in terms of rationality or even approximate rationality is unacceptable. This undermines Dennett's notion (1978, 1987) of the 'intentional stance', which requires agents to be rational in order to have states with semantic content. The mechanisms and internal states that underly rationality can sometimes interact in bizarre ways to produce totally different results. We need a theory that explains both the rational and the irrational behaviour on equal terms, for instance an account of an architecture composed of interacting information-processing subsystems, that sometimes function as required for rationality, but not always. Software engineers know how to build such systems, using not the intentional stance but the design stance applied to information-processing level descriptions (Sloman, 1994).

14.2. *Local vs. global semantic consistency*

For a really complex agent with a large set of belief-like substates S there may be no possible environment providing a model for the *total* set S, because the current beliefs are globally inconsistent. Similarly the desires may conflict with one another and with beliefs. People may want things which they know to be incompatible. The agent may be unable to detect all inconsistencies: for doing so reliably in large systems is computationally intractable, and therefore neither evolution nor robot designers can impose that requirement. In such systems semantic relations have to be local, or piecemeal: only fragments of the system have models, not the whole system. Perhaps this works because different subsets of the system are fully 'active' at different times, like the scientist who prays on Sundays or the kind father who bullies his employees.

14.3. *The irrelevance of history*

The helplessness of human neonates tempts many to assume their minds are empty. This may be part of the strong tendency to require concepts to have been derived from individual experience. But a newborn foal can run with the herd within hours, and could not possibly have learnt all the required concepts of 3-D structure and motion and action. So if we accept that it sees and that seeing is an intentional state, the interpretive concepts underlying that state need not come from the individual's interaction with the environment: the interactions of long-dead ancestors may suffice, as they do for the foal.

But even that cannot be a *logical requirement*. Suppose that by a highly improbable fluke of mutation an animal were born with the visual and action capabilities of a foal *without* this being the result of previous selective pressures. Would the new sport see or have intentions relating to the environment as well as a new foal? Surely the *current* internal structures, mechanisms, and causal links would suffice, for all practical purposes, without the normal causal history. (Whether such a mutation is likely to happen is irrelevant; cf. Young, 1994).

No doubt some philosophers will retort: 'this animal does not "Really" see, or think, or take decisions, despite appearances, because it does not have the right evolutionary history.' We should resist disputes about essentially trivial matters of 'correct' definition. To avoid such disputes, we can define two notions of 'see': one of which (to seeH) requires a normal historical source, while the other (to seeA) is a-historical. Apart from that there is no difference in the details of the capabilities, i.e. how well they enable the organism to survive. Those of us who use 'see' to mean 'seeA', have a ready-made way of talking usefully about new specimens whose perceptual ability is not rooted in evolutionary history. Those who insist on using 'see' to mean only 'seeH' will find it very awkward to describe.

14.4. *Semantics and inaccessible referents*

A requirement that semantic relations depend on causal links that preserve a correspondence between representing and represented things obviously fails for semantic states referring to remote parts of the universe, the distant past, the distant future, unrealized possibilities, etc. These referents are not capable of directly engaging causally with current beliefs or desires, though they may be linked through counterfactual conditionals about what would happen if the agent had a different location in space and time. However, if one tries to work out what would be the case if the agent were sufficiently close to the remote place or time for direct causal interaction, it may be impossible to decide what else would be the case: an extreme example of the 'Frame' problem. For agents that are capable of using a generative notation with inference techniques, it may be better to define the possible models in Tarskian terms, using a generative compositional semantics, with the restriction that the models contain submodels in the environment that act as causal loop-closing models, to select the right referents.

Not all organisms and machines have the internal architecture required for coping with this kind of semantic relation. For those that don't, any kind of semantics that they support will be simplified compared with human capabilities. Unlike Fodor (1987), we do not require all representing notations to be generative, although a system with generative capabilities will, of course, have more scope for creative intelligence and coping with unexpected situations, as well as thoughts and desires concerning remote places.

There need be no sharp boundary to the class of possible environments that are models of a sophisticated agent's beliefs or desires, i.e. the semantics for the internal states will be indeterminate in various ways. This in itself should not disturb us if we are interested in explaining human intelligence, since there is plenty of evidence that human languages (and probably internal representations too) are indeterminate in various ways. (For example, how big is a big man? How much water must fall on a rainy day? Is a circle an ellipse? Is it 3 o'clock on the moon? Are liquids mixtures or compounds? Where are the boundaries between species of birds?) Semantic indeterminacy is part of the human condition. It may be unavoidable in robots.

15. WORK TO BE DONE

The ideas presented so far concerning semantics are both tentative and lacking in precision. Considerable research is needed to clarify and extend them. In particular:

- Unlike the languages discussed by Tarski and most logicians there is no need for a fixed precisely delimited syntax to be used: intelligent systems can creatively extend the variety of representing structures they use, and humans frequently do this.
- The semantics assigned to particular notations by an individual need not be fixed: even one-off interpretations are possible (including 'let's pretend' games by children). It is tricky to fit this into an analysis that is very dependent on counterfactual conditionals, which, in turn, depend on lawlike generalizations. (This example of 'one-off' semantics refutes many philosophical theories of meaning!)
- The notation can include context-sensitive elements whose semantic role needs special treatment, like the indexicals whose denotation depends on the instance of use: 'this', 'now', 'I', 'we', 'he', etc.
- Semantic relations may depend not only on an individual's mechanisms and functional architecture, but also a social system or culture involving other intelligent individuals. This can determine the 'scope' of concepts, like 'valley', 'healthy', 'marriage', 'war', and 'honourable'.

16. CONCLUSION

Although computation has had a powerful catalytic effect in extending our ideas concerning possible mechanisms, we can now abandon the notion that the concept of computation is the only or even the central foundation for the study of mind. Instead we need to look at a whole variety of architectures and mechanisms, from the design standpoint, to see what kinds of more or less mind-like systems they can support. This was option (*c*) defined in the introductory section.

I've offered the beginnings of a conceptual map, albeit still a blurred and incomplete one, into which we can fit many kinds of natural and artificial mechanisms and processes that could be useful for intelligent systems. Some will be closely related to our precise notion of computation, and some will not. Whether they are or are not is of little importance for the question whether they provide the kind of functionality required for various sorts of intelligent capabilities, except where we are studying intelligent systems with particular computational requirements, e.g. proving theorems, making plans, etc.

I have not argued (like Searle) that a digital computer cannot understand symbols it uses. I simply draw attention to the need to consider a broader range of machine types than simply Turing-equivalent machines, for the purpose of explaining or designing intelligent systems that can function as effectively as we do in our world. We also need a range of mental concepts corresponding to each of our everyday concepts like 'understand', 'refer', 'believe', 'desire', 'perceive', etc. The different concepts will be grounded in capabilities supported by different architectures.

This is not a philosophical argument about 'correct' concepts to use, but an engineering argument about the appropriateness of different (animal or artificial) designs for different tasks. Exploring such relations (mappings between design-space and niche space) is part of the goal of AI (Sloman, 1995a). I claim that also provides the best framework for philosophy of mind.

I have shifted the emphasis away from computation towards a general notion of mechanism because it is hard precisely to define a concept of computation that is adequate as a non-circular, non-trivial foundation for explaining mentality. So the hoped-for single boundary between computations and non-computations is replaced by sets of features of computation-like mechanisms defining a *variety* of design boundaries with different implications, which we still need to explore. The notion of computation can then be replaced by a new taxonomy of designs, covering a more general class of architectures and mechanisms, which may lead us both to consider new designs and to improve our understanding of old ones.

On this basis we can explore a variety of more or less rich semantic notions, some relatively closely tied to causal links with the environment, some closer to the structural relations defined by Tarski (not to be confused with isomorphism!) and some linked to functional roles within the architecture. Mixtures of these different kinds of semantics can be instantiated in machines with different sorts of architectures and mechanisms.

Showing in detail how different subsets of machine types can support different forms of intelligence is a task remaining to be done, though some fragments are reported in work listed in the references. This work needs to be related to studies of human psychology, neuroscience, biological evolution, and comparative ethology.

REFERENCES

Ballard, D. H., and Brown, C. M. (1982), *Computer Vision*, Prentice-Hall: Englewood Cliffs, NJ.

Beaudoin, L. P. (1994), 'A Design-Based Study of Autonomous Agents', PhD thesis, School of Computer Science, University of Birmingham.

—— and Sloman, A. (1993), 'A Study of Motive Processing and Attention', in A. Sloman, D. Hogg, G. Humphreys, D. Partridge, and A. Ramsay (eds.), *Prospects for Artificial Intelligence*, IOS Press, Amsterdam, 229–38.

Clark, A. (1988), 'Computation, Connectionism and Content', in Yves Kodratoff (ed.), *8th European Conference on AI*, Munich.

Dennett, D. C. (1978), *Brainstorms*, Bradford Books, Montgomery, Vt., and Harvester Press, Hassocks, Sussex.

—— (1987), *The Intentional Stance*, MIT Press/Bradford Books, Cambridge, Mass.

Fields, C. (1996), 'Measurement and Computational Description', this volume, pp. 165–77.

Fodor, J. A. (1987), *Psychosemantics: The Problem of Meaning in the Philosophy of Mind*, Bradford Books, MIT Press, Cambridge, Mass.

Funt, B. V. (1980), 'Problem-Solving with Diagrammatic Representations', in *Artificial Intelligence*, 13/3: 201–30; repr. in R. J. Brachman and H. J. Levesque (eds.), *Readings in Knowledge Representation*, Morgan Kaufmann, Los Altos, Calif., 1985.

Haugeland, John (1985), *Artificial Intelligence: The Very Idea*, Bradford Books, MIT Press, Cambridge, Mass.

Nagel, E., and Newman, J. R. (1958), *Gödel's Proof*, Routledge & Kegan Paul, London.

Pylyshyn, Zenon W. (1984), *Computation and Cognition: Toward a Foundation for Cognitive Science*, Bradford Books, MIT Press, Cambridge, Mass.

Searle, John R. (1980), 'Minds, Brains, and Programs', in *The Behavioural and Brain Sciences*, 3: 417–24.

Sloman, A. (1971), 'Interactions between Philosophy and A.I.: The Role of Intuition and Non-Logical Reasoning in Intelligence', in *Proc. 2nd International Joint Conference on Artificial Intelligence*, London 1971; repr. in *Artificial Intelligence*, 2(1971), 209–25, and in J. M. Nicholas (ed.), *Images, Perception, and Knowledge*, Reidel, Dordrecht, 1977: 121–38.

—— (1978), *The Computer Revolution in Philosophy: Philosophy, Science and Models of Mind*, Harvester Press, Hassocks, and Humanities Press, New York.

—— (1985*a*), 'Why We Need Many Knowledge Representation Formalisms', in M. A. Bramer (ed.), *Research and Development in Expert Systems*, Cambridge University Press, 163–83; also Cognitive Science Research paper No. 52, Sussex University.

—— (1985*b*), 'What Enables a Machine to Understand?' in *Proceedings 9th International Joint Conference on AI*, Los Angeles.

—— (1986), 'Did Searle Attack Strong Strong or Weak Strong AI', in A. G. Cohn and J. R. Thomas (eds.), *Artificial Intelligence and Its Applications*, Wiley & Sons, New York.

—— (1987*a*), 'Reference without Causal Links', in L. Steels, B. du Boulay, and D. Hogg (eds.), *Advances in Artificial Intelligence-II* (Proc 7th European Conference on AI, Brighton, 1986), North-Holland, Amsterdam, 369–81.

—— (1987*b*), 'Motives, Mechanisms, and Emotions', in *Cognition and Emotion: i, Emotion and Cognition*, 217–33; repr. in M. A. Boden (ed.), *The Philosophy of Artificial Intelligence*, Oxford University Press, 231–47.

—— (1989), 'On Designing a Visual System: Towards a Gibsonian Computational Model of Vision, in *Journal of Experimental and Theoretical AI*, 1/4: 289–37; also available as Cognitive Science Research paper No. 146, University of Sussex.

—— (1992*a*), 'Prolegomena to a Theory of Communication and Affect', in A. Ortony, J. Slack, and O. Stock (eds.), *A.I. and Cognitive Science Perspectives on Communication*, Springer, Heidelberg; (also available as Cognitive Science Research, paper No. 194, University of Sussex.

—— (1992*b*), 'The Emperor's Real Mind', review of Roger Penrose's *The Emperor's New Mind: Concerning Computers, Minds and the Laws of Physics*, in *Artificial Intelligence* 56: 355–96; also Cognitive Science Research Paper, Birmingham University.

—— (1993), 'The Mind as a Control System', in C. Hookway and D. Petersen (eds.), *Philosophy and the Cognitive Sciences*, Cambridge University Press, Cambridge, 69–110.

—— (1994*a*), 'Explorations in Design Space', in A. G. Cohn (ed.), *Proc ECAI94, 11th European Conference on Artificial Intelligence*, Wiley, New York, 578–82.

—— (1994*b*), 'Computational Modeling of Motive-Management Processes', In N. Frijda (ed.), *Proceedings of the Conference of the International Society for Research in Emotions*, ISRE Publications, Cambridge, 344–8.

—— (1994*c*), 'Semantics in An Intelligent Control System', in *Philosophical Transactions of the Royal Society A: Physical Sciences and Engineering*, 349: 43–58.

—— (1995*a*), 'Exploring Design Space and Niche Space', in *Proceedings 5th Scandinavian Conf. on AI*, Trondheim, IOS Press, Amsterdam.

—— (1995*b*), 'A Philosophical Encounter: An Interactive Presentation of Some of the Key Philosophical Problems in AI and AI Problems in Philosophy', *Proceedings of the 14th International Joint Conference on AI*, Montreal.

—— (1995*c*), 'Towards a General Theory of Representations', in D. M. Peterson (ed.), *Forms of Representation*, Intellect Press.

Smith, B. C., 'The Semantics of Clocks', in James H. Fetzer (ed.), *Aspects of Artificial Intelligence*, Kluwer, Dordrecht, 3–31.

Tarski, A. (1956), 'The Concept of Truth in Formalized Languages', in *Logic, Semantics, Metamathematics*, trans. by J. H. Woodger, Clarendon Press, Oxford, 152–278.

Taylor, C. N. (1992), 'A Formal Logical Analysis of Causal Relations', D. Phil thesis, School of Cognitive and Computing Sciences, Cognitive Science Research paper No. 257, University of Sussex.

Turing, A. M. (1950), 'Computing Machinery and Intelligence', *Mind*, 59: 433–60.

Wright, I. P., Sloman, A., and Beaudoin, L. P., 'The Architectural Basis for Grief', presented at Geneva Emotions Week, 8–13 Apr. 1995.

Young, R. A. (1994), 'The Mentality of Robots', *Proceedings of the Aristotelian Society*, Supplementary Vol. 68: 199–227.

The Demise of the Turing Machine in Complexity Theory

IAIN A. STEWART

———◆———

INTRODUCTION

Computational complexity theory is essentially an aspect of recursive function theory involving the consideration of specified resources. These resources are usually those of time and space, where time and space are defined relative to the model of computation involved. Given that the model of computation used in recursive function theory is often the Turing machine (with most models related via the Church–Turing thesis, of course), it is not surprising that this model plays a central role in complexity theory, with the notion of time being the number of moves in a computation and that of space being the number of tape cells used. It is usually the case that restrictions are imposed on the Turing-machine model and that relationships between the classes of Turing machines so obtained are studied. For example, a well-known complexity class is P, the class of all deterministic polynomial-time Turing machines, obtained by imposing the restriction that this class should consist of those Turing machines which halt on all inputs and expend time polynomial in the length of the input string in any computation (the polynomial is fixed). Another well-known complexity class is NP, the class of non-deterministic polynomial-time Turing machines, defined 'similarly' to that above except that here the Turing machines are allowed to make non-deterministic guesses (we enclose the word 'similarly' in quotation marks as a simple comparison of the two models shows that one must eventually halt whilst the other need not do so: however, given that one intends to introduce non-determinism yet retain the polynomial-time bounds, then the model so obtained appears to be the natural analogue of the deterministic one). It is a long-standing open question in complexity theory as to whether the Turing machines in NP are strictly more powerful than those in P: this is usually referred to as the P = ? = NP problem.[1]

Whilst complexity theory is practised purely for aesthetic reasons, the consideration of complexity classes such as P and NP does have practical implications. For example, public-key cryptosystems have been devised based on the fact that if Turing machines in NP are strictly more powerful than those in P, then certain problems will take millions of years to solve using current technology. However, if this hypothesis is false then these public-key cryptosystems are easily broken. These cryptosystems are currently used by, for example, banks, for the secure transfer of funds, and so the consideration of the above (apparently pure) complexity-theoretic problem *could* make someone extremely rich, although probably somewhat illegally!

Given that the P = ? = NP problem (along with others concerning alternative complexity classes), when defined with respect to the Turing-machine model, appears to be extremely difficult (so difficult that even merchant bankers are not prepared to believe that it will be solved in the near future), many people have considered these complexity classes with respect to other models of computation. It turns out that when we consider these other (reasonable) models of computation and restrict these models to operate in polynomial-time, distinguishing between deterministic and non-deterministic such models, then we obtain the same complexity classes, P and NP. (We are now considering our models to be language recognizers, and so equivalently decision problem-solvers, and we are equating a given machine with the problem it solves: hence, complexity classes are classes of decision problems. It is the long-term goal of complexity theory to detail the inclusion relations between the naturally defined classes of problems arising from the consideration of resource-bounded Turing machines.) So the definition of these complexity classes appears to be, in some sense, model-independent. It is natural to ask whether these notions can be captured without reference to an obvious model of computation, and this is where the idea of logical specificity comes in.

---

[1] For more information concerning complexity theory, the reader is referred to R. Sommerhalder and S. C. van Westrhenen, *The Theory of Computability: Programs, Machines, Effectiveness*, and *Feasibility*, Addison-Wesley, 1988.

In recent years (the word 'recent' has different meanings as to whether one is a mathematician or a computer scientist), computer scientists have been infatuated with the problem of automated theorem-proving which involves the consideration of the logical specifications of problems. Whilst many remain sceptical as to how useful this approach will be, the consideration of the specificity of a problem has led to important new results in complexity theory.

In 1974, Fagin[2] published a paper detailing a characterization of the class of problems NP as those problems which can be specified using existential second-order logic. This led researchers, such as Immerman and Gurevich, to seek characterizations of other complexity classes as classes of problems specifiable in some logic. For example, complexity classes such as P and NL (the class of problems solvable by a non-deterministic logarithmic-space Turing machine) were characterized as being those classes of problems specifiable in first-order logic with successor and the least fixed-point operator, and first-order logic with successor and the transitive closure operator, respectively. This work led to the (positive) solution, by Immerman in 1988, of a twenty-year-old open problem concerning context-sensitive languages[3] (a problem which many had conjectured to have a negative solution, and had viewed as a problem with a degree of difficulty along the lines of the P = ? = NP problem).

It should also be mentioned that the well-known logical quantifiers $\forall$ and $\exists$ have also been used, in a paper by Wrathall, to characterize the polynomial-time hierarchy, PH (essentially the complexity-theoretic analogue of the Kleene hierarchy of recursive function theory). Moreover, probabilistic quantifiers, such as the one meaning 'for more than one half of the values the following holds', have been used to define probabilistic complexity classes, whose relationship with the more well-established complexity classes has been studied (this is particularly important given that certain 'hard' problems, for which no appropriate deterministic algorithm

---

[2] References and results concerning the logical specification of complexity classes can be found in I. A. Stewart, 'Logical and Schematic Characterization of Complexity Classes', *Acta Informatica* 30(1993): 61–87. We add that it is not necessarily the case that a result appearing in the text is due to the author of this reference.

[3] It should be pointed out that this problem was solved independently by R. Szelepcsenyi: see the reference given in note 2.

has been discovered, have been solved by algorithms which are allowed to 'toss a coin').

There are many advantages of characterizing a complexity class as a class of problems specifiable in a certain logic. One has already been mentioned: the new characterization provides additional insight (for example, Immerman's result mentioned above). But perhaps the most important, in our view, is that natural problems can be considered as problems *per se* and not, as is the case when our model of computation is the Turing machine, as encodings of problems over some finite alphabet, often the alphabet consisting of os and 1s. Consequently, information has no chance of being hidden by an encoding scheme.

At present, when developing some algorithm, the developer tends to think at a high level, and, indeed, the algorithm is usually presented in some high-level programming formalism, not as a Turing machine program (we say 'at present' as it may be the case that developers will learn to think differently in future; for example, with the advent of parallel computation). The Turing machine implementation has only been necessary when one wished to consider the complexity of the algorithm in more detail. However, specifying problems logically gives us a mathematically exact, machine-independent means for describing algorithms, whilst retaining the high-level structure of the problem, with this mathematical exactitude enabling us to examine the complexity of the problem. A logical specification is particularly amenable to manipulation, and so to improvement; for example, normal form theorems abound for various logics.

As we shall see, another advantage of this (high-level) logical specification is that we can often effectively transform the specification into an executable high-level program, and vice versa. The practical advantages are obvious, for what use is a Turing-machine specification of an algorithm when upon our desk-top sits a microcomputer able to run Pascal programs? Given the above relationship between logical specifications and high-level programs, and the fact that the detailed complexity of a logically specified problem can often be deduced from the specification, the writing appears to be on the wall as far as the Turing machine is concerned (well, as the main model of computation in complexity theory anyway). This new approach to ascertaining the complexity of problems gives us additional structure to work with, the power to manipulate specifications and programs more easily, and a practical means of automatically implementing our algorithms.

All this might lead one to believe that specifying problems logically can solve many of our complexity-theoretic problems. However, some qualification of the above discussion is in order. First, the problems under consideration must be of a certain complexity for the above effective procedure (taking specifications to programs) to work. In particular, they must be able to be solved by a polynomial-space Turing machine; that is, they must be in the complexity class PSPACE. Secondly, the program obtained by the above effective procedure is generally particularly unsubtle, with lots of scope for (non-effective) improvement. Thirdly, our logics are often such that the specification of a problem is tantamount to a description of the algorithm (for our logics are often obtained from first-order logic by adding on relational operators and well-known constructs from programming languages such as arrays).

Having possibly dispelled any initial elation by the previous paragraph, we shall now attempt to reinstate some. First, the complexity class PSPACE is extremely rich in that a lot of the naturally occurring problems of computational complexity theory reside in that class. Secondly, even though the program obtained, by an effective translation of a logical specification, is usually unsubtle, the prospect of (non-effectively) improving it compares favourably with that of improving a Turing machine program: a high-level program has obvious structure whereas a Turing machine program generally does not. Also, the theory behind the transformation from the logical specification to the program enables us to prove normal form theorems for both the logic and the program (with the prospect that lower bounds for certain problems may be deduced). Thirdly, by adopting the Turing machine as our primary model of computation, we often see the need to introduce new concepts, and consequently suffer from a 'can't-see-the-woods-for-the-trees' malady; that is, a logical perspective enables us to dispense with the novel, but in some cases unnecessary, introductions.

We end this introduction with a remark concerning the teaching of complexity theory. It is often the case that students do not see the need for the study of such a subject, especially as it is often based around what they see as an archaic model of computation such as the Turing machine. They often regard the complexity of a problem as a property dreamt up by the theoreticians to keep themselves in work, and take a lot of convincing that the subject has any relevance to modern-day computers (as do some of the more established members of the computing science fraternity). Teaching basic complexity theory using logical specification and a high-level analysis would, we believe, go far to dispelling some of these beliefs, especially as logic is widely believed to be an essential tool in computing science in general.

SOME DETAILS

Having, we hope, whet the reader's appetite for the mathematics behind the logical specification of complexity classes, we now endeavour to give an introduction to the topic, with a view to presenting some recent results. This account is concerned only with the mathematical niceties, and the reader is referred back to the introduction for the motivation.

A *vocabulary* τ is a tuple of constant and relation symbols, and a *finite structure* S over τ is a tuple consisting of a *universe* (that is, a finite initial segment of the natural numbers), together with constants and relations corresponding to the symbols of τ. We denote the set of all finite structures over τ by STRUCT(τ). For example, if τ_0 is the vocabulary consisting entirely of the binary relation symbol $\underline{E}$, then STRUCT(τ_0) can be considered as the set of all finite directed graphs (up to isomorphism).

We think of a *problem* as being a subset of structures of STRUCT(τ), for some vocabulary τ. For example, we might define a problem as being the subset of STRUCT(τ_0) consisting of those structures which, when considered as directed graphs, are connected.

It would be preferable for our problems to be specified in a rather more exact manner than a sentence of English. To this end, we consider first-order logic with equality, augmented with two new constant symbols, $\underline{o}$ and $\underline{max}$: this logic is denoted FO. We insist that given some formula $\phi \in$ FO and some appropriate structure S, the constants $\underline{o}$ and $\underline{max}$ are always interpreted as the first, that is o, and the last, that is $n-1$, say, elements of the universe of S, respectively (here, the universe of S is $\{o, 1, \ldots, n-1\}$ and we say that S is of *size n*). In future we do not distinguish between constants (etc.) and constant symbols (etc.), and so omit the underlining.

For example, consider the following sentence $\phi \in$ FO over the vocabulary τ_0:

$$\phi \equiv \forall x \exists y_1 \exists y_2 \exists y_3 [E(x,y_1) \wedge E(x,y_2) \wedge E(x,y_3) \wedge$$
$$y_1 \neq y_2 \wedge y_1 \neq y_3 \wedge y_2 \neq y_3 \wedge$$
$$\forall z[E(x,z) \Rightarrow [z = y_1 \vee z = y_2 \vee z = y_3]]].$$

If $S \in$ STRUCT(τ_0), then the interpretation ϕ^S of ϕ in S is valid if and only if the directed graph S is such that each vertex has out-degree exactly 3. If this is so, then we write $S \models \phi$. In general, we say that some sentence $\phi \in$ FO, over the vocabulary τ, *specifies* the problem $\{S \in \text{STRUCT}(\tau): S \models \phi\}$.

When used to specify problems, FO is extremely limited; for example, the problem $\{S \in \text{STRUCT}(\tau_0): S$ has an even number of vertices$\}$ cannot be specified in FO. Consequently, we choose to extend first-order logic in various different ways.

For one, we can introduce a binary relation symbol succ which is always interpreted as the successor relation; that is, $\text{succ}(x,y)$ holds in some structure if and only if $y = x + 1$. We can also introduce the transitive closure operator TC which, given a first-order formula ϕ regarded as being over k-tuples of variables x and y, enables us to form the relation $\text{TC}[\lambda x,y \ \phi(x,y)]$ which is interpreted as being the reflexive, transitive closure of ϕ (when ϕ is considered to represent a binary relation over k-tuples). We denote the logic formed by the addition of the successor relation symbol (resp. transitive closure operator) by $(\text{FO} + \leq)$ (resp. $(\text{FO} + \text{TC})$), and the logic formed by the addition of both by $(\text{FO} + \leq + \text{TC})$.

It should be clear that the problem $\{S \in \text{STRUCT}(\tau_0): S$ has an even number of vertices$\}$ can be specified in $(\text{FO} + \leq)$. Further, we can show that if $\phi \in (\text{FO} + \leq + \text{TC})$ is a sentence specifying some problem, over some vocabulary, then the same problem can be specified by a formula of $(\text{FO} + \leq + \text{TC})$, over the same vocabulary, of the form $\text{TC}[\lambda x,y \ \psi(x,y)](o, \max)$, where o (resp. max) are tuples of the constant symbol o (resp. max) and ψ is a quantifier-free first-order formula expressible in disjunctive normal form. For example, the problem $\{S \in \text{STRUCT}(\tau_0): S$ is connected$\}$ can be specified by the formula:

$$\phi \equiv \forall x \forall y TC[\lambda x, y \ E(x,y)] \ (x,y),$$

and, by the above remark, ϕ is equivalent to a formula of the form $TC[\lambda x, y \psi(x,y)]$ (o, max) (with ψ as above).

We can also show that the class of problems specifiable by some formula of (FO + $\leqq$ + TC) is exactly the complexity class NL. Similarly, by consideration of a deterministic transitive closure operator DTC, we can show that, as classes of problems, L = (FO + $\leqq$ + DTC), where L is the class of problems recognizable by a deterministic logarithmic-space Turing machine (we also mention that the class of problems specifiable by the logic (FO + $\leqq$ + LFP), obtained by augmenting (FO + $\leqq$) with a least fixed-point operator LFP, coincides with P).

In order to 'capture' the complexity class PSPACE by some logic, we amend (FO + $\leqq$) by introducing the notion of arrays to obtain the logic (FO + A + $\leqq$). In particular, to any well-formed formula of (FO + $\leqq$) can be tagged a set of array assignments, to obtain a well-formed formula of (FO + A + $\leqq$). These well-formed formulae of (FO + A + $\leqq$) can then be used to build more well-formed formulae of (FO + A + $\leqq$), using the usual connectives and quantifiers. For example, if $\phi \in$ (FO + $\leqq$) and $\{A[x] := y, B[u,v] := w\}$ is a set of array assignments, then $\phi \mid \{A[x] := y, B[u,v] := w\}$ is a well-formed formula of (FO + A + $\leqq$).

The semantics of (FO + A + $\leqq$) are, generally, rather complicated and so are omitted, suffice to say that the meanings of most formulae are straightforward and that the semantics of (FO + A + $\leqq$) are inherited by the logic (FO + A). The transitive closure operator can then be introduced as before (again, with complicated semantics) to obtain the logic (FO + A + $\leqq$ + TC). As an example as to how meaning is given to a formula of (FO + A + $\leqq$ + TC), consider the problem, over the vocabulary τ_o, specified by the formula:

$$TC[\lambda x, y, x', y' \phi(x,y,x',y')] \ (o, o, max, max),$$

where:

$$\phi \equiv [E(x,x') \land x' \neq o \land x' \neq x \land A[x'] = o \land y = o \land$$
$$y' = o] \mid \{A[x] := x'\} \lor [E(x,x') \land x' = o \land$$
$$\forall z(z \neq x \Rightarrow A[z] = o) \land y = o \land y' = max] \mid \{A[x] := o\} \lor$$
$$[x = o \land y = max \land x' = max \land y' = max] \mid \{\}.$$

Here, ϕ is the disjunction of three sub-formulae, each of which is a conjunction of simple predicates, possibly tagged with an assignment. Essentially, in some structure S of size n, ϕ represents a directed graph with vertices corresponding to binary tuples of elements of $\{0, 1, \ldots, n-1\}$, along with three rules for moving from one vertex to another; for example, according to the first rule above, if we are at the vertex (x, y) and:

$$E(x,x') \wedge x' \neq 0 \wedge x' \neq x \wedge A[x'] = 0 \wedge y = 0 \wedge y' = 0$$

holds for some vertex (x',y'), then we can move to the vertex (x',y'), and a 'global scoreboard', A, is altered according to the tagged assignment (this scoreboard entry may be referred to later by this and the other rules). So, for any structure $S \in \text{STRUCT}(\tau_0)$:

$$S \models \text{TC}[\lambda x,y,x',y' \ \phi(x,y,x',y')](0,0,\text{max},\text{max})$$

if and only if:

the directed graph S has a Hamiltonian circuit.

Now, having introduced our logics, we consider our high-level program specifications; that is, our *program schemes*. For some vocabulary τ, the class of program schemes $\text{NPSA}(\tau)$ is defined as follows:

(a) the *atoms* of $\text{NPSA}(\tau)$ consist of the variables and the constant symbols of $\tau \cup \{0, \text{max}\}$;

(b) the *assignment instructions* of $\text{NPSA}(\tau)$ are of the form:

var := atom, A[atom, . . . , atom] := atom, guess(var),

where atom and var are as expected and A is an array symbol;

(c) the *test instructions* of $\text{NPSA}(\tau)$ are of the form:

WHILE t DO $i_1, i_2, \ldots, i_k$ OD,

for some $k \geq 0$ and instructions $i_1, i_2, \ldots, i_k$, where t is a conjunction of simple tests, and their negations, of the form:

atom = atom, R(atom, . . . , atom),
atom = A[atom, . . . , atom],

with atom as expected, A an array symbol, and R a relation symbol of τ.

Each program scheme is a list of instructions of the above form, with the list beginning (resp. ending) with the instruction input($x_1, \ldots, x_k$) (resp. output($x_1, \ldots, x_k$)), for some variables $x_1, \ldots,$ x_k termed the *input/output variables*. We write:

$$\text{NPSA} = \{\rho \in \text{NPSA}(\tau): \tau \text{ is some vocabulary}\}.$$

Given some appropriate structure S, the interpretation of some program scheme ρ in S is obtained by replacing each constant and relation symbol of ρ by the corresponding constant or relation of S. We assume that the arrays and the input/output variables are all initially set at o, and that should an uninitialized variable be encountered then the program 'hangs forever'; that is, it does not terminate.

We can use our program schemes to specify problems as follows: for some program scheme ρ and appropriate structure S, we say that ρ *accepts* S, and write $\text{S} \models \rho$, if for some sequence of guesses (where the instruction *guess* appears), the program halts with the input/output variables set at *max*: consequently, each program scheme determines a problem. We denote by DPSA(τ) those program schemes of NPSA(τ) in which the instruction *guess* does not appear. As before, we can incorporate a successor operation $y := x + 1$ into our program schemes denoting the resulting class by, say, DPSA($\leqq$). Also, if we leave out the notion of arrays from the program schemes of NPSA($\leqq$), then we obtain the class of program schemes NPS($\leqq$) (the same goes for the other classes introduced above).

For example, consider the following program scheme $\rho \in$ NPSA($\leqq$)(τ_o):

```
input(x)
A[o] := max
WHILE x ≠ o DO
    guess(y)
    IF x ≠ y ∧ E(x,y) ∧ A[y] = o THEN
        A[y] := max
        x := y
    FI
    OD
z := o
x := o
```

```
WHILE x ≠ max ∧ z = 0 DO
  IF A[x] = max THEN
    x := x + 1
  ELSE
    z := max
  FI
OD
IF z = 0 ∧ A[max] = max THEN
  x := max
ELSE
  x := 0
output(x)
```

(We remark that we can concoct the usual IF-statements within the formalism of NPSA($\leq$), and that we present the program scheme in the usual programming style to improve readability.) Then clearly for some structure $S \in$ STRUCT(τ_0), $S \models \rho$ if and only if S has a Hamiltonian circuit.

It can be shown that the following classes of problems are all identical:

(FO + A + $\leq$ + TC), (FO + A + $\leq$ + DTC), NPSA($\leq$),
DPSA($\leq$), PSPACE,

as are

(FO + $\leq$ + DTC), DPS($\leq$), and L,

and

(FO + $\leq$ + TC), NPS($\leq$), and NL,

respectively. In fact, there is an effective procedure which, given some sentence ϕ of (FO + A + $\leq$ + TC), over the vocabulary τ, first of all converts it into normal form (that is, into a sentence of the form TC[$\lambda x, y \psi(x, y)$] (o,max), where ψ has no occurences of the operator TC and is quantifier-free) and then into a program scheme ρ of NPSA($\leq$) (τ), where the problem specified by ϕ and ρ is the same. (There is also an effective procedure for conversion in the other direction. The same goes for the logics (FO + $\leq$ + DTC) and (FO + $\leq$ + TC), and the classes of program schemes DPS($\leq$) and NPS($\leq$), respectively.)

We add that the complexity class P can be captured by a class of program schemes NPSS($\leqq$), where these program schemes are obtained from those of NPS($\leqq$) by the introduction of a stack, with the semantics as expected. It should not be difficult to define a logic, constructed similarly to (FO + A + $\leqq$ + TC), that captures P also and is related to NPSS($\leqq$) via an effective procedure as above. Notice that the introduction of non-determinism into the program schemes of NPSA($\leqq$) (and also NPSS($\leqq$)) does not give us added power.

We end by mentioning that we have used these classes of program schemes and logics to capture probabilistic complexity classes, such as BPL, BPNL, and BPP, as well as obtaining a characterization of the polynomial-time hierarchy PH. Using these characterizations, we have eliminated the need to introduce the notion of positive reducibility into a result of Schöning.

A Grammar-Based Approach to Common-Sense Reasoning

PETER MOTT

———•———

1. INTRODUCTION AND OBJECTIVES

There is at present a paradigm—or at least an almost paradigm—for the modelling of common-sense inference. It goes as follows. First, you translate an English sentence into a formal language, then you do inference using the rules and axioms of that system, then you translate back into English. There is a convenient division of labour here. Computational linguists will focus their concerns primarily on syntax. But they will, at least often, systematically associate logical formulae with their parsed sentences (e.g. Gazdar *et al.*, 1985; Pereira and Warren, 1980). In fact, from a computer science perspective, the grammars these linguists produce are compilers from English into logic. But the syntacticians do not do anything with their logic. That is left to philosophers and some AI workers concerned with common-sense inference. The philosophers (e.g. Cresswell, 1985; Lewis, 1970) use these logics to address the sort of questions concerning reference, selfhood, and the propositional attitudes which interest them. The AI-workers (e.g. McCarthy, 1986; McDermott and Doyle, 1980) use them in an attempt to represent common-sense reasoning.

My aim in this paper is to describe a different approach to common-sense reasoning, one that is based directly on the grammatical structure of English itself, and which thereby attempts to do without any intermediate formal logic. In the rest of this section I shall outline and defend this approach, which I call grammar-based inference (GBI), and in subsequent sections I will try to develop it as far as space allows.

Dan Dennett (1984) has criticized the non-monotonic logics developed in AI to represent common sense as 'cognitive wheels'. He means that they may be good solutions to the problems they address but they are not *Nature's* solutions; just as the wheel is a good solution to moving about but not one that Nature makes use of. But the analogy, as anyone who has taken a wheelchair at a high kerb will know, supplies more than Dennett apparently intends. For the wheel in fact is *not* a good solution to the general problem of getting about in a bumpy world, in fact it's a rotten one. I rather think that logics of common sense may be likewise condemned: they are not only unnatural but they are also no use for general purpose reasoning. There are three reasons for this opinion.

In the logic that Frege and Russell invented, validity and expressive power were the prime considerations, for they wished to use their logic as a tool to ground mathematics. But for common-sense reasoning in ordinary situations speed is a virtue quite as important as validity or expressive power. One might conceive of speed, validity, and expressive power as making competing demands on the finite computing resource. A more demanding conception of validity will require either less speed or less expressive power; a requirement for greater speed will have a cost in either validity or expressive power; and great expressive power will result in either a very slow computational process or a very forgiving conception of validity. Foundational studies want great expressive power and absolute validity. But common-sense reasoning wants reasonable expressive power and speed, and is prepared to accept a weaker conception of validity.

As an example consider the inference from *John hit Mary* to *Mary was hit by John*. This passive transformation is, I should say, a part of common-sense reasoning. Because *most of the time* it takes one from truth to truth, it is sufficiently reliable to be included. But sometimes passage from active to passive seems not to be truth-preserving. For example, consider the inference *Few people read many books* so *Many books are read by few people*.[1] The first sentence may be taken to assert that most people don't read much, while the second says that there are a lot of unpopular books. The second does not follow from the first. But the context is a tricky one, and it is not *patent* that the gloss I just gave is the

---

[1] The example is given by Winograd (1983), 559.

right one. If it matters that you get the readership right, then the best thing is leave common-sense reasoning out of it and build a model in first-order logic. But an inference should be allowed into common-sense inference when it is usually reliable and if, when it fails, it fails on improbable, contrived, or difficult cases.

Common-sense reasoning may also lack expressive power. It is said that there are some people who see no ambiguity in the sentence *Every boy loves some girl*. Certainly it is surprisingly hard to say, in English, what the two different meanings are (one may in the end be reduced to drawing a picture of the relation). But the sentence has only two quantifiers; deeper nestings would seem to be extremely difficult if not plain impossible in English. It is better to use predicate logic in contexts where delicate handling of multiple quantifiers is required. These considerations lead to the suspicion that non-monotonic logics, which are grounded in the tradition of predicate logic, may prove basically ill-adapted for handling common-sense reasoning. In short, their pedigree is wrong, they grew from the wrong design decisions.[2]

The second point is associated with this. Present logics for common-sense inference are good at *validating* conclusions drawn by other means but bad at *generating* them for themselves (Hanks and McDermott, 1987). This is a serious weakness in a model of common-sense inference. For example, suppose one is told that all the children at St Botolph's are girls and that Mrs Smith's eldest child is at St Botolph's. One can from these premises not only see that it follows that Mrs Smith's eldest child is a girl, one can also at once *draw* that conclusion.

The third point is harder to explain succinctly, but it is at least as important as the first two. Special purpose logics of common sense are not *extensible*. They may handle one sort of common-sense inference (typically the so-called 'default' inferences which we use when we say 'Tweety can fly' knowing only that he is a bird) but provide no obvious ways to extend the treatment to others. The assumption must be that any fairly comprehensive representation of common sense along these lines will be an aggregate of numerous special logics, an aggregate which will, one suspects, be computationally hopeless.

---

[2] Schlipf (1987) has shown that circumscription, perhaps the leading contender among non-monotonic logics, is in the general case computationally intractable.

There is a famous example of this in the work of the logician Richard Montague (Montague, 1974; Dowty *et al.*, 1981), the person above all who created the paradigm I mentioned at the outset. Montague specified a grammar for a fragment of English now called PTQ, then provided a systematic translation of each sentence of PTQ into his Intensional Logic, and then supplied a formal semantics for the Intensional Logic. This Intensional Logic is a frighteningly complex system, it is a typed lambda calculus after the fashion of Church (1940) with an additional modal and two tense operators, and a funny intensional thing all of Montague's own. The semantics involves both a type hierarchy and Kripke's possible worlds. This apparatus is needed to handle discourse involving propositional attitudes, necessity, and time. If common-sense reasonings about probability were to be included then there would be another layer of complexity; if default reasoning yet another and so forth. Eventually the enormous engine so constructed would completely seize up.[3]

These three problems: speed, weakness in finding consequences, and lack of extensibility may not be in the end decisive. But they are enough, I think, to motivate the search for an alternative approach to common-sense reasoning.

Natural language is certainly extensible and flexible enough to handle the varieties of common-sense inference because they are formulated in it in the first place. It is furthermore the instrument we actually use in common-sense reasoning, at least in so far as that instrument is available to us in consciousness. So it is natural to see whether we can do inference over natural language itself, instead of translating into some other formalism and then doing inference over that (and then translating back again). Parsimony suggests such an approach, as well as the consideration that if we *reasoned* in logic it is really to be expected that we would *talk* in logic too. As for speed, there is obviously a gain in eliminating translation to and from logic. Other reasons for hoping that GBI might be fast, and apt for finding conclusions instead of merely validating them, will emerge as the paper develops.

We have strong intuitions of *constituency*, that is intuitions about

[3] An example of what I mean is that in Montague's logic it is not a logical consequence of *John loves Mary* that *Something loves Mary*. You need a 'meaning postulate', that is a special axiom, to ensure this. What then would the inference to *Someone loves Mary*, with its default content that *John* is the name of a person, require?

which sequences of words in a sentence are the building blocks of the sentence. We recognize in 'Everyone who likes mice hates cats' that 'who likes mice' and 'hates cats' are constituents while 'likes mice hates' is not. Granted then that we have intuitions of constituency, why do we have such, what function do they serve? It is possible to make the epiphenomenal reply that they have no function at all, but are an inevitable side-effect of the generative power of natural language. That is, the only way we can have a learnable language with an infinite number of sentences is if they are built up hierarchically from smaller parts and these smaller parts are the constituents. But this is only half an answer. The generative power of language may explain why there *are* constituents—but it does not explain why we should be introspectively *aware of* them. I would propose a principle here: What you have conscious access to has a functional role supporting an activity that you conduct consciously. Thus our visual system is organized hierarchically but we have conscious access only to certain 'constituents' of it; namely those bits that represent external objects to us. And this access is used in the activity of walking about without bumping into things, an activity which is conscious. If we never moved from A to B except as in a dream, then according to the principle proposed we should have no conscious access to the objects in our visual field (any more than we have access to the various low-level structures involved in visual processing).

Since we have at least partial conscious access to the constituent structure of our language, we should look for a conscious activity that this access serves, and my claim of course is that this activity is inference. We have access to the constituent structure of English because we use that structure in reasoning (and reasoning is accessible to consciousness).

The objective, then, of GBI is to use the constituent structure of natural language to do inference.[4] We turn now to the question

---

[4] Peter Millican has suggested to me that GBI may in fact represent a return to the concerns of pre-Reformation logicians. For medieval logic stayed as close as it could to the forms of natural language (Latin), it took all inferences as within its purview, it preferred natural deduction to axioms, and the syllogism was its paradigm form. All these are true of GBI. The criticism of medieval logic that it provided an unmanageable multiplicity of forms—its 'damned particularity'—has little force now. All grammars of natural language reveal this very complexity, which suggests that medieval logic was just being realistic. It just lacked the computer hardware to make such realism manageable. For a succinct and delightfully lucid introduction to medieval logic see Broadie (1987).

that will occupy the rest of the paper, namely how it might be done. To begin with consider the three inferences below:

Today is Tuesday ∴ Tomorrow is Wednesday (1)
John is kissing Mary ∴ John is touching Mary (2)
John sees a fat man ∴ John sees a man. (3)

Validity, according to the old criterion, consists in the impossibility of the truth of the premisses together with the falsehood of the conclusion, and by that test all the above seem to be valid. But logic treats not of validity simply, but of validity in virtue of form. Are any of the above valid in virtue of their form?

For the first let d be a syntactic variable ranging over the days of the week, and for any day of the week d let $d+$ be the day after. Then the inference (1) is an instance of the valid form *Today is d ∴ Tommorow is d+*. Let *NP1, NP2*, be syntactic variables ranging over names. Then (2) is an instance of the valid schema *NP1 is kissing NP2 ∴ NP1 is touching NP2*. For the third let *NP, AP, NOM* be variables over noun phrases, adjective phrases, and nominals.[5] Then the inference is an instance of the valid schema *NP sees a AP NOM ∴ NP sees a NOM*. So they are all instances of valid schemas and hence all valid in virtue of their forms. But not all are within the scope of grammar-based inference. The mark of GBI is that its inference schema contain only variables for expressions that are grammatical constituents of English. Thus (2) and (3) fall under GBI but (1) does not. For the formalization given has nothing to do with grammar, while the obvious grammatical form of (1) is *NP1 is NP2 ∴ NP3 is NP4* which has numerous counter-examples.

The sentence *John knows Mary* is an instance of all of the schemas: *NP1 knows Mary, NP1 knows NP2, NP1 VP NP2*. Each of them qualifies as a form that may be used in grammar-based inference.

Traditionally, an argument can only be valid in virtue of a form provided that *no* instances of that form could have true premisses but a false conclusion. On that count the passive transformation is not valid—but it seems to be part of common-sense reasoning. I also suspect that natural language is just too flexible an instrument

---

[5] A nominal is a noun category of bar level 1 in X-bar syntax. This means that it is a phrase (i.e. not a single noun) but is still incomplete. A noun has bar level 0, a full noun phrase bar level 2. Examples of nominal are *fat man, last train to San Fernando, person who eats mussels*. See Radford (1988), 173.

to deliver any forms to which there are absolutely no counter-examples, so that unless a weaker notion of validity is employed GBI will be impossible. I propose then to mean by a *valid form* of GBI an inference form where all counter-examples to it are recondite or improbable. I offer no explicit definition of 'recondite or improbable' here, but if a counter-example takes a long time to think up (except for linguists) or is unlikely to occur in a common-sense context, then it is recondite or improbable. If, on the other hand, you can find counter-examples easily and in large numbers then the form plainly is not valid. There will be border-line cases.

In fact (3) above has a claim to be just such, for letting the adjective phrase be *alleged* or *toy* you derive errors. It does not follow from *John sees a toy soldier* that *John sees a soldier*. Such adjectives are sufficiently unusual to make us want to keep the inference, but not so unusual as to warrant dismissing the counter-examples as recondite or improbable. Is there a middle way?

In fact there is, for the 'overgeneration' of inferences thus threatened has a precise analogue in syntax and the solution—so-called feature-based grammars—can be adapted for grammar-based inference. In the present case we should complicate the inference schema by requiring that the adjective phrase was not 'syncategorematic'. In a common notation the schema would be:

NP sees a AP[SYN –] *NOM* ∴ *NP sees a NOM*.

Certain adjectives like *toy* would be marked [SYN +] and this feature would prevent the application of the schema.

Although a feature-based grammar will in the end be essential, to introduce it from the start makes for a lot of complication and obscures the main outline of the ideas I want to explain. So generally this paper ignores features, but the reader who sees a defect in a scheme proposed should check whether restriction by appropriate features would correct the defect.

2. ABOUT GRAMMAR, PHRASE-MARKERS, AND THE MECHANISM OF GBI

In this section I want to describe quite briefly and informally the sort of grammar that will be assumed for the remainder of the paper, and the mechanism of grammar-based inference. A more technical formulation appears in an appendix.[6]

A grammar comprise three things: words, grammatical categories, and production or phrase-structure rules. I consider these in turn. Categories are objects representing the informal categories of grammar; S for sentence, NP for noun-phrases, N for nouns, VP for verb-phrases, and so forth. These categories are structureless —as the 'truth-values' of logic are structureless. We are avoiding the complex categories of recent syntactical theories.

The set of words, the lexicon, is pretty much self-explanatory. It is just the set of words of the grammar. Each word is assigned to a grammatical category, which is done by adding the appropriate phrase-structure rules (e.g. $N \Rightarrow men$, which makes *men* a noun). One novelty of grammars for GBI is that the lexicon must include *variables* of each grammatical category (which I will write in italic followed by a numeral). If the word *Uther* is taken to be of the category NP, then there will be a rule $NP \Rightarrow Uther$. Additionally there will be noun-phrase variables $NP_1 \ldots NP_n$, which are noun-phrases in virtue of the rules $NP \Rightarrow NP_1 \ldots NP \Rightarrow NP_n$. These variables play an essential role in the process of grammar-based inference, as will be explained below.

Finally, of course we require a set of production or phrase-structure rules. These are expressions of the form $C_o \Rightarrow C_1 \ldots C_n$ where each C_i is either a grammatical category or a word. The rule $S \Rightarrow NP, VP$ is read 'A sentence may be composed of a noun-phrase followed by a verb-phrase.' (If that is the only rule expanding S then the 'may be' is replaced by 'is'.) A sequence of words $w_1 \ldots w_n$ (also called a *string*) selected from the lexicon is a sentence S provided that the sequence can be derived by the phrase-structure rules from the category S. Figure 1 shows a toy grammar at (*a*), a derivation of a sentence at (*b*) and a tree representation, a phrase-marker, of the derivation at (*c*). So *Uther sleeps* is a sentence because

---

[6] The following is very sketchy. The reader who wants the background to the ideas here might consult Shieber (1986) for feature structures from a computational perspective, Sells (1985) for a survey of syntactic theories that use them extensively, Radford (1988) for a general and detailed introduction to Transformational Grammar, and Burton-Roberts (1986) for the sort of simple grammar we are using in the rest of this paper. The current paradigm is perhaps Gazdar *et al.* (1985), but it is full of technicality and very difficult reading. Aho *et al.* (1986), 165–72 includes ample background material on formal language theory for the purposes of this paper.

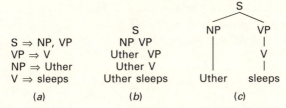

Fig 1. Toy Grammar, Derivation, and Phrase-Marker

it possesses a derivation from S. Note that a derivation proceeds by using the production rules to successively expand grammatical categories in terms of other categories or words. When you have only words you are finished (with the derivation, that is).

Derivations reflect the order in which the production rules are applied, so there can be several derivations of a single string. The phrase-marker (Fig. 1(*c*)) abstracts from this detail. Phrase-markers can also be presented in linear form. For example the one at 1(*c*) can be written out.[7]

$$\text{(S (NP } Uther\text{) (VP (V } sleeps\text{)))} \tag{1}$$

or as $(_S(_{NP}Uther) (_{VP}(_V sleeps)))$ to save white space.

Although linear format becomes unreadable even for moderately complicated phrase-markers it is easier to frame definitions with respect to it. (This is because word-order is implicit in a list, but has to be imposed additionally on a tree.) There are three definitions we need. First, a phrase-marker $\mathcal{P}$ is *of category* X provided that it is of the form (X . . .). A phrase-marker $\mathcal{P}$ is a *phrase-marker of* a string φ provided φ is exactly the list of words occuring in $\mathcal{P}$. Finally, if φ is any grammatical string then $\mathcal{PM}(\varphi)$ is the phrase-marker of φ.[8] So, for example, (1) above is of category S, it is a phrase-marker of *Uther sleeps*, and $\mathcal{PM}(Uther\ sleeps) = (1)$.

A word more about variables is in order before we finish this section. The grammar of Figure 1 is not completely stated there,

---

[7] Numbering of sentences begins anew in each section.

[8] This is not quite accurate. The phrase *John and Peter or Mary* is structurally ambiguous for it does not have a unique phrase-marker, since it may be taken to have either *and* or *or* as the main connective. A different sort of case is *sleeps* from the grammar in Fig. 2. It can be given both the phrase-marker (VP (V *sleeps*)) and (V *sleeps*), though obviously there is no structural ambiguity in a single word. In the present paper I ignore this complication, one may if one wishes construe $\mathcal{PM}(\varphi)$ as a choice function on the set of phrase-markers of φ.

for it will also include the words S_1, NP_1, VP_1, and V_1, and the rules $S \Rightarrow S_1$, $NP \Rightarrow NP_1$, $VP \Rightarrow VP_1$, and $V \Rightarrow V_1$ (and likewise for as many variables of each category as we may need). This means that:

$$(S \; (NP \; NP_1) \; (VP \; (V \; V_1))) \tag{2}$$

is a phrase-marker of the sentence $NP_1 \; V_1$ of the grammar. This sentence does not really 'mean' anything at all, the only use of it is that $\mathcal{PM}(NP_1 \; VP_1)$ could serve as a component in an inference schema. So, to take a wild example, we could have the schema $\mathcal{PM}(NP_1 \; VP_1) \; \therefore \; \mathcal{PM}(NP_2 \; VP_1)$. The effect of this is to allow us to pass from *Uther sleeps* to *Arthur sleeps* by making the appropriate substitutions in the schema. But this brings us to the mechanism of grammar-based inference, and this is best introduced in a more familiar context.

Officially the axiom schema $\mathcal{A} \rightarrow (\mathcal{B} \rightarrow \mathcal{A})$ stands for an infinite set of particular axioms. Among the members of this set is the formula $(P \& P) \rightarrow (Q \rightarrow (P \& P))$. But of course we don't come to know this by surveying any infinite set: we learn it by *pattern matching* the schema and the proposed instance. We call this process 'seeing that $(P \& P) \rightarrow (Q \rightarrow (P \& P))$ is of the form $\mathcal{A} \rightarrow (\mathcal{B} \rightarrow \mathcal{A})$'. The matching process consists in noticing that if $\mathcal{A}$ is replaced by $(P \& P)$ and $\mathcal{B}$ is replaced by Q in $\mathcal{A} \rightarrow (\mathcal{B} \rightarrow \mathcal{A})$ then we get $(P \& P) \rightarrow (Q \rightarrow (P \& P))$. Next, suppose we have an inference rule: $\mathcal{A} \& \mathcal{B} \; \therefore \; \mathcal{B}$. Given as premiss the formula $(P \vee Q) \& \neg R$ we infer using this rule that $\neg R$. We do this by matching $P \vee Q$ to $\mathcal{A}$, and matching $\neg R$ to $\mathcal{B}$. This binds the schematic letters so that the conclusion may be written out.

Now, instead of the formulae of sentence logic and the schemas derived therefrom, take phrase-markers of a grammar of English, and use schemas derived therefrom. What results is a system of grammar-based inference.

As an example, add to the grammar of Figure 1 the words *Arthur* and *and*, with the additional production rules $NP \Rightarrow Arthur$ and $CJ \Rightarrow and$ indicating that *Arthur* is a noun-phrase and *and* is a conjunction. Next add the rule: $S \Rightarrow S \; CJ \; S$ saying that two sentences conjoined make another sentence. The sentence *Arthur sleeps and Uther sleeps* has the phrase-marker:

$$(_S(_S(_{NP}Arthur) \; (_{VP}(_V sleeps))) \; (_{CJ}and) \; (_S(_{NP}Uther) \; (_{VP}(_V sleeps)))). \tag{3}$$

Of course *Uther sleeps* is a consequence of *Arthur sleeps and Uther sleeps*. This can be captured by a schematic rule for *and* like:

$$\frac{(S\ (S\ S\mathit{1})(CJ\ and)(S\ S\mathit{2}))}{(S\ S\mathit{2})} \tag{4}$$

To derive the phrase-marker $\mathcal{PM}$(*Uther sleeps*) from the phrase-marker $\mathcal{PM}$(*Arthur sleeps and Uther sleeps*) one proceeds essentially—there is one difference—as one did to apply the ordinary natural deduction rule just mentioned.

Instead of assigning the schematic sentence letters $\mathcal{A}$, $\mathcal{B}$ to formulas of sentence logic one assigns the category variables $S\mathit{1}$, $S\mathit{2}$, to phrase-markers of that category of the grammar of Figure 2. Or almost. In fact it is necessary to replace not just the category variable $S\mathit{1}$ but its phrase-marker $(S\ S\mathit{1})$ by a phrase-marker of the category S (otherwise one ends up with too many S's). This is, I confess, an inelegance but one I am not clear how to remove. In what follows I shall often be somewhat careless over this point. The exact nature of the replacements allowed is specified in the appendix. Thus, to conclude the example, in (4) let $(S\ S\mathit{1})$ be $(_S(_{NP}Arthur)\ (_{VP}(_V sleeps)\ )\ )$ and $(S\ S\mathit{2})$ be $(_S(_{NP}Uther)\ (_{VP}(_V sleeps)\ )\ )\ )$. Then the premiss of (4) becomes $\mathcal{PM}$(*Arthur sleeps and Uther sleeps*), i.e. (3) above. Thus infer the binding of $(S\ S\mathit{2})$ which is $\mathcal{PM}$(*Uther sleeps*), i.e. (1) above, as required.

Of course one hardly needs grammar-based inference to do sentence logic, but it is my claim that large tracts of common-sense inference can be handled using this approach.

3. THE SYLLOGISM REVISITED: A FIRST EXAMPLE

The two inferences (T1) and (T2) below are neither of them precisely syllogisms, but they are, I think, visibly 'syllogistic'. We easily reformulate the first premiss of (T1) as 'Every person who likes mice is a person who hates cats' and likewise for the second premiss (though which quantifier to insert is an old condundrum of the syllogistic, see Sommers (1982, 15 ff) for a solution).

> Everyone who likes mice hates cats
> Mary likes mice $\hspace{4em}$ (T1)
> ∴ Mary hates cats

Everyone who has received a benefit for at least six months should receive Long-Term Supplementary Rate.   (T2)

Mary has been receiving Widow's benefit for a year.

∴ Mary should receive Long-Term Supplementary Rate.

The second example will also fit into the syllogistic straitjacket, though the construal involved is much more extensive, and many 'suppressed' premisses are uncovered. But what most deserves comment about (T2) is not its complexity but its simplicity. It is an *easy* inference even though a formalization in first-order logic or an extension thereof will be long and slow and perhaps even difficult. The syllogism is a fast inference. Indeed, there are only finitely many valid syllogistic forms—so if we can constrain an inference to be a syllogism its validity can be checked quickly by scanning a list of forms. For this reason the apparent syllogistic form of these inferences is something which should not be given up lightly; rather we should seek to constrain as many inferences as possible into that form.

There is another point. In the brief heyday of the algebraic form of the syllogistic developed by Boole, Venn, and Jevons a common problem was to provide methods to discover the so-called *complete conclusion* of a collection of syllogistic premisses (a *sorites*). This was that conclusion which followed from all the premisses but from no subset of them, and it was a problem of discovery, not validation. Lewis Carroll was particularly ingenious at setting difficult problems of this sort—with twenty or more premisses sometimes (see W. W. Bartley, 1977). The perspective of discovery has since then largely dropped out of the purview of logic, so the syllogism provides a natural starting-point for restoring it.[9]

Consider the following inference schema (proto-Barbara):

$$\frac{\mathcal{PM}(every\ NOM_1\ VP_1)\quad \mathcal{PM}(NP_1\ is\ a\ NOM_1)}{\mathcal{PM}(NP_1\ VP_1)}. \tag{1}$$

If we now set $VP_1 = is\ a\ NOM_2$ *and* $NP_1 = every\ NOM_3$ we obtain the schema:

---

[9] But Kowalski (1977) in fact approaches logic from this old point of view—as the title of his book *Logic for Problem Solving* indicates.

$$\frac{\mathcal{PM}(\text{every } NOM_1 \text{ is a } NOM_2) \quad \mathcal{PM}(\text{every } NOM_3 \text{ is a } NOM_1)}{\text{every } NOM_3 \text{ is a } NOM_2}, (2)$$

which is as near as you can come, I suspect, to the mood BARBARA of the syllogism. It is also possible to generate DARII by letting NP_1 = *some NOM3*, and a fallacy of Illicit Process when NP_1 = *no NOM3*. So clearly the forms of common-sense reasoning require to be carefully constrained, but that is what one should expect.

The schema for the inferences (T1) and (T2) is also a variant of proto-Barbara, though not one that arises directly because of the odd word *everyone* which seems, grammatically, to be a proper name. We introduce the schema (R) *ad hoc*:

$$\frac{\mathcal{PM}(\text{everyone who } VP_1 \, VP_2) \quad \mathcal{PM}(NP_1 \, VP_1)}{\mathcal{PM}(NP_1 \, VP_2)}. \quad (R)$$

This schema will serve to handle the inference (T1), the first target inference. Given the premisses of (T1), to obtain the conclusion proceed in two steps: generate the phrase-markers of the premisses, then match them to a rule and draw the conclusion.

(i) First Step: Generate phrase-markers of premisses. A phrase-marker for the first premiss is:

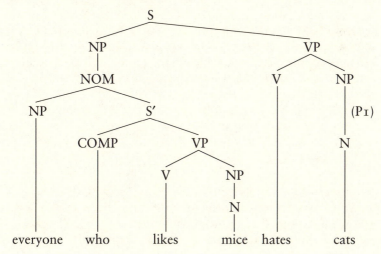

The phrase-marker of the second premiss is:

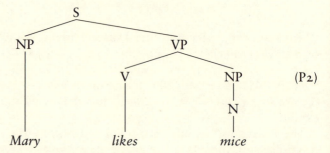

(P2)

(ii) Second Step: Match the given premisses to the premisses of the rule schema (R). The first premise is $\mathscr{PM}$(*everyone who VP1 VP2*). This is:

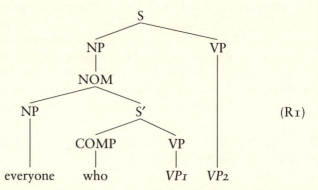

(R1)

If we let *VP1* be *likes mice*, or more exactly replace in (R1) the phrase-marker (VP *VP1*) by the phrase-marker (VP (V *likes*) (NP (N *mice*))) then (R1) matches (P1). The second premiss of the rule schema is $\mathscr{PM}$(*NP1 VP1*) which is:

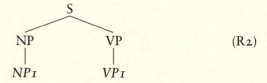

(R2)

In this case we let (NP *NP1*) be replaced by (NP *Mary*). We already have the replacement of (VP *VP1*) by $\mathscr{PM}$(*likes mice*), and we find that (R2) so instantiated matches (P2). Thus we can use the schema (R) to deduce $\mathscr{PM}$(*Mary hates cats*).

It is of course easy to recover the sentence *Mary hates cats* from the phrase-marker, for you only need to write out the leaves of the tree in the right order (or delete the brackets and categories if the linear format is being used). Thus grammar-based inference does not have any problem of finding an appropriate output form for its conclusions because the inference itself made use only of such forms.

4. TOWARDS THE SECOND EXAMPLE

The second target inference (T2) provides a much more severe challenge for GBI and will lead to two further ideas that have not yet been introduced: the relation of *involvement* and the procedure of *compounding*.

We begin just as in the previous example. A substitution σ is found to match the first premiss of (T2): *Everyone who has received a benefit for at least six months should receive LTSR*, with the major premiss of the rule schema (R).[10] To do this we easily see that *has received a benefit for at least six months* should replace VP_1, and *should receive LTSR* must replace VP_2. Thus we put:

$$\sigma \mathcal{PM}(VP_1) = \mathcal{PM}(\text{has received a benefit for at least six months}).$$

$$\sigma \mathcal{PM}(VP_2) = \mathcal{PM}(\text{should receive Long-Term Supplementary rate}).$$

This partially instantiates (R) but the minor premiss still has a variable in it, as does the conclusion. It has in fact become:

$$\mathcal{PM}(NP_1 \text{ has received a benefit for at least six months}).$$

Since we wish to match this to the minor premiss of (T2) we naturally do:

[10] LTSR is—or was—the Long-Term Supplementary Rate of Benefit. The example arose in early discussions of the Alvey-DHSS Large Scale Demonstrator project. It is part of a problem called the Widow's Trap. As the rules were then, a claimant would always receive the highest paying of all the benefits she might be entitled to. Widow's benefit was more than Short-Term Supplementary Rate. But LTSR could only be paid to those who had received STSR. So poor widows were caught in a trap. The problem was to build a system that identifies such traps while regulations are being drafted. These traps are neither recondite nor subtle—but there are a lot of regulations, and they tend to be overlooked. It was this problem that originally set me thinking about common-sense reasoning.

$\sigma\mathcal{PM}(NP\textsc{i}) = \mathcal{PM}(Mary).$

Thus $\sigma\mathcal{PM}(NP\ VP\textsc{i})$ is:

$\mathcal{PM}(Mary$ *has received a benefit for at least six months*$).\ (\textsc{i})$

This is then what we need to use the schema, and using it would give the result we want. Unhappily (1) is not the second premiss of (T2) which is in fact:

$\mathcal{PM}(Mary$ *has been receiving Widow's Benefit for a year*$).\ (2)$

So how can we get from (2) to (1) in order to apply (R)?

I take it that one can—at least as far as common sense is concerned—pass from (2) to (1). In fact one might explain this by a *sorites* as below, where each assertion implies the next:

> *Mary has been receiving Widow's benefit for a year.*
> *Mary has been receiving Widow's benefit for at least*
> *six months.* (3)
> *Mary has been receiving a benefit for at least six*
> *months.*
> *Mary has received a benefit for at least six months.*

But this series of inferences looks to me like a *post hoc* justification of the step from (2) to (1) rather than an account of how it might be done. I have two reasons for thinking this. First, simple introspection suggests that there is no such series of steps—as far as *sentences* are concerned only the first and the last appear to need formulation. That aside, there is very little computational point in replacing the problem of the single transition from (2) to (1) by the problem of making the three transitions above—for there is no genuine decomposition of the problem effected in (3). The sentential form of the *sorites* is otiose: what it really shows is a concealed process of inference over units smaller than sentences. In fact we pass from *a year* to *at least six months* because a duration of a year involves a duration of at least six months. Likewise we pass from *Widow's benefit* to *a benefit* because Widow's benefit involves (being a specific one) a benefit, and finally we pass from *has been receiving* to *has received* because your having been doing something involves your having done it. The formulations are not very tidy—the word 'involves' is about the best available for the relation at issue. This comes, of course, from Barwise and Perry (1983) who use the example that kissing involves touching. Anyway, these involvements support a relation between phrase-markers, a relation to which I give the same name 'involves' and notate by INV. For the example above we should want certain involvements:

$\mathcal{P\!M}$(*has been receiving*) INV $\mathcal{P\!M}$(*has received*).
$\mathcal{P\!M}$(*Widow's benefit*) INV $\mathcal{P\!M}$(*a benefit*).
$\mathcal{P\!M}$(*a year*) INV $\mathcal{P\!M}$(*at least six months*).

For the moment leave aside how these involvements are to be obtained, assume that they are just listed as *basic involvements* and as such are available to the inference process. The way they are used to derive (1) from (2) is as follows (the phrase-markers are drawn below in such a way as to point up their structural similarity). The object is to extend the involves relation to show that (2) INV (1). The procedure is this.

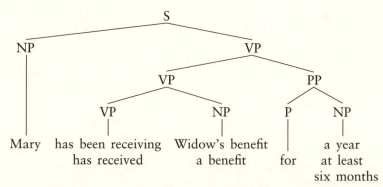

Compare the root nodes of the two phrase-markers. If they are not the same there is no involvement: return failure. If they are the same look first to see whether the phrase-markers are entirely the same. If they are then return success. If not look in the list of basic involvements. If you find the involvement there then again return success. In this case we have both (1) and (2) of the form (S (NP . . .) (VP . . .)), but no basic involvements with S. So next we see if the (NP . . .) of (2) involves the (NP ——) of (1), and if the (VP . . .) of (2) involves the (VP ——) of (1). If both do we return success, else we fail. Thus the process passes down the two phrase-markers, in this case succeeding because appropriate basic involvements are quickly found.

Notice that this process promises to be quick because it can execute in parallel since each stage looks only at the constituents available to it. This in turn is possible only because we do inference at a level lower than that of the sentence. I think such subsentential inference may be a key to obtaining good performance from a common-sense inference machine. Hence something like that may go on in us. But there are problems.

Not so much the difficulty of where all the involvements come from. Many can be stored, because we can remember quite a lot, and others can be derived by the very processes of GBI that we are investigating. That is, for example, the passage from $\mathcal{PM}$(*Widow's benefit*) to $\mathcal{PM}$(*a benefit*) should be handled in the same way as the passage from (2) to (1). I should imagine that involvements like $\mathcal{PM}$(*a year*) INV $\mathcal{PM}$(*twelve months*) will be simply stored, in fact they may be stored under a 'biconditional' version of INV which allows unrestricted substitution (a relation of synonymity, given in extension). Then the passage from $\mathcal{PM}$(*a year*) to $\mathcal{PM}$(*at least six months*) will take advantage of that stored involvement. No, the difficulty lies rather with the excessive liberality of the procedure of *compounding* just described. For what it says in general is that: (X $\mathcal{PM}(\varphi_1)$, $\mathcal{PM}(\varphi_2)$) INV (X $\mathcal{PM}(\psi_1)$, $\mathcal{PM}(\psi_2)$) whenever $\mathcal{PM}(\varphi_1)$ INV $\mathcal{PM}(\psi_1)$ and $\mathcal{PM}(\varphi_2)$ INV $\mathcal{PM}(\psi_2)$. This principle is true a surprising amount of the time but there are systematic counter-examples.

Certainly we should expect $\mathcal{PM}$(*man*) INV $\mathcal{PM}$(*animal*), hence by compounding $\mathcal{PM}$(*every man*) INV $\mathcal{PM}$(*every animal*). But in fact *every* reverses involvement, it doesn't pass it up the parse tree: you get instead that $\mathcal{PM}$(*every animal*) INV $\mathcal{PM}$(*every man*). Likewise negation *not* achieves this reversal. Because $\mathcal{PM}$(*every animal*) INV $\mathcal{PM}$(*every man*) we get that $\mathcal{PM}$(*not every man*) INV $\mathcal{PM}$(*not every animal*). Clearly grammar-based inference will have to modify the principle of compounding to take account of this.

There are in addition words which, it seems, just block involvement altogether. An example is the adjective *big*. For though $\mathcal{PM}$(*mouse*) INV $\mathcal{PM}$(*animal*) it does not follow that $\mathcal{PM}$(*big mouse*) INV $\mathcal{PM}$(*big animal*). Nor does it follow from *he came in with a big box of chocolates* that he came in *he came in with a big box* though presumably *box of chocolates* INV *box*. Big boxes of chocolates are, or anyway may be, small boxes. At present I am not sure how best to handle the issue of restricting the principle of compounding. One possibility is described in the appendix.

The procedure for handling the example (T2) is, then, to summarize, as follows. First, try the inference schema (R). This results in certain bindings of variables and poses the secondary problem of passing from (2) to (1). This can be solved by using the principle of compounding and certain basic involvements. Thus we can derive the conclusion of (T2) as desired.

These three: inference schemas, the principle of compounding, and the list of basic involvements, form the elements of a system of grammar-based inference.

5. CONCLUSION

As this discussion shows, grammar-based inference is not without problems and there are no doubt others that I have not seen. But it does seem to promise a useful approach to common-sense reasoning. For it uses the language we speak, is turned towards the form of logic that is most natural and came first historically, and it is oriented towards actually finding consequences rather than validating them. It is also easily extensible to new forms of inference, and should be apt for parallel implementation. Thus it gives some answer to the computational problem of how we can sometimes reason so quickly. There is a final motive for grammar-based inference, though it will not seem a good one to everybody. Our picture of reasoning tends to be monolithic; that reasoning is just one sort of thing rather than a hotch-potch of many as I am inclined to think. A distinguished topologist, I learn, used to irritate his colleagues by publishing pictures rather than proofs. It seems to me wildly unlikely that grammar-based inference could come any way near the sort of reasoning that underlay that performance, because GBI manipulates *words* and nothing else. To see the boundaries of the manipulation of words by finding the limits of GBI would perhaps be to learn something about cognition.

APPENDIX

The basic ideas of GBI have been described more or less informally in the paper. Here I want to try to specify the mechanism of GBI more concisely.

A *grammar* $\mathcal{G}$ is a triple <CAT, LEX, RULES> where CAT and LEX and RULES are non-empty disjoint sets of categories, words, and production rules respectively. A production rule is an expression $C \Rightarrow C_1 \ldots C_k$ where C is a category and $C_1 \ldots C_k$ are either categories or words. For each $C \in$ CAT there are variables $C1 \ldots Cn$ of category C in LEX. For each w in LEX there is a unique rule C ⇒ w; if w is a variable of category C then C ⇒ w is that rule.

A *phrase-marker* is a list defined inductively as follows:

(1) If C ⇒ w is a production rule, and w is a word then (C w) is a phrase-marker, and (C w) is *of category* C.

(2) If C ⇒ $C_1 \ldots C_n$ is a production rule, and $\mathcal{P}_1 \ldots \mathcal{P}_n$ are phrase-markers with $\mathcal{P}_i$ of category C_i ($1 \le i \le \cap$) then (C $\mathcal{P}_1 \ldots \mathcal{P}_n$) is a phrase-marker, and (C $\mathcal{P}_1 \ldots \mathcal{P}_n$) is *of category* C.

A grammar $\mathcal{G}$ generates a set of phrase-markers. I will refer to this set also as $\mathcal{G}$ and not take care to distinguish the grammar from the phrase-markers that it generates.

$\mathcal{P}$ is *a phrase-marker of* the phrase $\varphi = w_1 \ldots w_n$ provided that $w_1 \ldots w_n$ is what you get when you delete all the categories and brackets from $\mathcal{P}$. (cf. Cresswell, 1973). So the phrase-marker (S (NP *Uther*) (VP (V *sleeps*))) is a (in fact the) phrase-marker of the sentence *Uther sleeps*.

The problem is now to define a consequence relation to hold between a set X ⊆ $\mathcal{G}$ of phrase-markers and a phrase-marker $\mathcal{P}$, when $\mathcal{P}$ is a consequence of X according to the principles of GBI. This relation I call *involvement* and write X INV $\mathcal{P}$. As usual, $\mathcal{P}_1 \ldots \mathcal{P}_n$ INV $\mathcal{P}$ means $\{\mathcal{P}_1 \ldots \mathcal{P}_n\}$ INV $\mathcal{P}$.

The involvement relation is defined inductively as the smallest transitive and reflexive relation INV satisfying the clauses (I)–(IV) that follow.

(I) INV includes all basic involvements.

Basic involvements include no category variables. Examples are: $\mathcal{PM}$(*man*) INV $\mathcal{PM}$(*animal*), $\mathcal{PM}$(*year*) INV $\mathcal{PM}$(*twelve months*), $\mathcal{PM}$(*white lie*) INV $\mathcal{PM}$(*tall story*).

(II) INV includes all inference schemas.

These are distinguished from basic involvements by the presence of category variables. Again I give just some examples:

$\mathcal{PM}$(*S1 and S2*) INV $\mathcal{PM}$(*S1*).

$\mathcal{PM}$(*every NOM1 VP1*), $\mathcal{PM}$(*NP1 is a NOM1*) INV $\mathcal{PM}$(*NP1 VP1*).

$\mathcal{PM}$(*some ADJ1 NOM1*) INV $\mathcal{PM}$(*some NOM1*).

$\mathcal{PM}$(*very ADJ1*) INV $\mathcal{PM}$(*ADJ1*).

Involvements can be extended by two devices. First, INV is closed under a general rule of compounding:

(III) If $\mathcal{P}_1$ INV Q_1 & ... & $\mathcal{P}_n$ INV Q_n, then (X $\mathcal{P}_1 \ldots \mathcal{P}_n$) INV (X $Q_1 \ldots Q_n$).

As noted this rule is certainly too strong. I consider briefly one manner of restricting it below.

Let σ_0 be a map that assigns to each phrase-marker (X X1) some phrase-marker $\mathcal{P}$ of category X. Then extend σ_o to a *substitution* σ, defined for all phrase-markers as follows:

$\sigma(X\ X_I) = \sigma_o(X\ X_I)$	if X_I is a category variable.
$\sigma(X\ w) = (X\ w)$	if w is a word.
$\sigma(X\ \mathcal{P}_1 \ldots \mathcal{P}_n) = (X\ \sigma\mathcal{P}_1 \ldots \sigma\mathcal{P}_n)$	if $\mathcal{P}_1 \ldots \mathcal{P}_n$ are phrase-markers.

Now INV is closed under application of inference schemas:

(IV) If $\mathcal{P}_1 \ldots \mathcal{P}_n$ INV $\mathcal{P}$ then $\sigma\mathcal{P}_1 \ldots \sigma\mathcal{P}_n$ INV $\sigma\mathcal{P}$.

The rule of compounding may be replaced by various particular rule schemas which jointly achieve its effect as far as is wanted. Suppose that an application of (III) takes us from:

$$(NP \ldots)\ \text{INV}\ (NP\ \text{---})\ \text{and}\ (VP \ldots)\ \text{INV}\ (VP\ \text{---}) \qquad (1)$$

to:

$$(S\ (NP \ldots)\ (VP\ \text{---}))\ \text{INV}\ (S\ (NP\ \text{---})\ (VP\ \text{---})). \qquad (2)$$

To circumvent this particular application of (III) add the rule schema:

$$\frac{(NP\ NP_I)\ \text{INV}\ (NP\ NP_2),\quad (VP\ VP_I)\ \text{INV}\ (VP\ VP_2)}{(S\ (NP\ NP_I)\ (VP\ VP_I))\ \text{INV}\ (S\ (NP\ NP_2)\ (VP\ VP_2)).} \qquad (3)$$

Then given any particular involvements such as (1) above the rule (III) can be used with an appropriate σ to get the same conclusion (2) as before.

Note that (III) can only be used to pass from (1) to (2) because there is a production rule in the grammar $S \Rightarrow NP, VP$. For if there were no such rule there would be no phrase-markers of the form $(S\ (NP \ldots)$ $(VP\ \text{---}))$. So in designing a system of GBI one may go through all the production rules deciding in each case whether that rule preserves, reverses, or simply blocks the transmission of INV.

Obviously there is much greater scope for control here than with the global rule (III), but again there is a corresponding loss of speed.

Finally, a consequence relation is naturally thought of as restricted to sentences. This can be easily accommodated: a sentence φ *implies* a sentence ψ if $\mathcal{PM}(\varphi)$ INV $\mathcal{PM}(\psi)$.

REFERENCES

Aho, A. V., Sethi, R., and Ullman, J. P. (1986), *Compilers, Principles, Techniques, and Tools*, Reading, Mass.: Addison-Wesley.

Bartley, W. W. (1977), *Lewis's Carroll's Symbolic Logic*, Hassocks, Sussex: Harvester Press.

Barwise, J., and Perry, J. (1983), *Situations and Attitudes*, Cambridge, Mass.: MIT Press.

Broadie, A. (1987), *Introduction to Medieval Logic*, Oxford: Clarendon Press.

Burton-Roberts, N. (1986), *Analysing Sentences*, London: Longman.

Church, A. (1940), 'A Formulation of the Simple Theory of Types', *Journal of Symbolic Logic*, 5: 56–68.

Cresswell, M. J. (1973), *Logic and Languages*, London: Methuen.

—— (1985), *Structured Meanings*, Cambridge, Mass.: MIT Bradford Books.

Dowty, D. R., Wall, R. E., and Peters, S. (1981), *Introduction to Montague Semantics*, Dordrecht: Reidel.

Gazdar, G., Klein, E., Pullum, G., and Sag, I. (1985), *Generalised Phrase-Structure Grammar*, Oxford: Blackwell.

Hanks, S., and McDermott, D. (1987), 'Nonmonotonic Logic and Temporal Projection', *Artificial Intelligence*, 33: 379–412.

Kowalski, R. (1979), *Logic For Problem Solving*, New York: Elsevier North-Holland.

Lewis, D. (1970), 'General semantics', *Synthese*, 22: 18–67.

McCarthy, J. (1986), 'Applications of Circumscription to Formalizing Common-Sense Knowledge', *Artificial Intelligence*, 28: 89–116.

McDermott, D., and Doyle, J. (1980), 'Non–Monotonic Logic I', *Artificial Intelligence*, 13: 41–72.

Montague, R. M. (1974), *Formal Philosophy*, ed. R. H. Thomason, New Haven, Conn.: Yale University Press.

Pereira, F. C. N., and Warren, D. H. D. (1980), 'Definite Clause Grammars for Language Analysis: A Survey of the Formalism and a Comparison with Augmented Transition Networks', *Artificial Intelligence*, 13: 231–78.

Radford, A. (1988), *Transformational Grammar*, Cambridge: Cambridge University Press.

Schlipf, J. S. (1987), 'Decidability and Definability with Circumscription', *Annals of Pure and Applied Logic*, 35: 173–91.

Sells, P. (1985), *Lectures on Contemporary Syntactic Theories*, Stanford, CSLI Lecture Notes 3.

Shieber, S. M. (1986), *An Introduction to Unification based Approaches to Grammar,* Stanford, CSLI Lecture Notes 4.

Sommers, F. (1982), *The Logic of Natural Language*, Oxford: Clarendon Press.

Winograd, T. (1983), *Language as a Cognitive Process*, Reading, Mass.: Addison-Wesley.

13

Chaos: Its Past, Its Present, but mostly Its Future

JOSEPH FORD

———●———

The Roots of Tomorrow Visibly Entwine the Hours of Today.

The Evangelist of Chaos

In order to illuminate the significance of determinism in his Newtonian world, Laplace wrote, 'We ought then to regard the present
state of the Universe as the effect of its preceding state and as the
cause of its succeeding state.' Laplace's world was thus not only
determinate but also predictable, for, with sufficient knowledge
and skill he could be assured of accurately predicting not only the
motion of the solar system but the entire universe as well. For
decades, this *Weltanschauung* so permeated both popular and
scientific thinking that not even Poincaré's profound whimsy, 'The
notion of determinism is a fantasy due to Laplace', could shake
the faith of the devout. But eventually the pendulum did swing
and, while contemplating the wildly erratic properties of turbulent
systems, the mathematicians Ruelle and Takens directed attention
to a property which many now take to be the definition of chaos:
a chaotic system is one whose final state depends with exquisite
sensitivity upon its initial state. However, it was meteorologist
Edward Lorenz whose intuitive and picturesque 'butterfly effect'
laid bare the full meaning of 'sensitive dependence' to the man in
the street—specifically, today's weather in London can crucially
depend on whether one month ago a butterfly near Mount Kili-
manjaro flapped its wings two or was it four times before deciding

The author is pleased to have this opportunity to express his appreciation to the
National Science Foundation for the financial support provided for this work under
NSF Grant No. Phy-8722806.

not to depart the flower upon which it sat. But regardless of the specific description, 'sensitive dependence' always implies that two initially close system states diverge from each other at breakneck speed.

None the less, 'sensitive dependence' of itself only makes prediction difficult, not impossible. Here, the notion that determinism implies predictability is seriously eroded, not invalidated. In principle, measurement accuracy may be increased as needed though perhaps only as rapidly as government funding will permit. Regardless, practically speaking, short-term prediction is always feasible while long-term prediction can approach the impossible. But in what circumstances, if any, will prediction actually become totally impossible, as a matter of principle? To answer, let us consider the numerical computation of an orbit for a chaotic system exhibiting 'sensitive dependence', and now recall that 'sensitive dependence' means, no matter how accurate the initial data, orbital accuracy will steadily decay. To compensate for this decay, we must supplement the data initially given the computer. Specifically, if we wish to maintain constant accuracy in the calculation, we must input one additional bit of information for each bit of information lost to round off and/or truncation error. Of course, some loss of precision in orbital integration occurs for every dynamical system; however the calculation of a chaotic orbit loses accuracy at an astonishing rate, i.e. some fixed number of bits or decimal digits at each iteration. Thus, for orbital calculations having appreciable length, we must feed in just as much information as we get out! Consequently, for chaotic orbits our CRAY I or CYBER 205 machines have, without our notice, become nothing more than the world's most sophisticated Xerox machines. We now perceive that dynamical systems exhibiting 'sensitive dependence' have, in fact, been completely unpredictable, as a matter of principle, all along. Finally, recall that algorithmic information theory asserts that an output digit sequence is random if it cannot be computed by any algorithm (program) whose information content is less than that of the output. We can now, at last, present a definitive meaning for chaos: chaos is merely a synonym for randomness. Alternatively stated, a chaotic orbit is simply a realization of some random process. In summary, innate, irreducible, and uncomputable randomness actually appears first in classical mechanics not quantum mechanics as popularly believed. Put another tally in the Newton column! In closing this paragraph, we must emphasize that the word 'predictable' has been used in two seemingly contradictory senses. To illustrate, a one-dimensional random walk is most assuredly unpredictable in principle yet, knowing the walker's current position and step size, we can certainly provide bounded estimates on where he will be after the next step, the following step, etc. In physics, it is quite common to call this estimate a prediction. Henceforth, when confusion might arise, we shall speak of 'practical predictability' and 'theoretical predictability'.

Where now does all this leave Laplacian determinism? A chaotic Newtonian orbit is most assuredly deterministic, and yet, without internal contradiction, we may assert that it is also a realization of some random process. But a random process cannot be predicted. This is why, if we seek to compute a chaotic orbit, we find we are putting in just as much information as we get out. In essence, we can output a copy of the orbit only by inputting a copy of the orbit; we can find the answer only if we know the answer. This is not the stuff of which predictability is made. Laplace, of course, had no way of anticipating that orbital complexity could divorce predictability from determinism. Indeed, determinism itself disappears unless we maintain the fiction that man can measure and compute with infinite precision. Thus, Laplace is not alone in tacitly making unwarranted assumptions. Let us now discuss more of these assumptions.

Science assumes that Nature is closed, consistent, and single-valued, i.e. it is assumed that, when asked a question, Nature:

1. provides answers which are part of a closed logical system (e.g. Grand Unification),
2. provides answers which are mutually consistent, and
3. provides one and only one answer to each question.

Moreover, physicists generally believe that theory will eventually fit nature like a glove—closed, consistent, etc. Yet, the logic used by science cannot be proven to be either closed or consistent! The problem, of course, is Gödel's theorem on undecidable propositions. In this regard, IBM's Greg Chaitin has recently proven an equivalent of Gödel's theorem which is especially germane to the present discussion (See his 'Gödel's Theorem and Information', *International Journal of Theoretical Physics* 21 (1982): 941–54, and *Algorithmic Information Theory* (Cambridge: Cambridge

University Press, 1987))). Specifically, the essence of Chaitin's theorem is captured in the following paraphrase: 'A ten-pound theory can no more produce a twenty-pound theorem than a one-hundred-pound pregnant woman can birth a two-hundred-pound child.' What Gödel via Chaitin asserts is that there exist naturally occurring, simple questions whose answers are so complex they contain more information than exists in all our human logical systems combined. Such questions are Gödel's children. But where, a reader will surely ask, is one to find simple questions having such inhumanly complex answers? Why in physics, of course! Any question whose answer requires precise knowledge of a chaotic orbit is one of Gödel's children, for, being random, even a sufficiently long finite section of a chaotic orbit contains more information than all human logic. Dimly, we now perceive the emergence of a paradigm shift. The world of Laplace, Einstein, or even Schrödinger was horrendously complicated but it still seemed sufficiently ordered to lie within the realm of human understanding; the chaotic world described by Gödel and Chaitin, however, lies far beyond any hope of human comprehension. Like the Peace of God, it passeth all human understanding.

Thus, man is now seen to be not only a truly limited creature, but one who will never accurately recognize his world until he quits believing his skills are those of a lesser god. None the less, notions such as these lead many to inquire if the richness of man's existence will not be diminished if these limitations are found to be valid. *Au contraire*, quite the opposite is true. Recall that we would still not understand why the conductivity of quartz and copper differ by orders of magnitude, we would still not have the transistor and the laser, we would still have no fundamental understanding of superconductors and superfluids had we not, with Heisenberg, admitted that humans cannot accurately measure the simultaneous values of two conjugate variables. With each admitted limitation, man has grown richer in his understanding and control of his environment. And where might we look for the next significant limitation? Let us seek a promised root of tomorrow.

Specifically, let us begin by examining the influence of chaos upon the measurement process. To this end, consider an arbitrary macroscopic system whose time-evolving properties are to be determined experimentally. In order to ensure accurate measurements, Newtonian dynamics requires the existence of perfect clocks

and meter sticks which have either negligible or controllable interaction with the system. But clearly this postulate was made in
ignorance of chaos. Since chaos is ubiquitous at the macroscopic
level, the clock and meter stick as well as the given system itself
are chaotic in general. Interactions between chaotic systems create
effects which locally magnify exponentially with time; they cannot, therefore, be neglected even though initially small. Moreover,
because chaos means deterministic randomness, the effect of these
interactions is uncontrollable and unpredictable. Indeed, the effect
of one chaotic system weakly acting upon another appears as
random noise. A weak interaction among several chaotic systems
thus introduces a low-level random noise throughout the composite system. Hence, when we do not possess the non-interacting,
perfect clocks and meter sticks envisioned by Newton and when
we are forced to use weakly interacting chaotic substitutes instead,
the act of measurement introduces a small and uncontrollable
error into the quantity being measured. These arguments lead
one to suspect the existence of a generalized uncertainty principle
$\Delta A/A \geq \beta$ valid for all classical observables A, where ΔA is the
uncertainty in A and where β is a parameter depending perhaps on
system, measuring device, or observable. More speculative is the
notion that there exists a small, uncontrollable, irreducible, and
universal noise level due to chaos implying that $\Delta A/A \geq \alpha$, where
α is a new universal constant of nature. Finally, should these
possibilities find rigorous support, then the need to bring classical
and even quantum dynamics into accord with the new uncertainty
principle would become pressing. Thus far, this narrative, in common with most papers in this subject area, has treated chaos as if
it were an unmitigated disaster and the theory of chaos as if its
only proper function were the search for ways to protect man
from its deadly peril. The next paragraph reveals that chaos has
a brighter side.

Uncontrolled chaos is most assuredly a terrifying and devastat-
ing thing. Yet when controlled, the villainous chaos becomes
gentle, useful, even enchanting. And why should it not be so?
For in truth, chaos is merely dynamics freed from the shackles of
order and predictability. Dynamical systems released to randomly
explore their every possibility. To emphasize, order is totally dull;
chaos is truly fascinating. Who has not been mesmerized by the
chaotic arrivals of breaking ocean waves at a beach or the chaotic

dance of flames across the logs of a dying fire? Clearly, chaos can provide us with a virtuoso display of exciting variety, a richness of choice, a cornucopia of opportunity. Dare we hope that humans can harvest the richness without reaping its devastation? Here there is no choice. Man is increasingly facing problems of such enormous complexity that they lie beyond the scope of any deterministic solution. The only known hope lies in harnessing chaos, for only chaos can rapidly supply a wide variety of trial solutions from which a deterministic scheme can quickly select the correct or the best solution. In short, man can solve incredibly complex problems by letting controlled chaos do the work. We offer two examples which are not only useful themselves but which also point toward future uses. The first is nature's, the second is man's.

In setting up the scheme humans call evolution, nature wished to ensure in perpetuity the survival of life forms against every possible variety of natural catastrophe; in addition, nature wished to encourage the expansion of life into every possible ecological niche no matter how harsh or specialized. In principle, nature could have written a deterministic program to cope with the temporal unfolding of exceedingly complex, seemingly random patterns of life-affecting events, but that would have required an unacceptably inefficient or perhaps even an impossible solution. Instead, nature chose a highly effective technique which uses randomness (chaos) to defend against the unexpected. Specifically, nature uses random mutations to provide the wide variety of life forms needed to meet the demands of natural selection. In essence, evolution is controlled chaos or chaos with 'feedback'. Random mutations alone would correspond to nature indifferently rolling unbiased dice, but the added 'feedback' of natural selection and survival of the fittest, in effect, biases the dice so that, over many rolls, life-forms not only survive but with overwhelming likelihood they improve. Turning now to man.

Consider a military aircraft whose speed and complexity require that it be controlled by a computer which makes command decisions based upon information received from numerous sensing devices scattered about the plane. Clearly, the computer must be able to defend against misinformation received from failing or malfunctioning sensors, as might be especially likely in combat. In addition, the plane and its passengers must be defended against failure of the computer itself. The usual solution to this type of problem is to introduce redundancy through addition of several duplicate processors and sensors. Each processor then independently makes its decision, and majority rules. This ploy fails to work if, say, a decision depends on an altimeter reading and two or more of the processors read the altimeter at slightly different times. The readings may be similar but, close to the ground, slight differences could lead to disasterously distinct computer recommendations. To overcome this problem, why not let the processors communicate with each other? This represents a good step, for it immediately brings us face to face with the deterministically difficult but probabilistically solvable *Byzantine Generals' Problem*. By invoking this jazzy name, mathematicians make it clear they have taken notice of the commercial use physicists have wrung out of terms such as quarks, strange attractors, gluons, partons, and so ons. In the *Byzantine Generals' Problem*, a Commanding General must co-ordinate an attack involving numerous armies, each commanded by a general who reports to the one Commanding General. Clearly, all armies must attack in concert. In order to agree on the time and day of the attack, the Commanding General decides to poll his generals but, in so doing, he must defend against the ballots of a small, determined, but unknown group of traitors—the powerful Byzantine generals who will do anything in their power to thwart the will of the loyal majority. Taking the advice of his staff mathematicians, the Commanding General uses a strategy which repeatedly polls all of his generals. On all ballots, each general votes according to a rather elaborate procedure based on a coin toss (chaos) which optimizes the chances for the will of the loyal generals to prevail while thwarting all efforts of the Byzantine generals to subvert. This is accomplished in a fashion similar to that used by Las Vegas gambling houses to optimize their chances of success, independent of the strategy of the gamblers. Readers wishing to study the details of the actual solution to the *Byzantine Generals' Problem* are referred to a quite readable article in *Science* magazine (Gina Kolata, 'Order Out of Chaos in Computers', *Science* 223: 917–19, 2 March 1984). As reward for enduring the foregoing lengthy immersion in classical chaos, we now introduce the reader to the invigoratingly chilly breezes of controversy which surround the very existence of chaos in the quantum world.

Because quantum mechanics is presumed to contain classical mechanics as a special case and because classical systems are known to exhibit chaos, many investigators regard the existence of quantum chaos as an indisputable reality. But alas, twenty years of searching for quantum chaos has provided no examples; indeed, it has not even provided a definition! Two responses to this quandary have been proposed. The first suggests that, since there is no known chaos in the quantum world, there is no chaos in nature at the microscopic level; the second suggests that it would be much more fruitful for physicists to quit worrying about the existence of quantum chaos and concern themselves with quantum phenomena which correlate with the appearance of chaos at the classical level. Neither of these responses seeks to account for the remarkable success of quantum statistical mechanics which is founded on the proposition that chaos does exist in the microscopic world. Equally, both responses neglect whether chaos might emerge when the classical limit is approached. Although not widely acknowledged, there are strong differences of opinion here which make it quite clear that quantum mechanics is truly a house divided. Thus, we are looking for more than simple entertainment when we search for elements in our present knowledge which, more than others, might point toward a future resolution. In fact, there are several, but here we discuss only one.

Consider finite particle number, spacially bounded, quantum systems. The wave function Ψ, which determines everything of physical interest for all such systems, is known to be almost periodic in time. An *almost periodic function* F is one which undergoes aperiodic oscillations such that the function F, having achieved any value once, makes near returns to that value throughout all time. The function $[\sin(t) + \sin(t\sqrt{2})]$ is a simple but quite typical example of an almost periodic function. This almost periodic behaviour clearly implies that no member of this broad class of quantum systems is chaotic, despite the fact that many of the corresponding classical systems are fully chaotic, for the quantum motion is much too regular to even mimic chaos much less be chaos. Indeed, since this almost periodic motion persists for every value of $\hbar > 0$, no matter how small, it becomes natural to inquire if this class of quantum systems actually obeys the correspondence principle which, for the case at hand, asserts that chaos must appear when required by the classical limit. Many have suggested the following inventive resolution. One may anticipate that chaos (randomness) can occur in almost periodic motion at least during the initial time-interval before any near-period has occurred. Then, because it may be shown that the length of all near-periods become large as $\hbar$ becomes small, one may expect the original small seed of randomness (chaos) to grow to macroscopic size as $\hbar$ tends to zero. In this way, the lack of chaos at the deep quantum level can grow into the full randomness of classical chaos. This argument is quite ingenious, but it is also quite wrong.

An almost periodic wave function Ψ can always be written as a sum of trigonometric functions such as the $\sin(t)$ and $\sin(t\sqrt{2})$ above. Let us then regard each such trig term as specifying the position of a runner moving along a linear track between zero and one. At time zero, these runners occupy specified positions relative to each other, but as time goes on, since all runners move at their own speeds, they get 'out of phase' and their instantaneous positions appear to have no relationship one to the other. Yet if, at a given instant, we request each runner to reverse his velocity and then continue as before, we would find that the runners will eventually all occupy their original positions. This may seem a trivial point since both classical and quantal motion can always be reversed, in principle. However, even following a somewhat inaccurate, rather sloppy time-reversal, our runners will very nearly regain their initial configuration. Of course, the reversal cannot be too sloppily done, but absolute accuracy is not required. Indeed, there are actual laboratory systems which can be used to illustrate this 'easy' time-reversal phenomena. The essential point here is that such 'easy' time-reversals occur primarily only in systems which are non-chaotic. Specifically, in order to time reverse chaotic systems for any but the briefest time-intervals, one must use the extremes of accuracy. In summary, finite, bounded, quantum systems can, in principle, be shown by reversal to be non-chaotic no matter the smallness of $\hbar > 0$ and no matter that their classical counterparts be chaotic. The possibility that some future investigator will reveal these systems to be part of a larger Achilles' heel not previously detected in quantum mechanics now looms quite large indeed. And now on to the closing.

It is my sincerest hope that this brief article may induce a reader here or there to join the amateurs, the dilettantes, the connoisseurs, the aficionados, and the disciples of chaos as they seek to cope with the challenge facing us all. Chaos now presages the future as none will gainsay. But to accept the future, we must renounce much of the past, a formidable task indeed, for as Leo Tolstoy poignantly recognized, even brilliant scientists can seldom accept the simplest and most obvious truths if they be such as to contradict principles learned as children, taught as professors, and revered as sacred truths throughout their lives. How will *you* decide? Help with that decision is to be found in my article 'What Is Chaos, that We Should Be Mindful of It?' which appeared in *The New Physics*, edited by Paul Davies (Cambridge University Press, Cambridge, 1989), 348–72.

14

The Hierarchies of Knowledge and the Mathematics of Discovery

CLARK GLYMOUR

Philosophy before and after mid-century is united in a rejection of a central goal of traditional epistemology from Plato to Boole: a theory of discovery. Plato and Aristotle thought the goal of philosophy, among other goals, was to provide methods for coming to have knowledge. This same conception utterly dominated philosophy in the seventeenth century. It was Descartes' claim to have found such a method, and the disputes between him and his critics were in part over what it is to be a method of discovery at all. Leibniz not only advanced the conception of method, but provided a thesis about it that guided logical investigations into the twentieth century. In my view, the central eighteenth-century dispute in philosophy, between Hume and Kant, was fundamentally about whether we can have methods of inquiry that can be known to be reliable. The latter part of the century provided in Richard Price's interpretation of Bayes' probabilism yet another proposal for a universal method of discovery. English-speaking philosophers of the succeeding century were equally absorbed with discovery: John Stuart Mill popularized a method plagarized from Bacon and, in aid of a method for discovering causal relations from probabilities, George Boole made the largest advance in logical theory since Aristotle.

But after 1925 or thereabouts, there was in philosophy almost

I am indebted to Kevin Kelly for several years of happy conversation from which the perspective and views of this paper grew, for comments on a draft of the paper, and for constructing some of the illustrations. A fellowship from the John Simon Guggenheim Memorial Foundation provided the liberty to write this paper.

nothing more of methods of discovery. A tradition that joined together much of the classical philosophical literature simply vanished. From about 1930 to about 1960 philosophy of science was in fashion, and certain questions of epistemology—the existence of sense-data, for example, and the role of stipulations in our systems of belief—won the attention of even the most eminent philosophers. These were not the sorts of epistemological questions, however, that were the principal focus of epistemology for major philosophical writers before our century. And since the middle of the 1960s scarcely any major philosopher has thought even these epistemological questions worth much bother, let alone questions as to the best method of making discoveries or the limits of the discoverable. The latter questions are now commonly thought to be absurd and to make false and naïve presuppositions of one kind or another. As late as the 1980s a philosophical reporter could truly announce that most philosophers hold that there is and can be 'no systematic, useful study of theory construction or discovery'.[1] (In so far as they gave any heed to the question at all, the same might well have been said of most scientific practitioners: of statisticians, social scientists, economists, physicists.) The pre-eminent view among philosophers nowadays is that claims to knowledge, or to the possession of normative standards for methods of acquiring knowledge, are so much rhetoric, so much politics; truth, in so far as it is a useful notion at all, is relative to the conditions of the believer, and there are no matters of fact independent of the inquirer and the community.

In contrast, traditional epistemological questions were at the very heart of this century's revolutionary developments in logic and computation theory. From the mathematical logic of Hilbert, Gödel, and others, from the theory of computation created by Church, Post, and Turing, and from the theory of recursion there developed in the last twenty-five years a beautiful mathematical theory of methods of discovery and of the limits of knowledge, a theory that directly addresses the central epistemological concerns of the great philosophical tradition before this century. It is a theory about discovery that is nice in itself, of use to serious scientific concerns, and even applies to the concerns of the effete: it contains epistemological norms for those who hold that truth is

---

[1] W. H. Newton-Smith, *The Rationality of Science*, London: Routledge & Kegan Paul, 1981: 125.

relative to conceptual scheme. The subject has lain almost completely hidden from the view of philosophers and practitioners. I did not come upon it until fifteen years ago, after I had written a book on epistemology that concluded by calling for the creation of a theory whose fundamentals had already existed for fifteen years. My aim is to tell you something about the development of this subject, and to discuss some of its applications.

THE PLATONIC-POSITIVIST EPISTEMIC HIERARCHY

Plato's *Meno* presents a view about inquiry and discovery that has had an enduring appeal. In that dialogue the Socratic task is to learn truths of a special kind. From a logical point of view, what is to be learned, for example about the nature of virtue, is a universal biconditional sentence without disjunction that can serve as an appropriate definition, e.g. of 'is virtuous'. The learning is by example and counter-example. Socrates presents examples of virtuous things and their features, and examples of things that are not virtuous and their features; the correctness of the data of the examples and counter-examples is never in doubt. What is it that Plato requires in order for someone to have discovered in this way the answer to the question, 'What is virtue?' To know the answer, one must hit upon the correct definition of virtue, and *know* that one has done so. One must have the kind of certainty that amounts to a dogmatism, and reserves no right to alteration: *opinion* can change, knowledge cannot. How such knowledge is possible is the point of Meno's challenge to Socrates: How will Socrates recognize the truth when he comes upon it? Plato's answer appeals to an internal oracle that somehow guarantees the correctness of certain definitions.[2] Without the oracle, nothing is firm save the examples and the counter-examples.

In the 1930s, philosophical conceptions of discovery were essentially Plato's but without the oracle. It was supposed that there are some matters that are simply data, and either permanently or contextually fixed. They are the 'sense data' or 'observation statements' or 'protocol sentences'. They met the Platonic criterion for

---

[2] For a more detailed discussion of the *Meno* see C. Glymour and K. Kelly, 'Thoroughly Modern Meno', in J. Earman (ed.), *Pittsburgh Studies in Philosophy of Science*, Berkeley and Los Angeles: University of California Press, 1992.

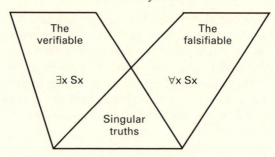

FIG 1. The positivist hierarchy

the discoverable: once accepted in the context of some inquiry, one could be sure that they would not be abandoned. Only two other kinds of discoveries met that criterion: mathematical truths, and sentences verified by the data. With only a little logical knowledge, philosophers in this period understood the verifiable and the refutable to have special logical forms, namely as existential and universal sentences respectively. There was, implicitly, a positivist hierarchy (see Figure 1). Positivists such as Schlick confined science and meaning to singular data and verifiable sentences; 'anti-positivists', notably Popper, confined science to the singular data and falsifiable sentences. In both cases, what could be known or discovered consisted of the singular data and verifiable sentences, although there is a hint of something else in Popper's view. In Popper's conception inquiry consists of conjecturing falsifiable sentences and attempting to falsify them; Popper in effect agreed with Plato that knowledge requires a kind of unalterability, but unlike Plato he did not think that the process of science obtains knowledge. Popper and the positivists agreed that there could not, in any case, be an *algorithm* for carrying out scientific inquiry. Why not?

In the Platonic conception, an algorithm for scientific discovery must be a procedure that examines data and, after a finite time, announces the truth. Whenever the procedure results in such an announcement, it must be correct. There must be no possibility of revision. The Platonic conception of an algorithm for discovery was also the philosophers' conception in the twentieth century, but the philosophers did not hold with oracles. They rightly believed that no such algorithm is possible for the claims of science. There are algorithms of this kind that will reliably conclude when

universally quantified formulas are false, but none that will conclude when they are true, and science is filled with what appear
to be universal claims. That is one reason for denying that there
is an algorithm for scientific discovery. Another is the changes
in physics that had taken place in the three decades before 1930,
and that were familiar to many philosophers. If there were an
algorithm for discovery, one could only think that the practice
of science embodied a social version of it. And if there were such
an algorithm embodied in scientific practice, then most certainly
by the latter half of the nineteenth century that algorithm had
announced the truth of Newtonian physics. John Tyndall, for
example, announced in popular lectures that the framework of
physics was fixed forever; all that remained to do was to find
the various force laws. The years between 1905 and 1926 utterly
demolished Tindall's claim. A further reason for thinking that
empirical discovery could be subject to algorithm was the author-
ity of Albert Einstein, who with charming inconsistency claimed
both determinism in human affairs and that scientific theories are
'free creations'. For Popper—who quite confused a psychological
question with a mathematical issue—it sufficed to quote Einstein
to disprove the possibility of a discovery algorithm; for Carnap it
sufficed to quote Popper quoting Einstein.

THE ENTSCHEIDUNGSPROBLEM AND ALGORITHMS FOR MATHEMATICAL DISCOVERY

Frege's remarkable logical achievement was a theory of proof;
a proof theory for what is now known as first-order logic is
explicit in the *Begriffschrift*. Two questions naturally arose for
which Frege provided no answer: Is the system of proof complete? Is there an algorithmic procedure that will, for any formula,
decide whether or not it is provable? The importance of these
questions is, of course, epistemological. Hilbert and others suggested that a positive answer to the two questions would show
that it is in a sense in principle possible to carry out Leibniz's
vision. If Hilbert and Ackermann's proof theory, for example,
were complete and admitted a decision procedure, then there
would exist a method to discover the consequences of any first-
order axiomatization.

Not long after the questions had been clearly formulated, Gödel answered the first question affirmatively, and gave reason to think the answer to the second question is negative. Church and Turing settled the question altogether. In so far as the philosophical community took note of the epistemological significance of these results, they cemented the conviction that there can be no such thing as algorithms for empirical discovery, and no interesting theory about them. And yet from a logical point of view, because of Gödel's completeness theorem, the undecidability of the validity of first-order formulas did not quite kill the idea of an algorithm for mathematical discovery. Rather, it throws into clear relief an epistemological idea about what it is to come to know something, an idea that is quite different from the Platonic and the Positivist conception.

Consider trying to discover whether or not a certain first-order formula Φ is valid. Since Hilbert and Ackermann's system is complete, if Φ is valid there is a proof of it. Since there is a decision procedure that decides whether or not a finite sequence of formulas is a proof, and since the collection of all finite sequences of well-formed formulas can be effectively enumerated, we can imagine a procedure that examines each finite sequence of formulas in such an enumeration in turn, and checks to see whether or not it is a proof of Φ, and stops when a proof is found. Call this procedure P. The procedure P will eventually find a proof if in fact Φ is valid. Otherwise the procedure will continue on forever. Suppose now that we adopt the following rule for formulating hypotheses as to whether or not Φ is valid:

> If at stage n, P does not say that a proof of Φ has been found, conjecture that Φ is not valid.

Is this an algorithm for acquiring knowledge about logical truth? Clearly not, if your conception of what it is to know is Plato's. Using this algorithm, if Φ is not valid, there is no time at which you can be certain of that fact, no time at which you can rock back and say, 'No further evidence is needed.' But the rule for formulating conjectures has a property that suggests a different conception of what it is to know: *Using this rule, there is some finite stage after which your conjectures as to whether or not Φ is valid will always be correct.* Eventually you will be right forever after, although if Φ is not valid you will never know when that stage has arrived, and you will never be able to dispense with further evidence. Perhaps that is all *knowledge* requires. Perhaps you know the truth about the validity of Φ if you are disposed to conjecture by a rule that has this convergence property and you have in fact reached a stage after which conjectures made according to that disposition are always correct. Call this sort of relation *knowledge in the limit*.

I doubt that there is one true account of what it is to know, but certainly this is an interesting knowledge relation, and one we can have even when we can't have the sort of knowledge Plato required. When can we have knowledge in the limit, and when not? We have just seen that we can have it for the validity of any first-order sentence. When can we have it for empirical issues? There's a good question.

TURING, PUTNAM, AND GOLD

The epistemological idea about knowledge in the limit is implicit in many contexts in the twentieth century. Abraham Robinson remarked that something like it is to be found in Gödel's proof of the completeness theorem. But the articulation of the idea came almost simultaneously in the 1960s from two independent sources, Hilary Putnam and E. Mark Gold. It seems likely that Putnam took the idea from Hans Reichenbach and combined it with reflections on Turing's conventions for the output of a computing machine. In Putnam's words:

we know what sets are 'decidable'—namely, the recursive sets (according to Church's thesis). But what happens if we modify the notion of a decision procedure by (1) allowing the procedure to 'change its mind' any finite number of times (in terms of Turing machines: we visualize the machine as being given an integer (or an *n*-tuple of integers) as input. The machine then 'prints out' a finite sequence of 'yesses' and 'nos.' The *last* 'yes' or 'no' is always to be the correct answer); and (2) we give up the requirement that it be possible to tell (effectively) if the computation has terminated, i.e. if the machine has most recently printed 'yes', then we know that the integer put in as input must be in the set *unless the machine is going to change its mind*; but we have no procedure for telling whether the machine will change its mind or not.

The sets for which there exist decision procedures in this widened sense are decidable by 'empirical' means—for, if we always 'posit' that the most recently generated answer is correct, we will make a finite number of mistakes, but we will eventually get the correct answer. (Note, however, that even if we have gotten to the correct answer (the end of the finite sequence) we are never *sure* that we have the correct answer.)

Instead of requiring that the sequence of 'yesses' and 'nos' be finite and non-empty, we may require that it should always be infinite, but that it should consist entirely of 'yesses' (or entirely of 'nos') from a certain point on; the class of predicates obtained ... is easily seen to be unchanged.[3]

Gold called such sets 'limiting recursive', Putnam called them the extensions of 'trial and error predicates'. Gold's terminology has stuck. Gold and Putnam each proved the same main theorem: A set is limiting recursive if and only if it is in Δ_2 in the arithmetic hierarchy. Gold proved a similar result for recursive functionals. Putnam's proof, which I paraphrase as follows, is easy and instructive.

Recall that the Δ_2 sets in the arithmetical hierarchy are the following: A set S is Σ_2 if there is a formula $\exists x \forall y R(xyz)$ such that R is a recursive predicate of triples of numbers and S is the set of all numbers satisfying the formula. A set is Π_2 if its negation is Σ_2. If you drive the negation through the quantifiers in a Σ_2 formula you get a formula that is universal existential with a recursive predicate. A set is Δ_2 provided that it is both Σ_2 and Π_2. In other words, a set is Δ_2 provided that there is a formula $\exists x \forall y R(xyz)$ such that R is a recursive predicate of triples of numbers and S is the set of all numbers satisfying the formula, and also there is a formula $\exists x \forall y P(xyz)$ such that P is a recursive predicate of triples of numbers and the complement of S is the set of all numbers satisfying that formula.

Suppose that S is an arbitrary set of numbers, and there is a Turing machine T that for every number n converges in the limit to 'yes' if n is in S and converges to 'no' if n is in the complement of S. The predicates 'T on input x converges in the limit to "yes"'; and 'T on input x converges in the limit to "no"' can each be formalized in number theory, e.g. $\exists m \forall n \; n > m \rightarrow T(x,n) = 1$ and $\exists m \forall n \; n > m \rightarrow T(x,n) = 0$, where '$T(x,n)$' denotes a total recursive function. So they are each in Σ_2. Since by assumption T must for

---

[3] H. Putnam, 'Trial and Error Predicates and the Solution to a Problem of Mostowski', *Journal of Symbolic Logic*, 30 (1965): 49–57, at 49. Gold's paper, 'Limiting Recursion' is in the same issue, 28–48.

any input converge to 'yes' or 'no' and cannot forever vacillate, 'T on input x converges to 1' is satisfied by a value of x if and only if for every stage y of computation such that $T(x,y)$ is not 1, there is some later stage z for which $T(x,z) = 1$. So 'T on input x converges in the limit to "yes"' is also equivalent to $\forall y \exists z[T(x,y) \neq 1 \rightarrow (z > y) \ \& \ T(x,z) = 1)]$. So the predicate is also Π_2. Hence S is a Δ_2 set.

Suppose, conversely, that S is a Δ_2 set. Then S is a set of numbers that satisfy $\exists x \forall y R(xyz)$ for some recursive R and the complement of S is the set of numbers that satisfy $\exists x \forall y P(xyz)$ for some recursive P. Let $T1$ be a Turing machine that computes (in the usual way) $R(xyz)$ and let To be a Turing machine that computes (in the usual way) $P(xyz)$. Given input z, the set of all triples xyz can be effectively enumerated. Let $(n,m,z)_i$ denote the ith triple in some such enumeration. For each i, using $T1$ a machine $T11$ can check effectively whether or not $\exists x \forall y R(xyz)$ is true in the set of all triples $(n,m,z)_h$ for $i \geq h$. Let the output of $T11$ be 1 for the ith set of triples if $\exists x \forall y R(xyz)$ is thus satisfied and o otherwise. Similarly, using To a machine Too can check effectively whether or not $\exists x \forall y P(xyz)$ is true in the set of all triples $(n,m,z)_h$ for $i \geq h$. Let the output of Too for the ith triple be 1 if $\exists x \forall y P(xyz)$ is thus satisfied and o otherwise. Now let $T(z,n)$ be the machine that on input z gives an infinite string of outputs whose nth, $T(z,n)$, is 1 if $T11(n)$ is 1 and is preceded by a longer uninterrupted string of 1s than is $Too(n)$, and let $T(z,n)$ be o otherwise. $T(z,n)$ is the machine that computes S in the limit.

Although tied to computation, the idea behind Putnam's proof has a more general epistemological significance. Suppose given any triple of objects $<u,v,w>$ you have some way of determining whether or not they satisfy $R(xyz)$. Never mind about computers, just some way. Suppose, over some domain, you can investigate each triple of objects making the determination as you go. Then if $\exists x \forall y R(xyz)$ is true, you can know in the limit that it is: just keep guessing 'yes' if the formula is satisfied for all triples (with z) you have seen so far, and 'no' otherwise. If the formula is true after a finite time you will find a value of x that in fact stands in the relation $R(xyz)$ for all values of y, and you will be correct in your guess ever after; if the formula is false, you will either converge to 'no' or change from 'yes' to 'no' or back again infinitely often. And if it is the case that if formula F is true you can know it in the limit, and also that if ¬F is true you can know it in the limit, then by running the two inquiries jointly you can know in the limit whether or not F (and likewise whether or not ¬F) is true. It looks as though what you can know in the limit is characterized by existential and universal quantification over what you can know in the Platonic way.

CONFIRMATION RELATIONS AND LANGUAGES

How does one get from the characterization of the limiting recursive sets of numbers to an understanding of empirical questions for which discovery methods do and do not exist? There was a direct route, which was not taken. Hilary Putnam seems to have come to the idea through two prior papers about limitations on the reliability of Carnapian confirmation functions.[4] His arguments assumed in effect that there is a collection of possible relational structures, and the learning procedure is given, singular fact by singular fact, the diagram of some structure in the collection. At each stage the learner must either guess a hypothesis or alter the probabilities it assigns to the hypotheses in light of the evidence. The question is whether the machine can eventually output the truth, or eventually always give the true hypothesis: a probability (or degree of confirmation) greater than $1/2$. These papers are wonderfully prescient in seeing that confirmation theories are cogs in possible learning algorithms and in struggling to form a framework in which to evaluate such algorithms. They were unfortunately wrong in their optimism. Writing in 1963, Putnam saw that there was a rich structure to investigate and assumed that logicians and philosophers of science would turn to uncovering it. By and large save for his own work and Gold's that didn't happen, and by the time Putnam's vision was realized, confirmation theory no longer interested philosophers.

Gold applied the idea of limiting recursion to issues motivated by Chomsky's work rather than by Carnap's: the problems of language learning. The application is quite natural. Chomsky was concerned with Universal Grammar—the grammatical features shared

---

[4] See his essays on Carnap and 'Probability and Confirmation', repr. as chs. 17 and 18 of vol. 1 of his collected papers, *Mathematics, Matter and Method*, Cambridge: Cambridge University Press, 1975.

by all possible human natural languages—and a principal constraint on that hypothetical grammar was that, whatever the set of possible human natural languages might be, it must be possible for a human to learn to parse any language in that collection. What collections of languages meet that condition?

Gold reformulated the question this way. Give the well-formed sentences of a language Gödel numbers. Then, syntactically, a language L can be represented as a recursive set of numbers. One way to view a parser for the language is then as a Turing machine or other program that decides for any number whether or not it is the number of a grammatical string in the language. We can effectively enumerate the Turing machines, giving each program a number or index. Learning to parse a language implies that one has identified, at least implicitly, the index of a program for deciding the set of well-formed strings of that language. Suppose that the would-be learner receives the well-formed strings of the language in some order, and never receives (or ignores) strings that are not in the language. Every string in the language eventually occurs, and a string may occur any number of times, even infinitely often. Suppose after each string is received the learner guesses a program (or an index for a program) that he conjectures will parse exactly the unknown language. For what collections of languages does there exist a learner who, no matter which language is the correct one and no matter in what order the data are received, will obtain limiting knowledge of the index of a program to parse the language?

Gold showed that there are simple collections of languages that cannot be learned in the limit by any possible learner, not even by one free of computational constraints. A famous and simple example is the collection consisting of all finite subsets of N together with N.

Gold's paper was followed in the next twenty years by a great deal of work on language learning. The assumptions about data and convergence criteria were altered in various ways, notions of approximation introduced, relations among the paradigms were studied extensively, the effects of methodological strictures on the capacities of learners were studied, and ever more psychologically realistic learning constraints were investigated. Many of these results are presented in Osherson, Stob, and Weinstein's *Systems That Learn* (MIT Press, 1986). One of the fundamental results

of this literature was obtained by Dana Angluin ('Inductive Inference of Formal Languages from Positive Data', *Information and
Control* 45(1980): 117–35), who provided a characterization of
necessary and sufficient conditions for any subset of the collection
of recursively enumerable languages to admit a learner that could
identify any language in the collection in the limit no matter the
order in which the strings of the language were presented as data.
Of course these collections of alternative languages were necessarily countable.

LEARNING THEORIES

Despite the interesting methodological structure of the studies of
language learning in the limit, it was not evident just how to make
it apply to the questions with which we began concerning methods
of empirical discovery. The movement back to Putnam's original
concerns began with Angluin's student, Ehud Shapiro.[5] Recall our
discussion of the problem of deciding validity, and the existence
of procedures that will decide validity in the limit. In the same
way, there are procedures that will decide entailment in the limit.
This suggests a sort of Popperian approach to discovery: formulate
a hypothesis, gather evidence in the form of singular sentences
and see if, in the limit, all of the evidence can be deduced from
the hypothesis and no denial of any evidence sentence can be so
deduced. Somehow order the possible hypotheses so that their
testing, gathering further evidence, changing conjectures appropriately, etc., can be dovetailed. Shapiro described algorithms of
this sort that find a true finite axiomatization of all of the atomic
sentences true in a structure when such an axiomatization exists.
The predicates occurring in the hypotheses must be the same as
those occurring in the evidence.

Suppose we consider a collection of relational structures for a
language. Imagine that one of the structures, we know not which,
characterizes our actual circumstances. Whichever world is actual,
we will receive from it a sequence of singular facts characterizing
the diagram of the structure. The order of the sequence of data

---

[5] E. Y. Shapiro, *Algorithmic Program Debugging*, Cambridge, Mass.: MIT
Press, 1983.

is not subject to our control. Generally we want something other than a true finite axiomatization that entails all of the true atomic sentences. What might that be?

It might be that we want to know which theory within a certain class of alternative theories is correct. Suppose so. We could learn a theory in the limit in at least two different senses. In one sense, called *EA* or uniform learning, we learn a theory by converging in the limit to a conjecture for that theory (or if the theory is not finitely axiomatizable and we insist that the outputs of our conjecturing process be finite objects, to a program for computing a set of axioms for the theory). So there exists a point after which all of our conjectures about the identity of the true theory are correct. In another sense, called *AE* or non-uniform learning, we could learn a theory by converging in the limit piece by piece. That is, for every theorem of the theory there exists a point after which every theory conjectured entails that theorem, and for every sentence that is not a theorem of the theory there exists a point after which no theory conjectured entails that sentence. Kevin Kelly and I characterized by syntactic classes the cases for first-order theories in which the true alternative can (and cannot) be identified in the *EA* or *AE* sense, either by Turing-computable learners or by learners that embody arbitrary functions—learners who have powers that transcend the computable. Later work extended the classification for *AE* theory learning to cases in which quantified sentences occur in the data.[6]

Another thing we might want in empirical inquiry is the answer to a specific question. We might consider discovery problems set up closer to those Putnam envisaged, in which a question is posed by a first-order sentence whose truth value is to be determined, data are obtained from an unknown structure in a collection of alternative structures, and conjectures are made as to the truth or falsity of the sentence in the unknown structure. This case was investigated by Dan Osherson and Scott Weinstein,[7] who distinguished a number of alternative senses of convergence to the truth: the learner can converge to the correct truth value for Φ if Φ is

---

[6] K. T. Kelly and C. Glymour, 'Convergence to the Truth and Nothing but the Truth', *Philosophy of Science*, 56(1989): 185–220, and 'Theory Discovery from Data with Mixed Quantifiers', *Journal of Philosophical Logic*, 19(1990): 1–33.

[7] D. N. Osherson and S. Weinstein, 'Paradigms of Truth Detection', *Journal of Philosophical Logic*, 18 (1989): 1–42.

true but possibly fail to converge otherwise; converge to the correct truth value if Φ is false; or do both. They showed that for learners with 'free will' AE theory learning is possible if and only if there is a learner who can converge to the truth for any sentence in the language of the theory. Importing methods from the investigation of language learning, they showed that various methodological principles, such as consistency and conservatism, restrict the scope of the reliability of any Turing-computable learner. And, by the same means, they characterized the conditions for which it is possible to obtain knowledge in the limit about the truth of a sentence, provided the number of alternative relational structures is countable and the learner is required to succeed on all possible orderings of the complete data true in a structure.

This work on learning theories had two obvious points of weakness, shared in principle by the work on language learning. First, the collections of alternative structures or theories over which discovery is possible may be *uncountable*. There are, for example, uncountably many distinct purely universal theories, but there is a learner (in fact a Turing-computable learner) that will learn (AE) any purely universal theory. But the characterizations of necessary and sufficient conditions for knowledge in the limit, whether of languages or of the truth or falsity of first-order formulas, were restricted to cases in which the number of alternative structures is countable. Second, all of the investigations considered, whether of language learning or theory learning, assumed that every possible ordering of the data could occur. The learner is never permitted to have prior knowledge restricting the order in which the data arrive. In fact that is quite implausible both for language learning and for theory learning. To fully understand knowledge in the limit, these two artificial restrictions needed to be removed. Recent work by Kelly has removed them by returning to the original ideas in Gold's and Putnam's papers.

THE HIERARCHIES

Suppose that the facts that may occur as data, whether the strings in a language or singular or quantified formulas satisfied in a structure, are encoded as numbers. Then an infinite data sequence is an ω sequence of numbers. So a data sequence can be thought of as a function from ω to ω, assigning to each finite ordinal the datum that occurs there. Now consider the set B of all such sequences. Extensionally, any property of data sequences is a subset of B. For example, if the data are from languages, then for any language there is a subset of B corresponding to the set of all infinite sequences of strings from the language; if the data are from a relational structure, then for any structure there is a subset of B corresponding to the set of all infinite sequences of singular data. This suggests that the way to avoid the limitation of previous investigations to circumstances in which the data from a language or structure can occur in any order is to investigate which properties of data sequences can be known in the limit. That is, instead of thinking in terms of identifying languages or identifying relational structures or learning theories, let us ask the more general question: when can we know in the limit that the data sequence we are investigating has a specific property? If we know the answer to that question, the answers to other questions will follow as special cases.

Gold's and Putnam's papers suggest the following idea: what you can know to be true in the limit is what you can get by quantifying existentially and universally over what you can know Platonically. Some analogies transform this suggestion into guides for investigating the possibility of knowing properties of data sequences in the limit: what you can know Platonically is just the initial segments of data sequences. Quantifying existentially is analogous to taking infinite disjunctions, which is analogous to taking infinite unions. Quantifying universally is analogous to taking infinite conjunctions, which is analogous to taking infinite intersections. We can describe a hierarchy of collections of subsets of B using an analogy. Consider any subset S of B for which there is a set of initial segments such that all and only data sequences in B having those initial segments are in S. Call the collection of such subsets Σ_1. Consider the collection of subsets of B each member of which is the complement of some set in Σ_1. Call this collection Π_1. Let Δ_1 be the intersection of Σ_1 and Π_1. Now consider the collection of all subsets of B that are (countable) unions of sets in Π_1. Call this collection Σ_2. Consider the collection of all subsets of B that are (countable) intersections of sets in Σ_1. Call this collection Π_2. Let Δ_2 be the intersection of Σ_2 and Π_2. Continue in this way forever and ever again. The result is a hierarchy that is closed upwards, the Borel hierarchy.

The sets in Σ_1 correspond to those properties such that if a sequence has such a property some computationally unbounded learner can eventually have Platonic knowledge that it does. (Just wait until one of the initial segments characteristic of the set appears.) The sets in Π_1 correspond to the properties such that if a sequence fails to have the property, some computationally unbounded learner can eventually have Platonic knowledge that it fails to have the property, i.e. that it has the complementary property. The properties such that some unbounded learner can have Platonic knowledge of whether or not the data sequence under investigation has that property are given extensionally by sets in Δ_1.

We might suspect that the knowledge in the limit available to a computationally unbounded learner corresponds to sets in Δ_2 in the Borel hierarchy. That is what Kelly proved. In fact he proved something stronger. We can think of 'background knowledge' as given by a subset K of B. Starting not with the sets of data sequences that share an initial segment but instead with intersections of such sets with K, we can build a relativized Borel hierarchy. Kelly has shown that if P is any subset of B, a computationally bounded learner with background knowledge K can know in the limit whether or not a data sequence is in $P \cap K$ if and only if $P \cap K$ is in Δ_2 in the hierarchy relativized to K.

And what if discovery must be done by computationally bounded agents? The key to the solution to that question lies in Gold's use of the recursive functionals. Consider a Turing-machine learner at work on a sequence from B. There is actually some w sequence the learner is receiving as data, and at each stage the learner outputs either 1 or 0. So the learner can be thought of as a partial recursive functional $T\,[t,n]$ where t is the infinite sequence, and hence really a function from w to w, and n is the stage of data presentation. A Turing-machine interpretation of such a functional is as a machine that can, for any t and n, receive the first n values of t before producing an output. We are asking, in effect, not which sets of numbers are computable in the limit, but which sets of functions from the natural numbers to the natural numbers are computable in the limit.

Now just as there is a recursion-theoretic (arithmetic) hierarchy for sets of numbers, there is a recursion-theoretic (arithmetic) hierarchy for sets of functionals. A functional of type (k,j), is just a finite sequence of k functions from w to w and j numbers. A relation is a set of functionals all of the same type. We can think of relations of type $(1,0)$ as subsets of B. The recursion-theoretic hierarchy can be constructed analogously to the Borel hierarchy, but using quantifiers rather than unions and intersections. In the same way, starting with background knowledge K, one can construct a relativized hierarchy. Kelly proved that a Turing-computable learner with background knowledge K can know in the limit whether or not a relation obtains if and only if the relation is Δ_2 in this hierarchy. The same result is implicit in Gold's Theorem 4.

Together these results yield general characterizations for Turing-computable and for computationally unbounded learners both of language learning in the limit and of detecting the truth or falsity of a first-order formula in the limit. The characterizations are not limited to cases in which the number of alternative structures or languages is countable, and they do not require that one assume that every ordering of the data is possible.

Kelly's results don't close the subject; they open it up for application and investigation. For example, Kelly derives a characterization of conditions under which the truth or falsity of a given first-order hypothesis can be known in the limit; one of the surprising consequences is that if any such problem can be solved by a computationally unbounded learner, it can also be solved by a Turing-computable learner. So far as deciding in the limit the truth or falsity of a given first-order sentence, the Turing computability of the learner is no handicap. But that is not so when we consider the AE learning of theories. We have only limited knowledge of when theories can be learned AE by a Turing-computable learner. We will come across a number of other open questions in what follows.

RELATIVISM

Whenever something is a lot of work folks are bound to look for reasons why it isn't worth the effort. There are lots of complaints about limiting analyses of learning that seem mere excuses. For example, that no one cares what happens in the long run. The reply is twofold: first, that short-run results are much to be desired but require strong background knowledge that we often fail to have, and, second, if you can't know the truth in the long run, you can't know it in the short run either. Another is that the results and techniques can't be applied to 'real'—meaning other people's—problems. We'll see that they can be indeed. Still other excuses appeal to some relevant factor of inquiry that is not explicitly represented in the formal representations—experimentation, for example. The response is that it is in principle straightforward to include experimentation in the framework, and work to that end is already under way.

But there is a further objection that is more fundamental and that is surprisingly interesting. Suppose one denies, with many prominent contemporary philosophers, that there is any one common world of inquiry. Suppose one denies that there are any facts of experience to serve as data that are independent of the inquirer. Instead one holds that, depending on what one believes, on one's history, on the community to which one belongs, or other factors, there will be different data. Even suppose that depending on such factors the very character of logic may change. Then all of the results I have so far described are otiose; they do not apply, they are 'inoperative'.

These are the suppositions that dominate contemporary philosophical discussion. Their champions conclude that there are no such things as epistemological norms, because there are no such things as intelligible epistemological goals. I find these views enormously distasteful. Each time I read or hear some plump and comfortable academic saying such things I am overcome by images from *Darkness at Noon*. But that is no reason not to think about the epistemology of relative truth. It turns out to have an astonishing and intricate structure, altogether unseen and unexplored either by its advocates or its critics.

Suppose that the world of experience is a function of some feature of the inquirer. Even the most radical critics of science rarely hold that what one experiences depends on what one believes or does and on nothing else. So the world of experience is a function of features of the inquirer and of features, we know not what, that are not subject to the inquirer's power. For brevity let us call the first set of factors the 'conceptual scheme' of the inquirer and the second set of factors the 'world in itself'. Then the world of experience is a function of conceptual scheme, which is subject to the inquirer's choice and decision, and of the world in

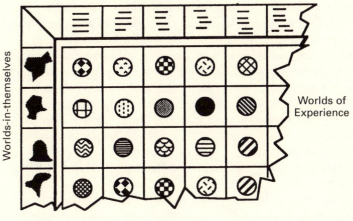

FIG 2.

itself, which is not. We can think of the world in itself abstractly as simply a function that for each possible conceptual scheme determines a world of experience (see Figure 2).

Now if truth is relative and cannot be formed entirely by your will, then one traditional epistemological goal becomes impossible: evidence cannot be expected to produce agreement among different inquirers. But the notion of invariant truth unites agreement with another goal, getting to the truth, and when the possibility of getting to agreement is eliminated, the possibility of getting to the truth, even the relative truth, remains. A perfectly intelligible epistemological goal is to find the relative truth for you about some question. Since we do not want to presuppose anything about logic, let a question be given simply by some finite string S over some finite set of elements. Each pair consisting of a world in itself and a conceptual scheme determines a status for the string: it is meaningful and true, meaningful and false, or meaningless. As the inquirer changes conceptual schemes the status of S changes.

A whole range of questions suddenly appears. We can think of a discovery problem as given by a set of possible worlds in themselves and a set of possible conceptual schemes, with each member of their Cartesian product determining a world of experience. Suppose the inquirer receives data from any world of experience, just as in non-relativist discovery problems, but when he changes conceptual schemes, the world of experience from which he thereafter receives data also changes, depending on which world in itself is the actual one. Can the inquirer know the truth value of S in the limit? That might mean: can he find a conceptual scheme in which S has a truth value and stay in that conceptual scheme forever and converge to the correct truth value for S? Or it might mean: can he reach a point after which his changes of conceptual schemes have no effect on the truth value of S and after which his conjectures about that truth value are correct? Or it might mean: is there a point after which S always has a truth value and the inquirer always guesses the correct truth value for S, even though (because the inquirer changes conceptual schemes) the truth value of S may change?

It is easy to construct simple examples of relativistic learning problems in which none of these kinds of knowledge can be obtained. Moreover, these different senses of knowledge in the limit are strictly inequivalent; there are problems that are solvable in the last sense but not in the second, and problems solvable in the second sense but not in the first. One can show that restrictions on conceptual schemes restrict the capacity for knowledge in the limit in each of these three senses. For example, there are problems involving an infinity of possible conceptual schemes that cannot be solved by any learner who is limited to a finite number of alternative conceptual schemes.

For the case in which the number of alternative conceptual schemes is finite, Kelly and I characterized the relativist discovery problems that are solvable in each of these three senses of 'knowledge in the limit'. For each conception of convergence there is a universal learner that will solve any problem solvable by any learner. In order to guarantee success, some fairly intricate strategies must be followed in deciding when to gather further evidence using a particular conceptual scheme and when to change conceptual schemes. If you believe yourself to be in a relativist system and your goal is to get to the relative truth for you, then the features of such strategies are epistemological norms.

Relativists might complain that they don't know which relativist system they are in, so they can't apply the norms, and a norm that cannot be applied is no norm at all. Can they learn which relativistic system they are in? Perhaps they think that which relativistic system one is in is relative to his conceptual scheme.

Can one then learn the relative truth value of strings interpreted as claims about which relativistic system one is in? It would seem so in some cases if one follows the norms. But to follow the norms one must know which meta-relativistic system one is in. We can continue this way forever, just as with the Tarski language hierarchies. Unless a relativist thinks he can get out of the game, there is an epistemic norm for him.

These results only begin to touch the interesting questions about the epistemology of relative truth. Consider that much else could be relative to the inquirer's conceptual scheme, including the very history of the inquirer's conjectures. Consider the troubles that can result for those who attempt to learn theories *AE* in a relativistic system, when the truth is a function of the theory one conjectures.

APPLICATIONS

One person's application is another person's theory. What potential applications are there of these epistemological ideas to other enterprises?

The history of philosophy

The epistemological ideas about discovery that emerged from logic and the theory of computation are closely tied to history of philosophy, and they can be used to look back upon that history. The effect is to illuminate very different aspects than one finds in the histories of professional historians of philosophy. The convention, for example, is that Plato's Meno paradox is a paradox about reference. It is not. Bacon's *Novum Organum* is essentially a concept-learning procedure, whose reliability can be described and compared with contemporary procedures. Kant's antimonies of reason are for the most part valid arguments about what cannot be known in the limit.

Philosophy of science

What remains of general methodological discussions in philosophy of science consists largely either of arguments over 'rational' relations between theory and evidence or historicist recommendations for assessing scientific traditions and research programs. If the principal point of inquiry is to get to the truth, or to get to certain kinds of truths, then these discussions typically establish nothing about the connections between the methodological notions that are advocated and the goal of inquiry. Considerations of when knowledge is and is not possible in the limit, and by which inferential strategies, keep the connection. Consider just a few examples.

Philosophers of science dispute when evidence is 'relevant' to a hypothesis. There are probabilistic accounts that follow a subjectivist framework and treat evidence as relevant for someone if it changes his degree of belief in the hypothesis; there are logical accounts, such as hypothetico-deductivism and my own 'bootstrap' account of evidential relevance. Each of these accounts looks like so much logical or probabilistic sociology, and the disputes among them often look like equivocations. Consider whether a class of possible evidence sentences is 'relevant'. If the goal is knowledge in the limit, and someone is following a particular strategy, a particular rule for conjecturing, then evidence in the class can be relevant for him for a particular discovery problem provided that his limiting behaviour would be different if evidence from that class were deleted from each possible data sequence. In a more robust sense, a class of evidence is relevant to a discovery problem provided that the problem can be solved when that class of evidence is included in the data sequences, but when the problem is altered by removing evidence of that class for each sequence, knowledge in the limit can no longer be obtained. These features of evidential relevance turn out to be purely logical matters.

Methodologists dispute whether theories should always be consistent with the data and with background knowledge; whether the process of theory formation and alteration should be conservative and not make changes unless the current theory is contradicted by the evidence; whether theories should be simple in one or another sense. Each of these methodological principles will entail a cost for computationally bounded learners: there will be knowledge that can be obtained in the limit but not by any learner who abides by the methodological restrictions. Just where the costs lie remains to be investigated.

The extant results about knowledge in the limit connect directly with the concerns in philosophy of science that originally motivated Putnam's investigations. Putnam, recall, proved that for any

'Carnapian' confirmation function for a sufficiently rich language there is a possible true sentence that never receives degree of confirmation as large as 1/2, no matter how much positive evidence of the hypothesis is presented. We can now see the same sort of thing much more generally. Suppose a probabilitistic learner who changes probability distribution by conditionalizing on the evidence (or by any other means) converges to probability greater than 1/2 for a sentence S if and only if that sentence is true. Then an obvious corollary of Kelly's characterization is that the evidence sequences satisfying S must be Σ_2 in the appropriate hierarchy. For example, if the evidence is singular and the set of structures consists of all countable structures for the language, then the sentence must be logically equivalent to a sentence with a series of existential quantifiers followed by a series of universal quantifiers. So it is easy to give sentences and collections of possible structures such that no probabilistic learner can converge to probability greater than 1/2 in just the structures in which the sentence is true.

Artificial intelligence

Thinking about limiting knowledge can sometimes be useful in understanding what a machine-learning program does and doesn't do. One example will suffice.

Patrick Winston developed a well-known automated system for learning relational concepts from examples. The program will, for example, learn the concept of an arch from examples of facts about systems of blocks that are and are not arches (see Figure 3). In terms of non-logical predicates 'x is a block', 'x supports y', 'x touches y', 'z is a part of u', we could define *arch* by

$\forall u \exists x \exists y \exists z \forall w [Arch(u) \leftrightarrow x$ is a part of u and y is a part of u and z is a part of u and x supports z and y supports z and x does not touch y and if w is a part of u then w is identical with x or w is identical with y or w is identical with z].

Consider whether any system could know in the limit whether or not this formula is true in a structure from data consisting of singular facts. Since the sentence is not Σ_2, we know that is impossible. How then does Winston's program manage to learn the concept? The answer is that the data the program is given are not confined to singular facts, but include universal data. The program is told,

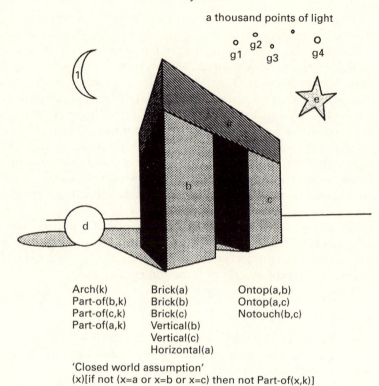

a thousand points of light

g1   g2   g3   g4

Arch(k)	Brick(a)	Ontop(a,b)
Part-of(b,k)	Brick(b)	Ontop(a,c)
Part-of(c,k)	Brick(c)	Notouch(b,c)
Part-of(a,k)	Vertical(b)	
	Vertical(c)	
	Horizontal(a)	

'Closed world assumption'
(x)[if not (x=a or x=b or x=c) then not Part-of(x,k)]

FIG 3.

for example, that a certain list of parts is *all* of the parts of an object. The hypothesis is Π_1 relative to universally quantified data.

The enterprises of 'circumscription', 'closed world assumptions', and so forth that have occupied so much effort in artificial intelligence appear to be simply a variety of methods for restricting the connection between data and hypotheses so that finite singular data will tacitly contain universal information. There is nothing objectionable in giving a machine (or a person) universally quantified data or data otherwise quantified, and one may for reasons of application be interested in finding one or another set of axioms that permit such information to be given indirectly through apparently singular data. But there is no reason to obscure the very simple epistemological structure at stake.

Cognitive science

Mathematical cognitive psychology contains a number of 'impossibility' theorems that assert the indistinguishability of certain hypotheses from evidence of certain kinds. Features of short-term memory phenomena, for example, can provably be accounted for either by serial or by parallel processes. The literature on response times contains a number of such results.[8] Results of this sort are valuable in sorting out which of our allegiances are 'working hypotheses' or 'metaphysical background' for which we cannot hope to get empirical evidence of certain kind. They teach us that we must either be tolerant even as we pursue our conviction, or else we must look to other forms of evidence to establish our case.

One of the first applications of limiting analyses was of this sort. Gold considered a 'black box' containing an unknown Turing machine. You can put an input into the box and you will get an output. You can repeat the process with different inputs, forever. Suppose after each trial you attempt to conjecture the future behaviour of the machine. Is it possible to be right in the limit? Is there a strategy for conjecturing such that there will be some time after which the conjectures about the future behaviour of the machine are correct? Gold proved there is not. If we have the computational power of Turing machines, then behavioural evidence cannot reliably predict behaviour even in the limit. If, however, it is known that the black box can contain only some (unknown) finite automaton, then its behaviour can be predicted.

A consequence of Kelly's characterization is a reflection that is almost intuitively obvious but so far as I know otherwise unremarked: it is impossible to determine from input–output behaviour whether or not a system is computationally bounded at all. That is, from data consisting of initial segments of the graph of an unknown function, one cannot reliably determine in the limit whether or not the function is computable.

Cognitive neuropsychology

Cognitive neuropsychology aims to discover something about the functional architecture of human cognition principally from data about normal human capacities and abnormal incapacities.

8 See R. D. Luce, *Response Times*, Oxford: Oxford University Press, 1986.

Schematically, the theories neuropsychologists produce are directed graphs with input vertices and output vertices. A capacity is a list of inputs and an output such that there is a path from each of the inputs to the output. Different capacities can overlap in their set of inputs, and different capacities can have the same output. The internal vertices of a hypothetical graph represent 'functional modules' where cognitive processing is supposed to take place.

There are currently hot debates among neuropsychologists over the structure of inference and the relevance of evidence in neuropsychology. Some argue that the structure of testing is hypothetico-deductive, some that it is a matter of bootstrapping. Some argue that studies of statistical relations of incapacities in groups of subjects are relevant data, and some argue that they are not. Some argue that dissociations—the occurrence of an incapacity and a capacity together in an abnormal subject—are the most important data, others that double dissociations—the occurrence of an incapacity and a capacity in one subject and the reverse in another subject—are the crucial evidence. Some argue that associations— the fact that certain incapacities or capacities always occur together —are just as important as dissociations.

There is a natural structure in these issues that might usefully be clarified by thinking through the issues in terms of what can be known in the limit. The neuropsychologists' problems are about knowledge in the limit, rather than about Platonic knowledge, because they do not at any point know that the array of observed combinations of capacities and incapacities exhausts the possibilities. Misfortune might at any time present a new subject with a new combination. Depending on background assumptions, observed combinations can be used to exclude various architectures, and strategies that take advantage of our knowledge of learning in the limit may offer the possibility of increased reliability. At the very least, the learning-theoretic framework should move the focus from arguments over methods of argument to the fundamental question of the reliability of inference and data acquisition strategies.

Economics

One place in which a kind of relativism does obtain is the social sphere. What one does or says can have an effect on the truth value of what one claims. Consider only stock market prognosticators. Games have a similar feature, in which one player's expectations for an opponent's behaviour depend on what the first player decides to do. Results about learning in the limit are a kind of a game in which the inquirer plays against a demon: the demon tries to deceive the learner in the limit, the learner tries not to be deceived. If there is a strategy for the learner such that the demon cannot succeed if the strategy is followed, we say the discovery problem is solvable; if there is a strategy the demon can follow such that no matter what strategy the learner follows he will be wrong in the limit, we say the discovery problem is unsolvable. In the relativist setting the relations between the inquirer and the demon are more nearly symmetrical. A completely symmetrical version of learning in the limit would be a setting for the investigation of infinite games, with and without computationally bounded players.

CONCLUSION

There is a great deal more to be discovered about discovery, much of it undoubtedly not about knowledge in the limit. We should by all means seek to discover what can be known in the short run with sufficiently strong background knowledge and to understand how to measure the complexity of discovery and the interaction of probabilistic ideas with computation and complexity. But we ought not for a moment to take seriously the claim that there is no systematic, rigorous, informative theory of discovery. There is a very handsome, simple theory, and it has an excellent pedigree. Readers who want to see it should consult Kevin Kelly's *The Logic of Reliable Inquiry*, Oxford University Press, 1985.

INDEX

ACE (Automatic Computing Engine) 27
Ackermann, W. 269–70
Aho, A. V. 240, 253
Allen, J. 38
Anderson, J. R. 16, 39–40
Angluin, Dana 276
Archimedes 129–30
Aristotle 129, 265
ascriptional stance 72–9
Ashby, W. R. 166, 167, 176
associative priming 16–18

Bacon, Francis 265, 285
BACON 98–9
Ballard, D. H. 16, 206, 217
Bartley, W. W. 244, 253
Barwise, J. 248, 253
Bayes, Thomas 265
Baylor, G. W. 84, 101
Beaudoin, L. P. 209, 217, 219
belief-like states 206–12
Benacerraf, Paul 116, 118, 122
Benioff, P. 172, 176
black-box computability 6, 143–63
Bloom, B. S. 87, 101
Bletchley Park 1, 59–60
Boole, George 244, 265
Borel hierarchy 279–81
Bostock, David 122
Bowie, G. Lee 122
Boyer, David L. 109, 122
Bradshaw, G. L. 98, 101
brain, see cerebral hemispheres
Bratko, Ivan 42
Broadie, A. 237, 254
Brouwer, L. E. J. 130
Brown, C. M. 206, 217
Burton-Roberts, N. 240, 254
butterfly effect 255–6
Byzantine Generals' problem 261

Carnap, Rudolf 269, 274
Carroll, Lewis 244
cerebral hemispheres 39–41, 43–6

Chaitin, Greg 8, 257–8
chaotic systems 8–9, 169, 255–64
Chase, W. G. 86, 93, 101
chess playing programs 70, 79, 84–7, 89–90
Chihara, Charles S. 119, 122
Chomsky, N. 162, 163, 274
Church, Alonzo 4, 9, 110–11, 137–9, 163, 236, 254, 270
Church–Turing thesis 6, 137–64, 168, 221, 271
Churchland, P. S. 165, 173, 177
circumscription 235, 288
Clark, Andy 184, 217
Clark, H. H. 93, 101
Coder, David 122
Colby, K. M. 58
common-sense reasoning 8, 233–53
complexity theory 7, 221–32
    see also polynomial time
computability, see black-box computability, quantum computability, Turing machine computability
computational process 6–7, 165–76, 179–217
confirmation 274, 286
consciousness 31–51, 65, 71–9, 90
continuity (cf. discreteness) 158–9
creativity 97–9
Cresswell, M. J. 233, 252, 254
Cummins, R. 174, 175, 176

decomposable systems, see structure of systems
De Groot, A. D. 84, 101
DEEPTHOUGHT 84–5
DeLong, H. 173, 176
Dennett, Daniel C. 4, 32–3, 35–6, 47, 63–8, 79, 107–9, 122, 161, 163, 212, 217, 234
Descartes, René 265
desire-like states 206–12
determinism 257
Deutsch, David 6, 145–7, 159, 162, 163
Dietrich, E. 176

discovery, theory of 9, 97–9, 244,
265–91
discreteness and non-discreteness
182–3, 206
see also continuity
divine spark 5, 126–33
see also insight
DOCTOR 58
Dowty, D. R. 236, 254
Doyle, J. 233, 254
Dreyfus, Hubert L. 12, 23
Dummett, M. A. E. 107

Eccles, John C. 34–5, 41, 44
Edelman, G. M. 174, 177
Einstein, Albert 269
Enderton, H. B. 146, 163
effective computability, *see* Turing
machine computability
ELIZA 55, 58
Entscheidungsproblem 6, 269
EPAM 88
Epimenides 104
Euclid 127–30
Euler, Leonhard 134
expert systems 88–9

Fagin, R. 223
falsifiability 268
Feigenbaum, E. A. 88, 101
Feldman, J. A. 16
Fernando, Emmanuel Q. 122
Feynman, R. 172–3, 176
Fields, Chris 6–7, 159, 163, 165–77,
183, 184, 217
flight, artificial 13–15, 57–8
Fodor, J. A. 165, 175, 176, 214, 217
Ford, Joseph 255–64
Fowler, D. H. 129
Frame problem 214
Frankfurt, H. G. 65, 79
Frege, Gottlob 134, 269
French, Robert M. 2, 11–26, 29–30,
41, 55, 162, 163
Funt, B. V. 182, 217

Galton, Antony 6, 137–64
Gandy, Robin 1, 2, 125–36, 141–2,
163
Gazdar, G. 233, 240, 254
Gilmartin, K. A. 87, 102
Glover, Jonathan 123
Glymour, Clark 9, 110, 265–91

Gödel, Kurt 4, 9, 104, 111, 126–7,
131–2, 135, 137, 163, 180, 266,
270, 271
Gödel's theorem 58, 103–22, 130–1,
257–8
Gold, E. Mark 9, 271–5, 278,
279–81, 289
Good, I. J. 110–12, 123
Gorman, R. P. 172, 176
grammar, formal 251–3
grammar-based inference 8, 233–53
Grice, H. P. 65, 76, 79
Griffiths, A. P. 64, 79
Grossberg, S. 171, 177
Gurevich, Y. 154, 163, 223

Halle, Morris 38
Hanks, S. 235, 254
Hanson, William H. 107, 123
Harel, D. 152, 163
Harnad, S. 171, 174, 177, 203
Haugeland, John 183, 217
Hayes, J. R. 87, 96, 101
Heisenberg, Werner 258
Hermes, H. 139, 163
Hilbert, David 6, 266, 269–70
Hilef, F. D. 58
Hinton, G. E. 172, 177
Hodges, A. 59
Hofstadter, Douglas R. 16, 18, 20,
24, 107–8, 110–12, 119–20,
123
Hopcroft, J. 175, 177
Hume, David 265
Hunnicutt, M. S. 38
Hutchins, E. 37
Hutton, Anthony 120, 123

imitation game, *see* Turing Test,
Turing on 'Computing Machinery
and Intelligence'
Immerman, Neil 223, 224
insight 94–5
see also divine spark
intelligence, *see* consciousness,
personhood, Turing Test
intelligent systems 190–1, 199–202
intentional stance 4, 63–9, 212
see also ascriptional stance,
representational stance
intentional systems 63–5
intuition 86–7, 97–8
ISAAC 96

James, William 46–7
Jauch, J. M. 167, 177
Jefferson, Professor 30–1
Jevons, W. Stanley 244
Johnson-Laird, Philip N. 38

Kalmár, L. 141, 155–6, 163
Kant, Immanuel 265, 285
Kaplan, C. A. 94, 101
KARDIO 42–3
KEKADA 98–9
Kelly, Kevin T. 267, 277–87, 291
Kenny, A. J. P. 123
Kinsbourne, M. 47
Kirk, Robert 123
Klatt, D. 38
Kleene, S. C. 110–11, 139, 155, 164
Klein, E. 233, 240, 254
knowledge in the limit 9, 271–81
Koch, C. 165, 173, 177
Kosslyn, S. M. 93, 101
Kowalski, R. 244, 254
Kraemer, H. C. 58
Kripke, Saul 236
Kuhn, Thomas 59
Kulkarni, D. 98, 101

Lakoff, George 24
Langley, P. 98, 101
language learning 90–1, 96–7, 274–6
language processing 95–7
    see also grammar-based inference
Laplace, Pierre-Simon de 255, 257–8
Larkin, J. H. 92–3, 102
Lavrac, N. 42
learning 274, 276–8
    see also language learning, machine
    learning
Leibniz, G. W. F. 265
Lewis, David 123, 233, 254
limiting recursive sets 271–5
linguistics, computational 233
Lorentz, Edward 255
Lucas, John R. 5, 58, 103–24, 126,
    130–1, 133–4, 147
Luce, R. D. 289

McCarthy, J. 233, 254
McClelland, J. L. 16, 172, 177
McDermott, D. 233, 235, 254
machine learning 287–9
    see also Turing on machine learning
MacKay, Donald 136

Mackie, J. L. 123
Marr, D. 165–6, 177
Martin-Löf, P. 134
MATER 84–5
measurement 6–7, 8, 165–76, 258–9
mechanism 103–22, 125–36
medieval logic 237
    see also syllogism
memory, short-term 87–8, 289
mental pictures 92–4
Meyer, D. E. 16
Michie, Donald 1, 2–3, 29–51, 55
Mill, John Stuart 265
Millican, Peter 237
Minsky, M. L. 139, 154, 164
Montague, R. M. 8, 236, 254
Moore, E. F. 166, 177
motivation 99–100
Mott, Peter 7–8, 233–54
Mozetic, I. 42

Nagel, E. 180, 217
Narayanan, Ajit 3, 63–79
Negroponte, Nicholas 48–9
neural nets, *see* parallelism
Newell, A. 82, 88, 102
Newman, J. R. 180, 217
Newton-Smith, W. H. 266
Novak, G. S. 93, 96, 102
NP (non-deterministic polynomial
    time), *see* complexity theory
numbers, Babylonian and Greek views
    of 127–30

Ornstein, R. E. 48
Osherson, Dan N. 275, 277

Paige, J. M. 93, 102
parallelism 181–2, 194
    see also seriality and parallelism
PARRY 58
parsing 275
Parsons, H. McIlvaine 45
Peano Arithmetic 107, 131
Penrose, Roger 5, 9, 130–1, 133–6
Pereira, F. C. N. 233, 254
Perry, J. 248, 253
personhood 4, 63–8
Péter, R. 147, 149, 156, 164
Peters, S. 236, 254
Plato 265, 267, 285
Platonic conception of inquiry
    267–70

pluralization 38–9
Pnueli, A. 156–7, 164
polynomial time 152–5
　see also complexity theory
Popper, K. R. 35, 41, 44, 268, 269
positivist conception of inquiry
　267–70
Posner, M. I. 40
Post, Emil L. 131, 266
Price, Richard 265
Pullum, G. 233, 240, 254
Putnam, Hilary 9, 116–17, 123,
　271–9, 286–7
Pylyshyn, Z. W. 165, 177, 183, 217

quantum computability, *see* quantum
　mechanics
quantum mechanics 6, 9, 135, 159,
　167–9, 172–3, 182, 184, 261–3
Quine, W. V. O. 134

Radford, A. 238, 240, 254
rating games 18–22
ratio 127–30
reactive systems 156–8
recognition of features 86–7
Reeke, G. N. 174, 177
Reichenbach, Hans 271
relativism 281–5
representation 91–5, 173–5
representational stance 69–71, 78
response times 289
Richards, I. A. 96
Richman, H. B. 88, 102
Robinson, Abraham 271
Robinson Arithmetic Q 107
Rogers, H. 154, 164
Rucker, Rudy 107, 123
Ruelle, D. 255
rule induction 40
Rumelhart, D. E. 16, 172, 177
Russell, Bertrand 48

Sag, I. 233, 240, 254
Sayre, K. M. 174, 177
Schank, R. C. 58
Schlick, M. 268
Schlipf, J. S. 235, 254
Schvaneveldt, R. W. 16
search, selective heuristic 85–6, 88–9
Searle, John R. 30, 33–5, 76, 79, 90,
　126, 171, 177, 181, 216, 217

Sejnowski, T. J. 165, 172, 173, 176,
　177
Sells, P. 240, 254
semantic facilitation, *see* associative
　priming
seriality and parallelism 87–8, 289
Sethi, R. 240, 253
Shapiro, Ehud Y. 276
Shieber, S. M. 240, 254
Siklóssy, L. 91, 96, 102
Simon, Herbert 1, 4, 81–102
Sleazak, P. 123
Sloman, Aaron 7, 159, 164, 179–219
Smart, J. J. C. 123
Smith, B. C. 181, 219
Smolensky, P. 172, 177
Sommerhalder, R. 222
Sommers, F. 243, 254
Stewart, Iain 6, 7, 154–5, 164,
　221–32
Stob, Michael 275
Stoy, J. E. 173, 177
Strawson, P. F. 64, 79
structure of systems 82–3, 191,
　194–8
subcognition 2, 15–26, 35–41
Suber, Peter 25
superarticulacy 3, 41–3
syllogism 8, 243–51
　see also medieval logic
symbol-grounding problem 174–5,
　203
Szelepcsenyi, R. 223

Takens, F. 255
Tanenbaum, A. S. 165, 177
Tarski, A. 204–6, 215, 216, 219
Taylor, C. N. 186, 189, 219
Thom, René 135
Thorp, J. W. 123
Tolstoy, Leo 263
transfinite ordinals 110–12
transformational systems, *see* reactive
　systems
Trevarthen, Colwyn 32, 46
Turing, Alan 1
　the Church–Turing thesis 137–40
　cognitive compatibility 29
　'Computing Machinery and
　　Intelligence' 2–4, 11–13, 25,
　　29–33, 53–4, 59–62, 66, 77,
　　125, 199
　epistemological relevance 266, 271

limitations of computability 4–6, 9, 103, 164, 270
logic programming 28
machine learning 3, 28
programmable digital computers 27–9
see also Entscheidungsproblem
Turing machine 7, 221–32
see also mechanism and Turing machine computability
Turing machine computability 6–7, 137–63, 168, 271–2, 280–1
Turing Test 1–4, 11–26, 27–51, 53–62, 65–6, 76–7, 199
'Turing's Theorem' (Gandy) 141–2
see also Turing on the Church–Turing thesis
'Turing's Theorem' (Lucas) 103
see also Turing on limitations of computability
Tyndall, John 105, 269
typing 40

Ullman, J. P. 175, 177, 240, 253
Ullman, S. 165, 177
uncertainty principles 258–9
UNDERSTAND 96
user interface design 48–9

Venn, John 244
verifiability 268
von Neumann, John 104, 146, 164, 167, 177

Walcott Sperry, Roger 43
Wall, R. E. 236, 254
Wang, Hao 107, 109–11, 117–20, 124, 138–9, 164
Warren, D. H. D. 233, 254
Webb, Judson C. 112–13, 124, 151, 164
Weber, Sylvia 58
Weinstein, Scott 275, 277
Weizenbaum, J. 55
Westrhenen, S. C. 222
Whitby, Blay 3, 4
Whitehead, A. N. 36
Whiteley, C. H. 124
Winograd, T. 234, 254
Winston, Patrick 287–8
Wittgenstein, Ludwig 24, 126
Wrathall, C. 223
Wright, I. P. 219

Yazdani, M. 57
Young, R. A. 213, 219

ZBIE 96–7
Zytkow, J. M. 98, 101